I0763091

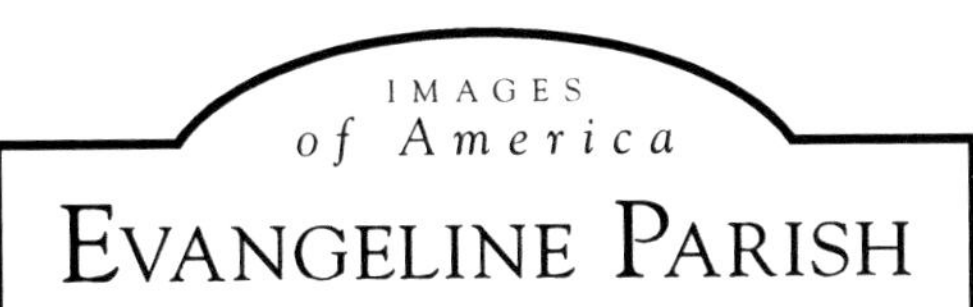
IMAGES
of America
EVANGELINE PARISH

On the Cover: Ville Platte's Main Street is seen about 1905, as enthusiasm was building to create the Parish of Evangeline. Although the town was small, it was poised to grow with the new parish. The street is unpaved, but newly dug ditches help control runoff. Sidewalks are being laid for the convenience of pedestrians. Commerce is good, as indicated by the many stores along the street. (Courtesy of Pam McGee.)

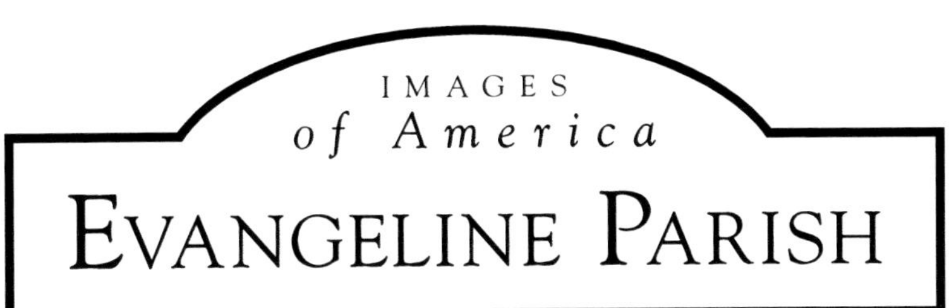

Jane F. Vidrine and Jean S. Kiesel

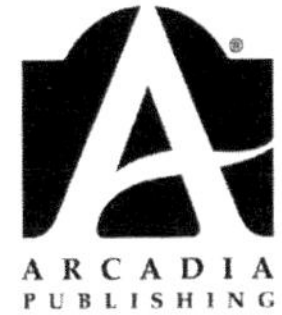

ISBN 987-1-4671-1178-2

Published by Arcadia Publishing
Charleston, South Carolina

Printed in the United States of America

Library of Congress Control Number: 2013951274

For all general information, please contact Arcadia Publishing:
Telephone 843-853-2070
Fax 843-853-0044
E-mail sales@arcadiapublishing.com
For customer service and orders:
Toll-Free 1-888-313-2665

Visit us on the Internet at www.arcadiapublishing.com

To the people of Evangeline Parish, who love their heritage.

Contents

ACKNOWLEDGMENTS

In preparing this book, we have benefited from the assistance of many people; in fact, without their help, we never could have succeeded. First and foremost, we thank our supervisor, Dr. Bruce Turner, for his full support during this project. Thanks are due to the entire Special Collections staff and the Dean's Office of the Edith Garland Dupré Library at the University of Louisiana at Lafayette for their generous support as well.

The people of Evangeline Parish have been so generous in sharing their photographs and their knowledge; we cannot thank them enough. Special thanks go to Pam McGee, who spent countless hours guiding us, encouraging us, and providing many photographs from her own collection. She also pointed us to many others who had photographs and information to share. We are also grateful to Lynn Landreneau for her support and assistance.

We would like to also thank the Ville Platte Mayor's Office, Ville Platte Chamber of Commerce, Evangeline Sheriff's Office, Evangeline Parish Library, Pine Prairie Village Hall, Diocese of Lafayette Archives, UL Lafayette Center for Louisiana Studies, Evangeline School Board Office, Evangeline Clerk of Court, and the *Ville Platte Gazette*, especially David Ortego for all his help.

Many residents of Evangeline Parish shared their photographs and stories for this book. These include Bernice Ardoin, JoAnn Burnett, Rayford and Delores Chapman, Mitzi Duos Cochrane, Joyce Coreil, Bobby Dardeau, Richard Deshotel, Deen Fontenot, Sister Helen Fontenot, Rollins G. Fontenot, Wendel Fuselier, Kathleen DeVille Godchaux, Kathryn Lebleu Guillory, Alice Bacon Guillotte, Sandra Himel, Annette Duos Johnson, Jackie Jones, Leah Kiesel, KVPI Radio, Warren Lafleur, Janis Landreneau, Allison "Sonny" Launey, Runnie F. Matte, Linda McGee, Jo Anna Miller, Kermit Miller, Mike Miller, Clarence Rivers, David Simpson, Elvin Soileau, J.D. Soileau, Kathleen Eastin Soileau, Teresa Van Atta, Barbara Johnson Vautrot, Tim Veillon, J. Kilren Vidrine, Vietnam Veterans Chapter No. 632, and Merlyn Yielding. If we have left anyone out, please be assured that we value your contributions highly. This book could not have been written without your help.

Thanks go to Arcadia Publishing, especially our editors Jason Humphrey, Mary Margaret Schley, and Maggie Bullwinkel for their valuable assistance.

Finally, we especially want to thank our families, Roland R. Vidrine and Leah and Sara Kiesel, for their love and support during this project and always.

INTRODUCTION

Evangeline Parish, located in central Louisiana, encompasses the hills and piney woods of the northern part of the state as well as the prairies and wetlands of the south. Culturally, too, Evangeline merges the English-speaking families who settled the northern part of the parish and the French-speaking groups who settled in the south.

During Colonial times the area was part of the Opelousas Post, governed from the outpost at Opelousas. The fort was established by the French to guard against Spanish encroachment from Mexico. After Louisiana was ceded to Spain in 1763, the Spanish colonial government promoted settlement around the post. The land was well suited for agriculture, and the prairies were ideal for raising cattle. Some of the first settlers in Evangeline Parish were retired French soldiers from the Illinois country who preferred to move to Spanish territory rather than remain in Illinois under British rule when France lost nearly all her colonies in North America after the French and Indian War. At about the same time, the first English-speaking families began settling farther north in the piney woods around Bayou Chicot, the first English settlement west of the Mississippi River. Settlement on the prairies of southwest Evangeline Parish came later. A few Acadian families moved onto the prairies in the early 1800s, living on isolated homesteads, tending cattle and raising crops to feed their families.

Evangeline Parish does not include any of the major waterways that would have provided the principal means of transportation from Colonial days until the coming of the railroad. Consequently, settlement came late to the area. William Darby's map of Louisiana, published in 1815, shows a road (more likely a rudimentary trail) between Opelousas and Alexandria, roughly following the route later taken by US Highway 167. A few small settlements were located along this road in what later became Evangeline Parish: McDaniel and Hanchett to the north, and Fontenot farther south. These settlements bore the names of important residents, probably the largest landowners or keepers of inns or stores, and would later be known as Turkey Creek, Bayou Chicot, and Ville Platte, respectively. The names also give a good indication of the ethnicity of the people who settled each area: Anglo-Saxons in the north, French to the south. The topography indicates how Ville Platte (French for "flat town") got its name, for old beds of the Red River made hills around Opelousas and Bayou Chicot, while the land in between is quite flat.

Evangeline was one of the last parishes established in Louisiana. It was long a part of St. Landry Parish, but as the population grew in the late 19th century, the parish seat's distant location became more burdensome. It was 70 miles or more to Opelousas from some sections of the parish, a journey that could take two days by horse and buggy over bad roads. Yet it was necessary to go there to pay taxes, get a marriage license, pursue a lawsuit, or file any number of official documents. Furthermore, political interests in the southern part of St. Landry dominated parish politics and were accused of neglecting issues more important in the northern section. Interest in creating a new parish surfaced around 1890. Advocates in Bayou Chicot, Pine Prairie, and Ville Platte held citizens' meetings to promote the idea, but they could not get the necessary support. The idea continued to attract attention, however, while political leaders from other parts of St. Landry lobbied the legislature in opposition. By 1905, interest in forming a new parish was so great that opponents held a mass meeting in Opelousas, while proponents met in Ville Platte. P.L. Fontenot, who represented the area in the state legislature, introduced legislation creating Evangeline Parish in 1908. It passed both houses unanimously and was signed by Gov. J.Y. Sanders, but it was declared unconstitutional by the state supreme court a few days later. More mass meetings followed, culminating in a special election on April 12, 1909, to decide the question. The vote was in favor of division, with Ville Platte chosen as the parish seat. Fontenot introduced new legislation, more carefully drawn up, in the 1910 session of the legislature, and it became law.

The new parish was named for Evangeline, the heroine of Henry Wadsworth Longfellow's epic poem about the expulsion of the Acadians from Nova Scotia. In the poem, Evangeline Bellefontaine is on the point of marrying her beloved, Gabriel Lajeunesse, when the British round up the Acadians and ship them off to various English colonies. The two lovers are separated. Evangeline searches for Gabriel for many years, unsuccessfully. Finally, she joins the Sisters of Mercy in Philadelphia, working among the poor. While tending to the sick during an epidemic, she at last finds Gabriel among the victims. They are reunited, just as he succumbs. Many residents of Evangeline Parish are descendants of the Acadians and treasure the poem as part of their heritage.

According to the 2010 census, the population of Evangeline Parish is about 34,000. The parish is 69 percent white and 28 percent African American, with the rest identifying themselves as members of other ethnic groups or of mixed heritage. The median age is 36—slightly higher for women, slightly lower for men. Principal industries include education, health care, social services, agriculture, retail trade, and construction. But statistics leave out much.

The people of Evangeline Parish live in small communities. They can often trace their ancestry to the people who founded those communities a century or more ago. Names that belonged to the earliest settlers, like Fontenot, Vidrine, Soileau, Savoy, Lafleur, Johnson, Coreil, Guillory, Ortego, Manuel, Landreneau, Campbell, Clark, and Tate, are still prevalent in the parish. The French name for Evangeline Parish is *La Paroisse d'Evangeline*. Citizens referred to the parish by its French name for many years, and some still do today.

Evangeline Parish residents are family-oriented and value their heritage. Residents here love to tell stories of their ancestors, passing the tales along to their children. They work hard in order to enjoy the things that really matter: spending time with family and friends, sharing good food and traditional music, hunting and fishing, camping, and passing a good time at festivals, parades, and high school sporting events. These hardworking people teach their children that education and work are necessary in life.

Evangeline Parish has a rich past, and its residents know their history and cherish it. This book is not a definitive history of the parish; that remains to be written. We hope readers will enjoy this book for what it is, a sampler of the people, places, and events that belong to that history.

One

Communities

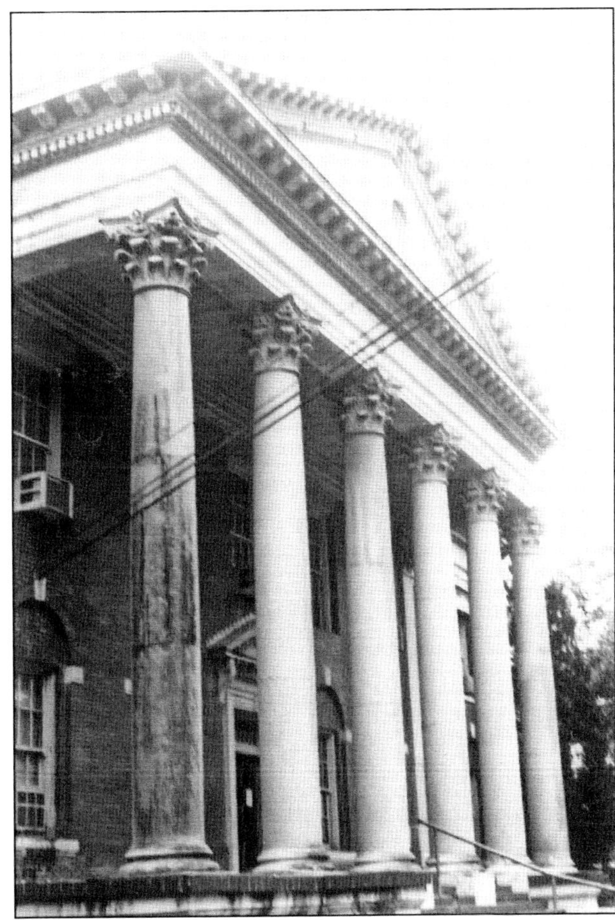

The original Evangeline Parish Court House was built in 1912 at a cost of $100,000. It housed all parish government offices including the police jury, sheriff, assessor, clerk of court, and school board, until the expansion of government programs during the New Deal. Renovations and additions to the building kept it in service until the mid-1970s. (Courtesy of Center for Louisiana Studies, UL Lafayette.)

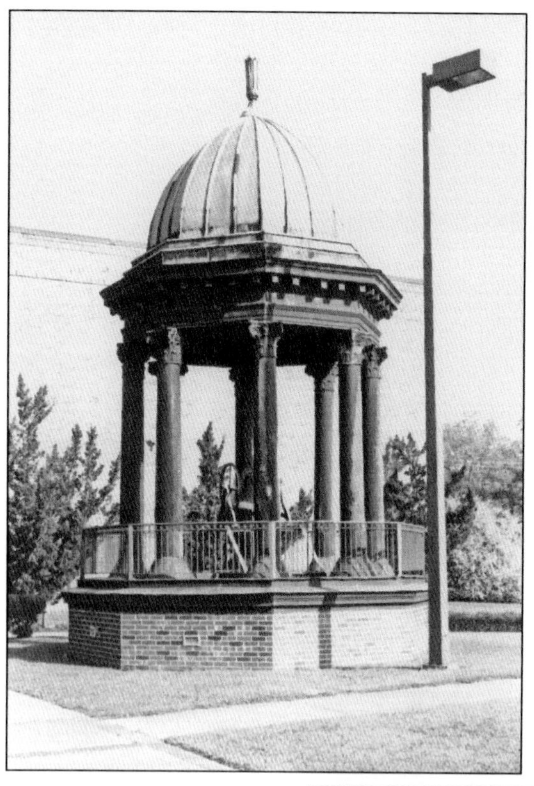

The cupola and bell that adorned the roof of the original Evangeline Parish Court House were salvaged when the building was demolished. They now grace the lawn in front of the new courthouse. The original structure stood in front of the new one, a block off Main Street in Ville Platte. (Courtesy of Center for Louisiana Studies, UL Lafayette.)

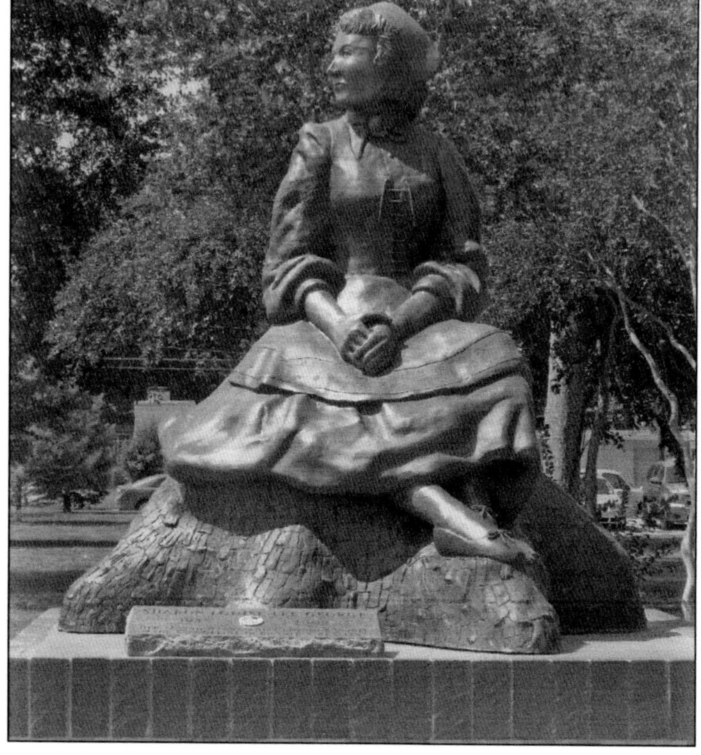

Evangeline Parish was named for Evangeline, the heroine of Henry Wadsworth Longfellow's epic poem about the expulsion of the Acadians. This statue of Evangeline was created in 2011 as part of the parish's centennial celebration. It is located at 200 Court Street, in front of the parish courthouse. (Courtesy of Jane Vidrine.)

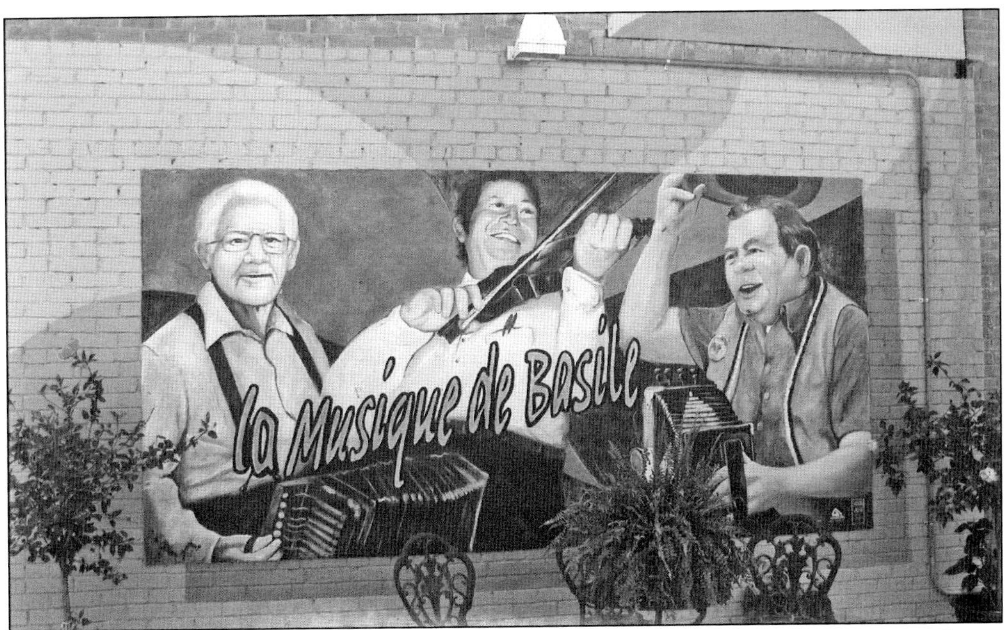

Basile is located in southwest Evangeline Parish. It has long been a center for Cajun music, being the home of such luminaries as Nonc Allie Young, Dewey Balfa, and Nathan Abshire (depicted here from left to right). Basile hosts the Louisiana Swine Festival each fall, encompassing events like a boudin-eating contest and a greased-pig chase. In the spring, it also hosts a Courir du Mardi Gras. (Courtesy of Center for Louisiana Studies, UL Lafayette.)

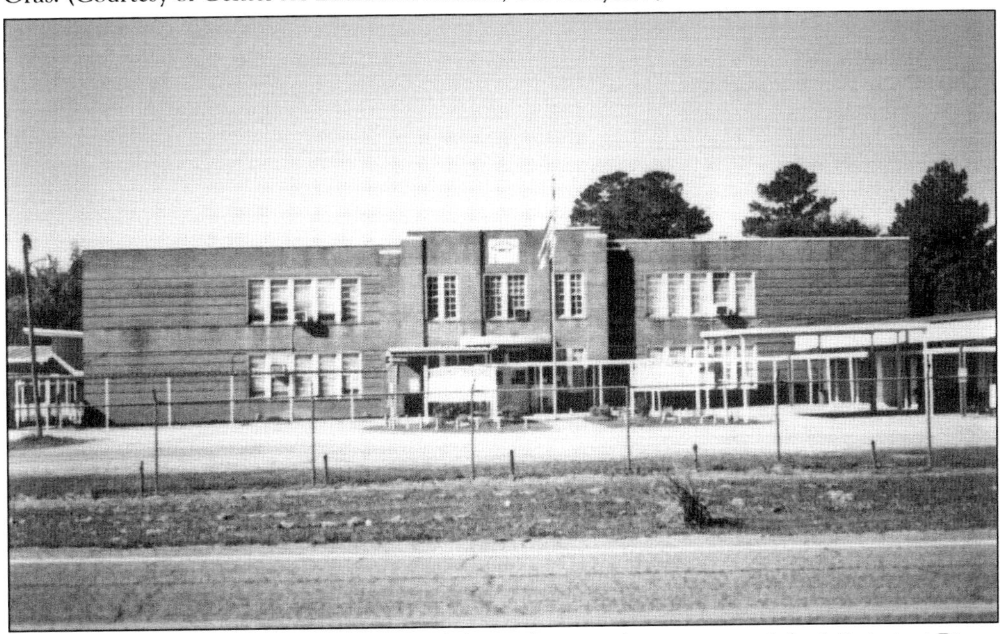

Bayou Chicot claims to be the oldest English-speaking settlement west of the Mississippi River. The first settlers came prior to 1783. It was a prosperous community in the 1800s, with many fine homes as well as a hotel, a post office, gristmills, tanneries, blacksmith shops, churches, schools, and even a medical school. Little remains today except the school (shown here), fire station, and the Baptist church. (Courtesy of Jean Kiesel.)

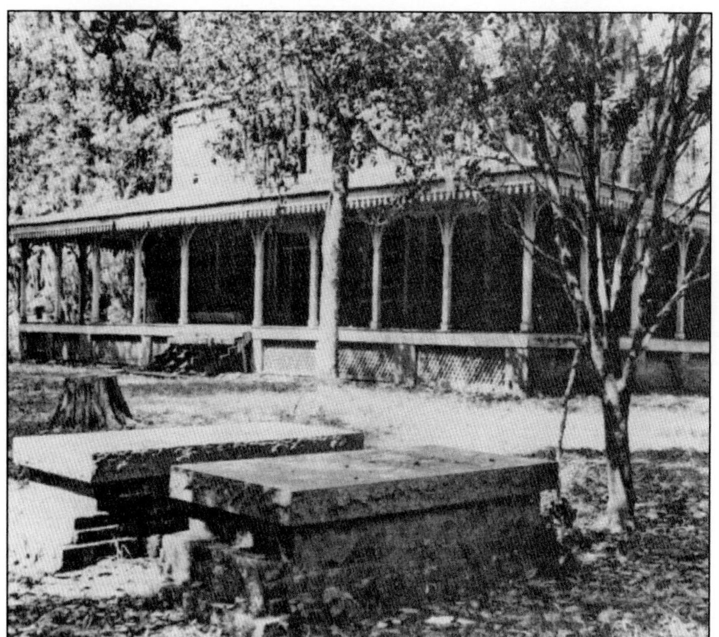

This house in Bayou Chicot was originally built by the Akinhead family. About 1870 it was purchased by Dr. Josiah Hawkins, a medical doctor from Georgia. He added the elaborate woodwork. Besides practicing medicine, Dr. Hawkins also trained many students who went on to practice medicine in Evangeline Parish and surrounding communities. This was common before the establishment of medical schools. (Courtesy of *Ville Platte Gazette*.)

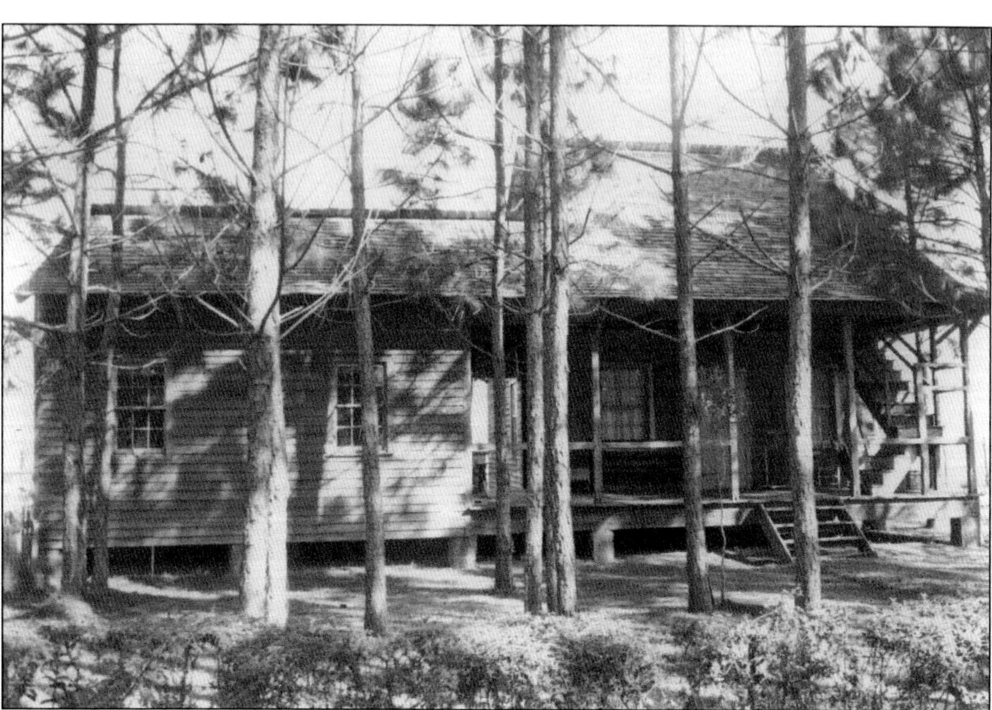

This old house in the Bayou Chicot area seems to represent the two cultures of Louisiana that merge in Evangeline Parish. The right half is a traditional Acadian-style home like those found throughout southern Louisiana, with its outside staircase and deep gallery. It is connected to the left half by a dogtrot, common in the Anglo north but rarely seen in the south. (Courtesy of *Ville Platte Gazette*.)

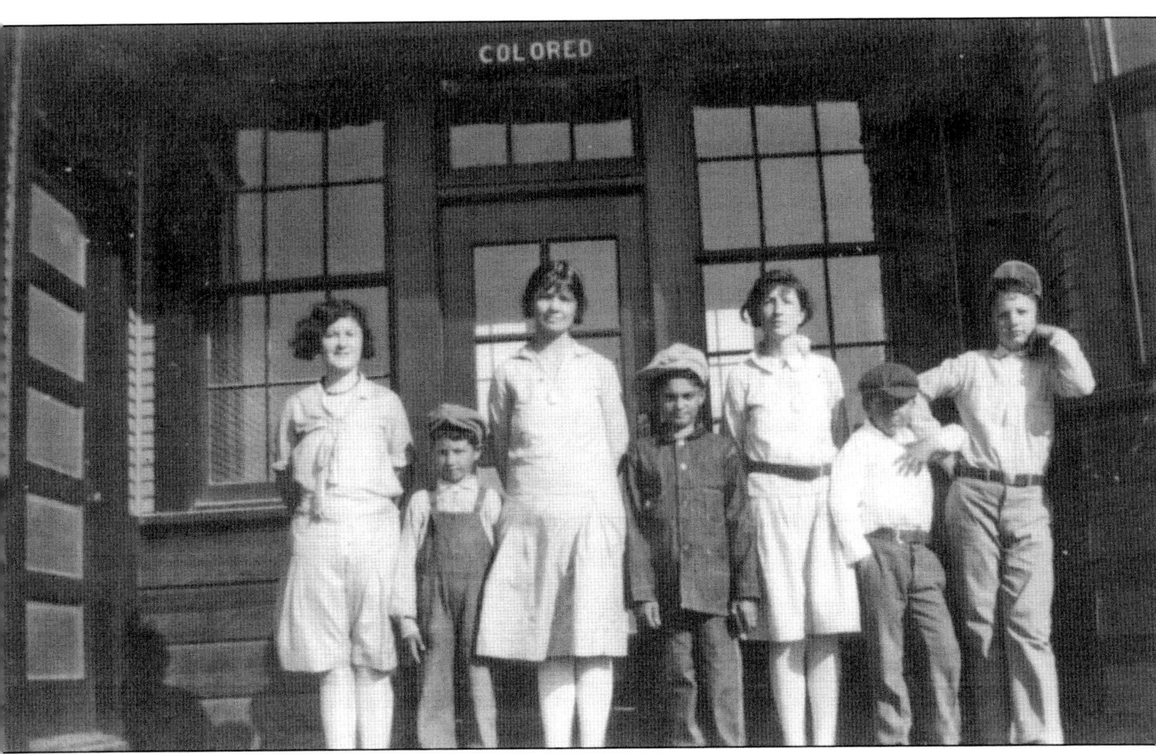

Chataignier is another very old settlement in Evangeline Parish. The first settlers came before 1800, when Louisiana was still a Spanish colony. The Catholic church in Chataignier was established as a mission of Opelousas in 1856, and the first known school opened in 1858. The post office was established in 1879, but the village was not incorporated until 1973. The Texas & Pacific Railroad line that connected Eunice and Bunkie ran through Chataignier, giving the community rail service in the 1920s. Shown here in front of the depot are some local children. They are, from left to right, Ament and Abel Fontenot; Eola, Chester, and Hilda Rozas; Eray Ardoin; and Otis Fontenot. (Courtesy of Kathryn Lebleu Guillory.)

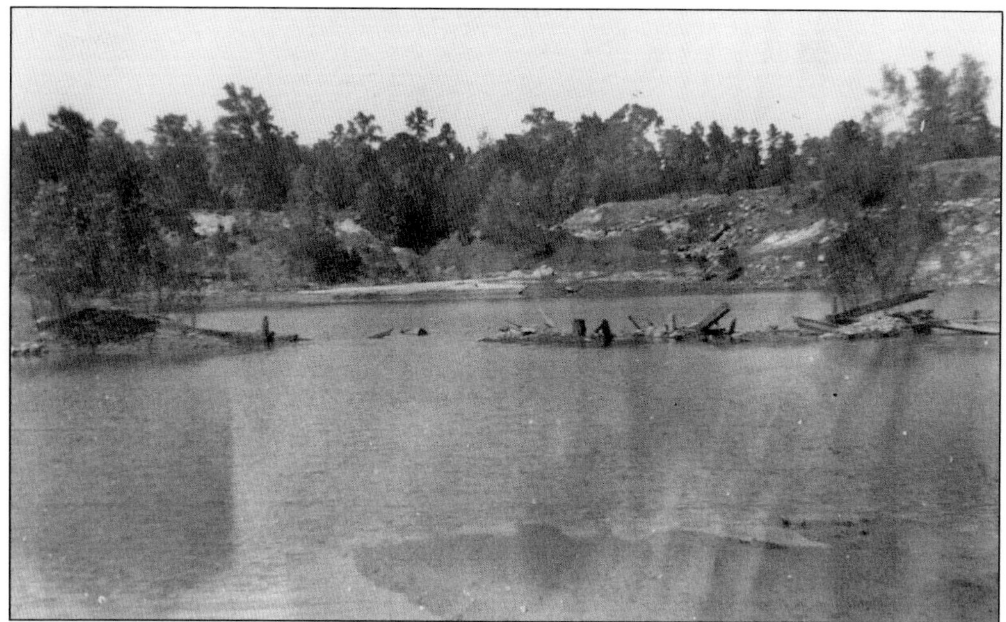

The beach in Easton was a popular swimming hole for years. It was formed from an old limestone quarry known as the Rock Pit. Originally, the quarry was a private operation begun in the 1930s to supply gravel for road construction. A railroad spur ran to Easton to carry the gravel. During World War II, the quarry was used to train Army engineers on heavy equipment. (Courtesy of Clarence Rivers.)

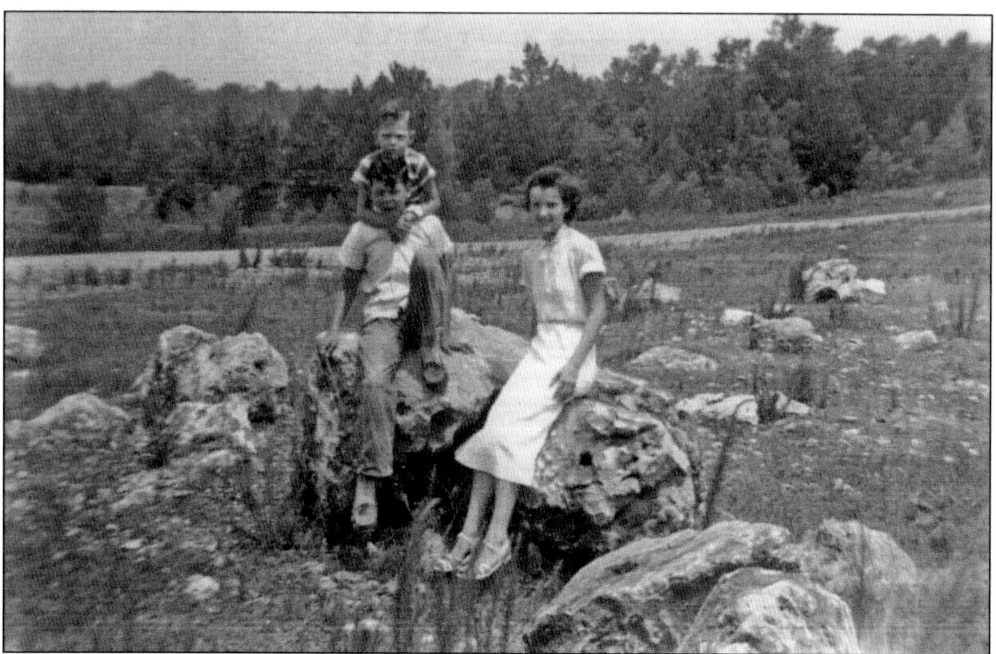

Kenneth, Bryan (in rear), and Wilda Morgan pose at the Rock Pit, the old limestone quarry near Easton, about 1950. The hole in the rock was for placing a dynamite charge to break up the rock. The Rock Pit was used to train Army engineers during World War II. There was a large camp on top of the hill for white soldiers, and another nearby for blacks. (Courtesy of Clarence Rivers.)

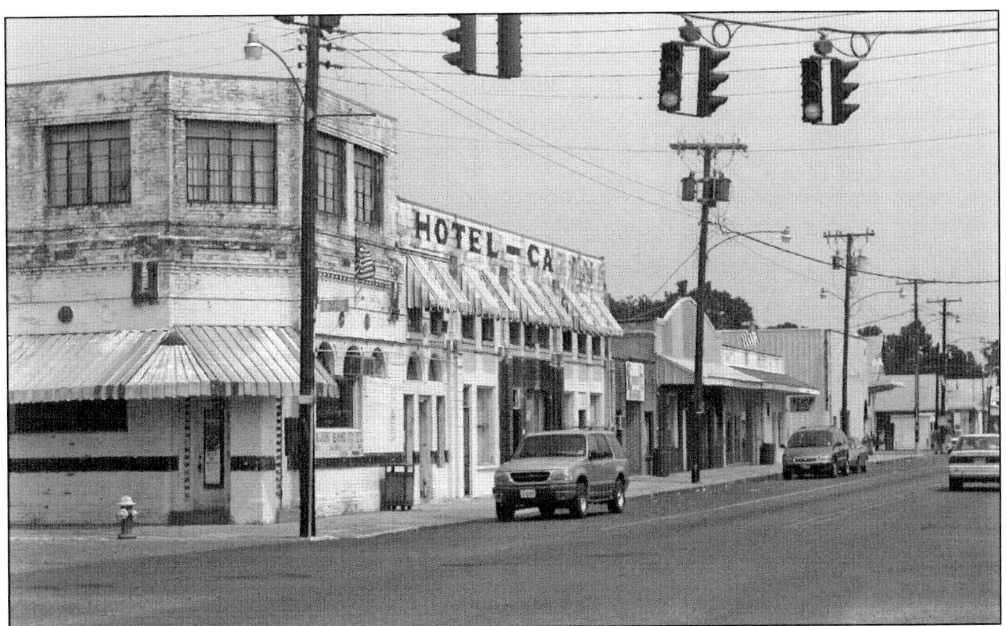

The town of Mamou was laid out in 1907 by C.C. Duson, who along with his brother W.W. Duson did much to develop the prairies of southwest Louisiana. It prospered during its first two decades, but fell on hard times during the Depression. Today, it is known for its country Mardi Gras celebration and as a center for Cajun music. (Courtesy of Center for Louisiana Studies, UL Lafayette.)

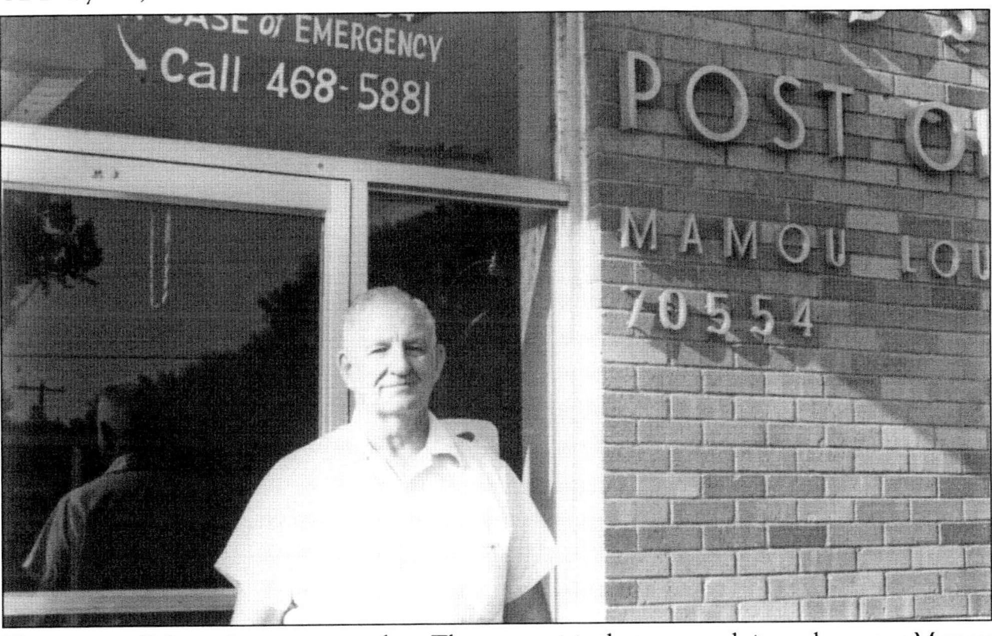

The origins of Mamou's name are unclear. The vast prairie that surrounds it was known as Mamou Prairie since the late 18th century. English speakers called it the Mammoth Prairie. "Mamou" is also the local name for the coral tree, whose leaves, roots, and berries were used in folk medicine. Here, former mayor Warren Pierrotti stands in front of the Mamou post office. (Courtesy of *Ville Platte Gazette*.)

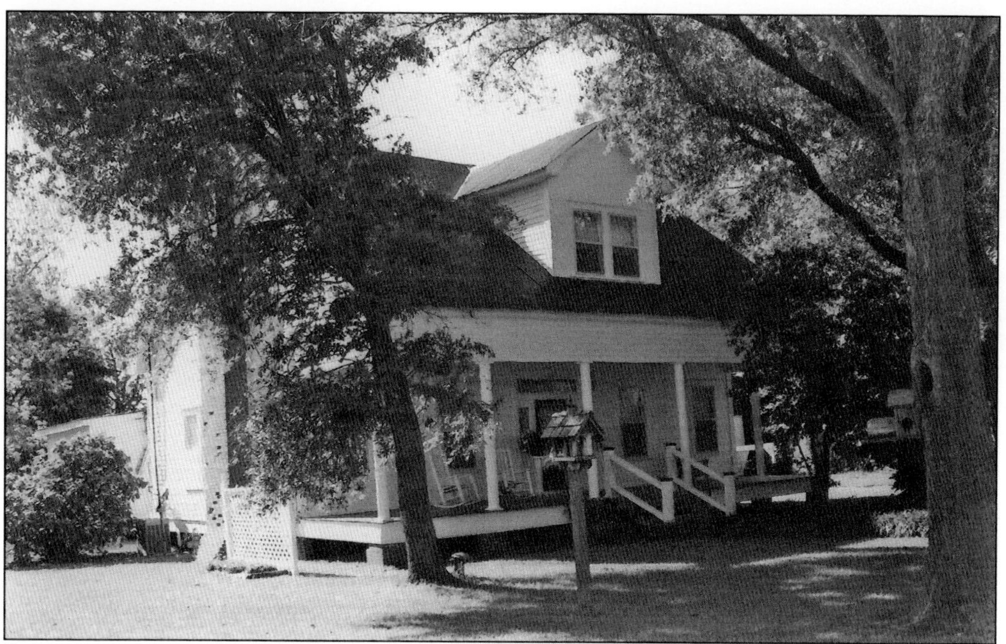

Land for the town of Pine Prairie was donated by Eloi Campbell, who also gave land for the Methodist and United Brethren churches. His son Harvey built this home on the south end of town in 1907, near what is now Highway 13. The house has been renovated extensively in recent years by Dot Stevens, the current owner. (Courtesy of Pine Prairie Village Hall.)

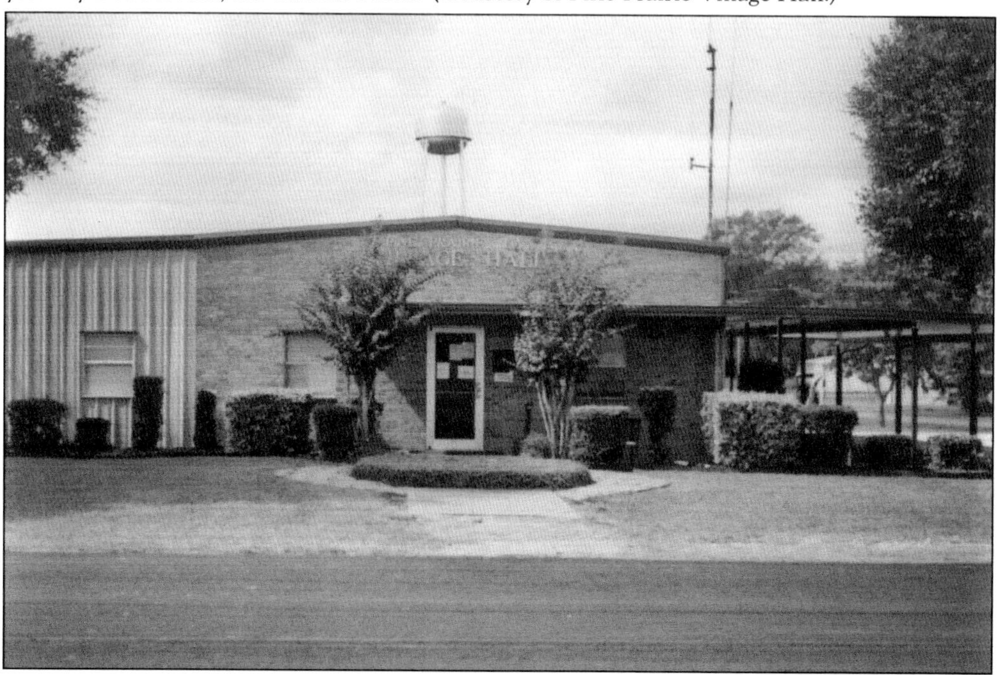

Pine Prairie, a village of about 1,000 residents, is located near the center of Evangeline Parish. The village hall was built in 1983 using federal revenue-sharing funds. It had offices for the mayor, chief of police, and village clerk, and a meeting room for the village council. The fire station is adjacent to the hall, and the nursing home is just down the street. (Courtesy of Jean Kiesel.)

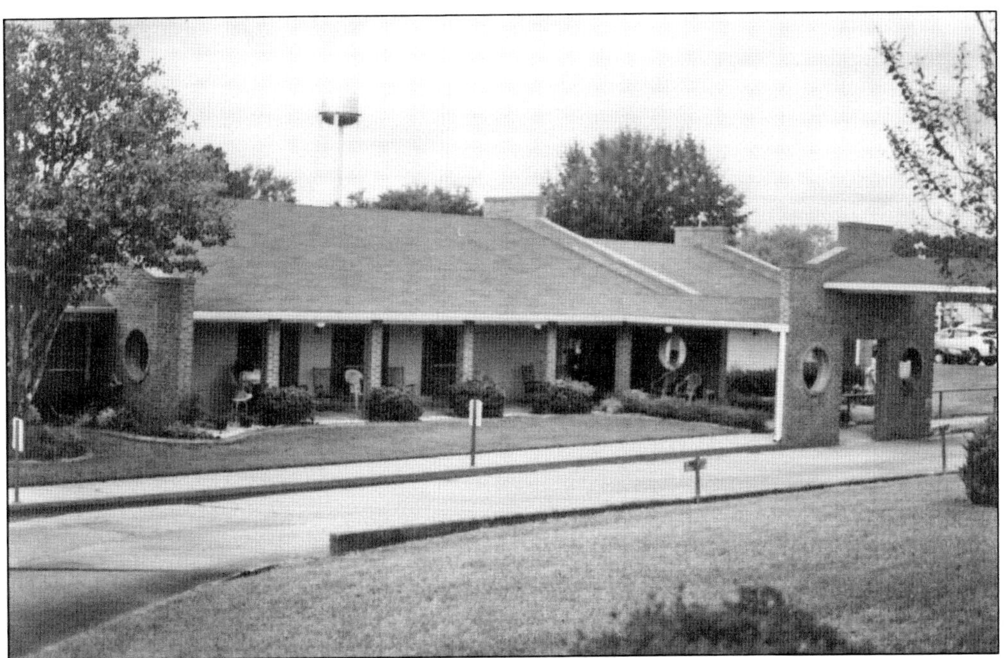

Pine Prairie is home to Prairie Manor Nursing Home, established in 1986 to keep people in need of skilled nursing care in their own community. It is owned by the community and run on a not-for-profit basis. Each spring, Pine Prairie hosts the Boggy Bayou Festival, the proceeds from which go to benefit the nursing home. (Courtesy of Jean Kiesel.)

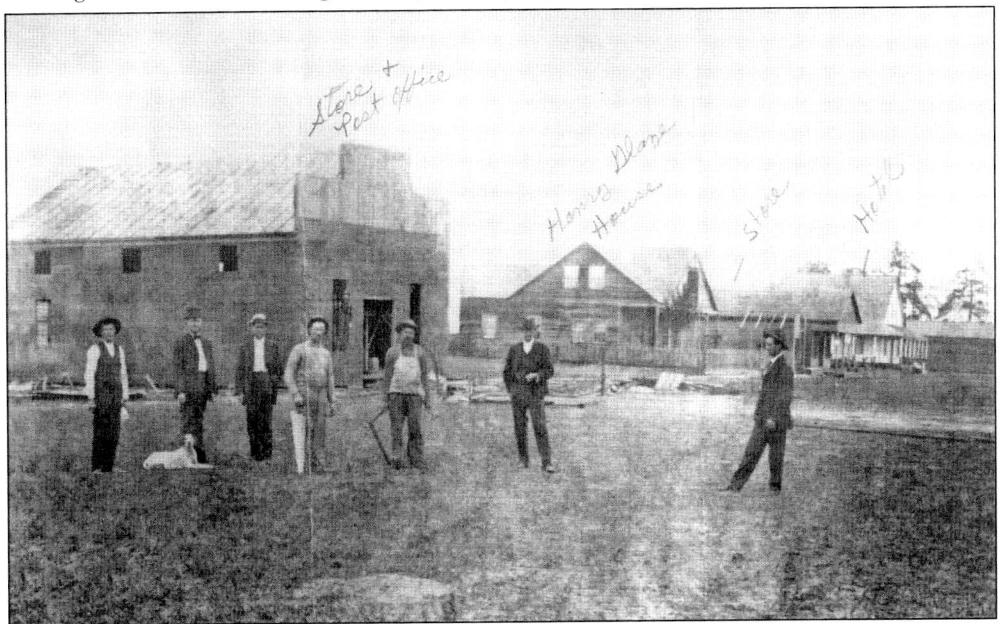

Pine Prairie apparently experienced something of a building boom around the turn of the last century, as captured in this photograph. The row of buildings shown here include, from left to right, A.B. Whittington's general store and post office, Henry Glaze's house, another store, and a hotel. Whittington's store was a local landmark for many years. (Courtesy of Pine Prairie Village Hall.)

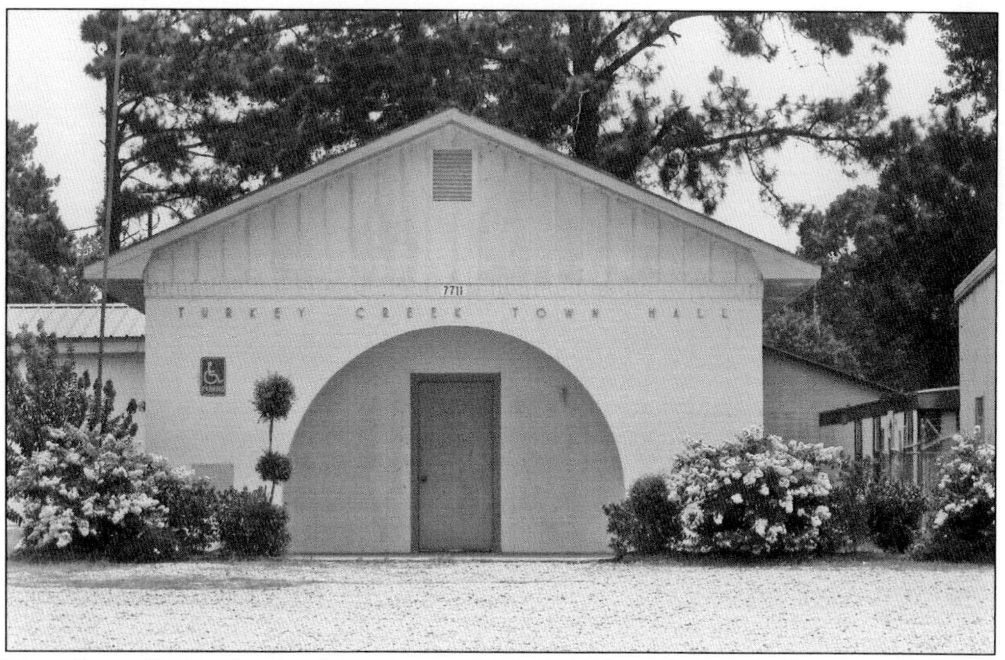

The village of Turkey Creek is located in northern Evangeline Parish, on the stream of the same name. At one time it was a center of the logging industry, with several sawmills located in the woods surrounding the town. It had an elementary school as early as 1845 and a college in the late 1870s. (Courtesy of Center for Louisiana Studies, UL Lafayette.)

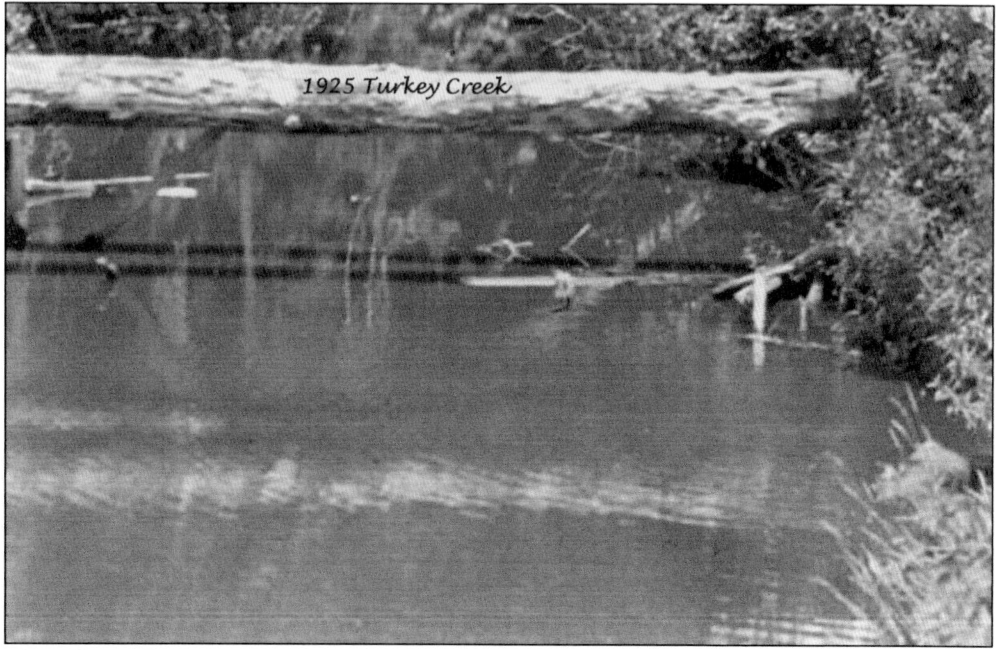

The village of Turkey Creek is located near the stream of the same name. The creek may have gotten its name because the first settlers found an abundance of game along its banks, or because it has three branches that spread out like a turkey's foot. The stream is pictured here in 1925. (Courtesy of Richard Deshotel.)

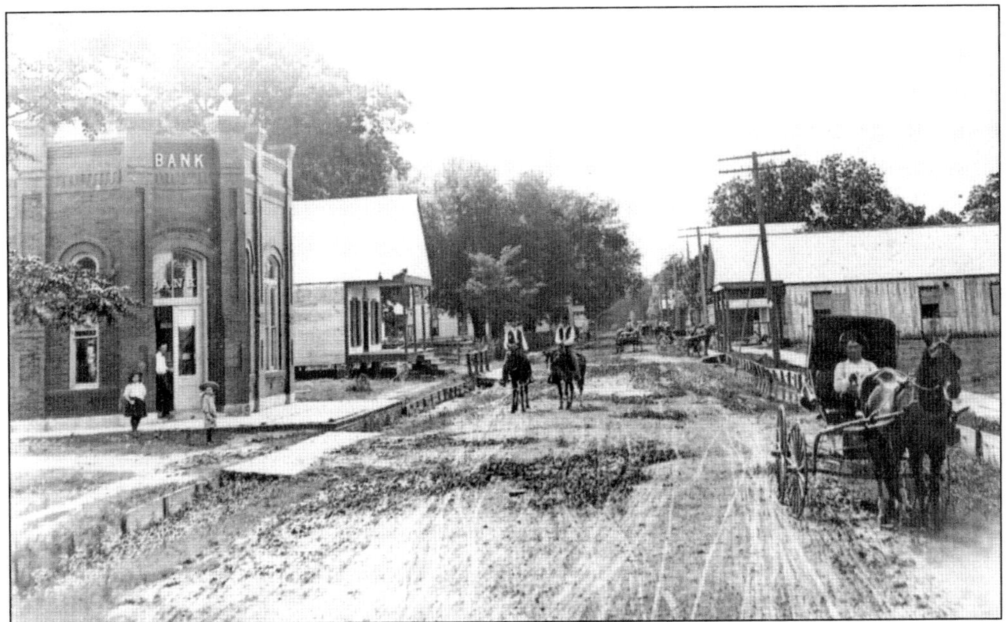

Ville Platte's Main Street in 1905 was still unpaved, but it was showing signs of progress. The Bank of Ville Platte (left) proudly occupies the first brick building in town. Standing in the doorway is Ulysse Lafleur. On horseback are its first president, Rene L. Derouen (left), and Louis Marius Coreil. The girls near the bank are Belle Stromer (left) and Henrietta Lebas. Driving the buggy is Remi Ardoin. (Courtesy of Pam McGee.)

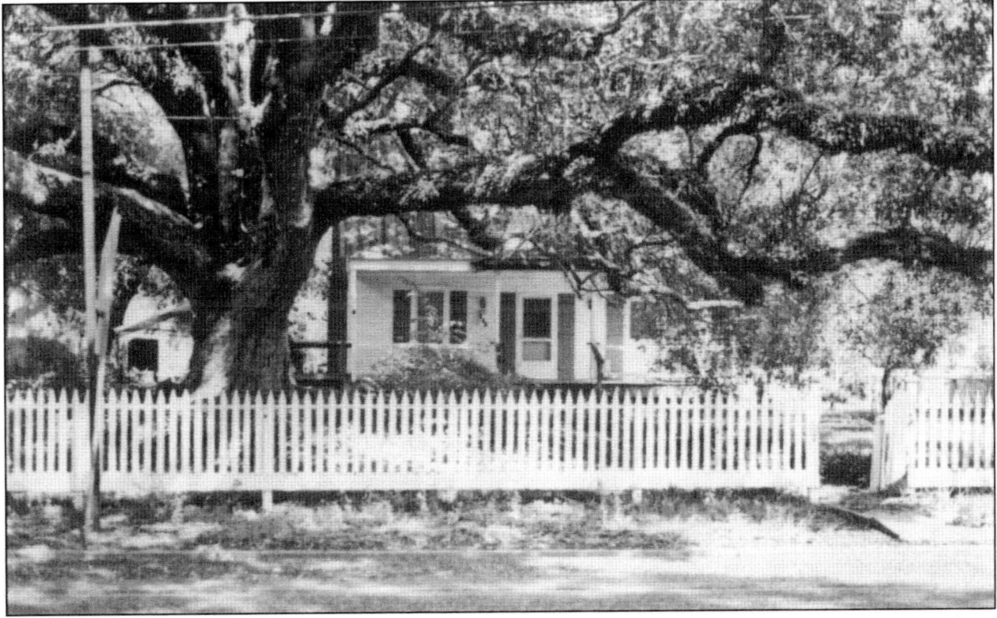

The Jean Marie Laran House in Ville Platte is one of the few buildings in Evangeline Parish to be listed in the National Register of Historic Places. The single-story raised cottage was built in 1883 by Jean Marie Laran, a carpenter who had emigrated from France. The house faces Main Street and stands across from Sacred Heart Catholic Church. For several years it housed the local historical museum. (Courtesy of Jean Kiesel.)

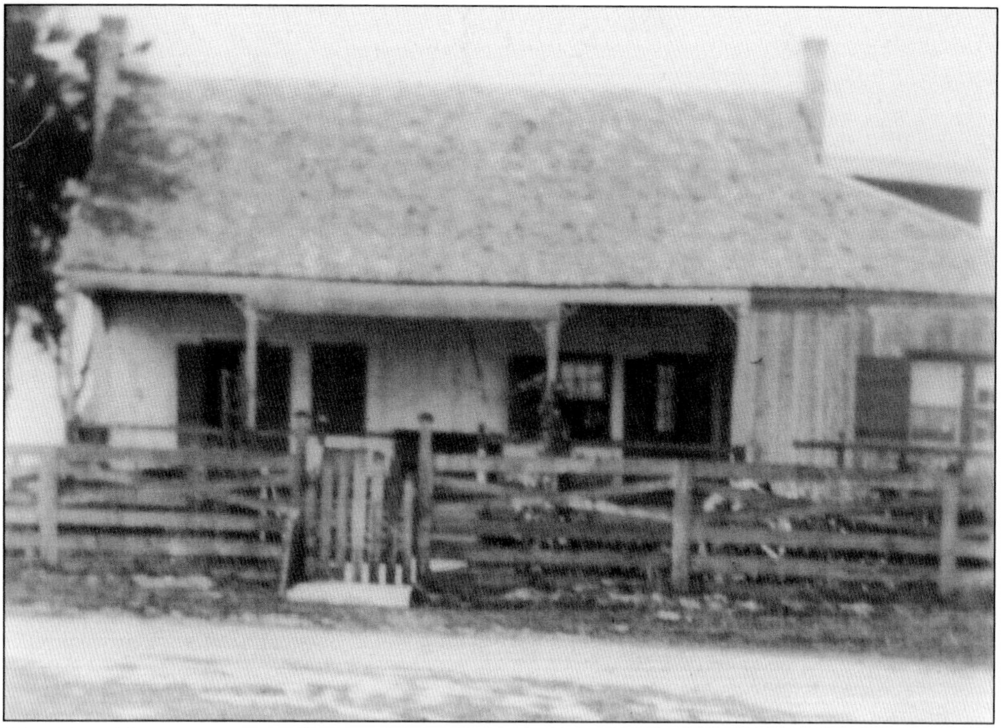

The Coreil house was initially located on Main Street in Ville Platte before it was moved to Evangeline Drive. Built by Barthelemy Marius Coreil, the founder of the Coreil family in Evangeline Parish, the home was 36 feet square. Once it was at its final location, the family added on to the house. Part of it is still used as a residence today. (Courtesy of Lynn Landreneau.)

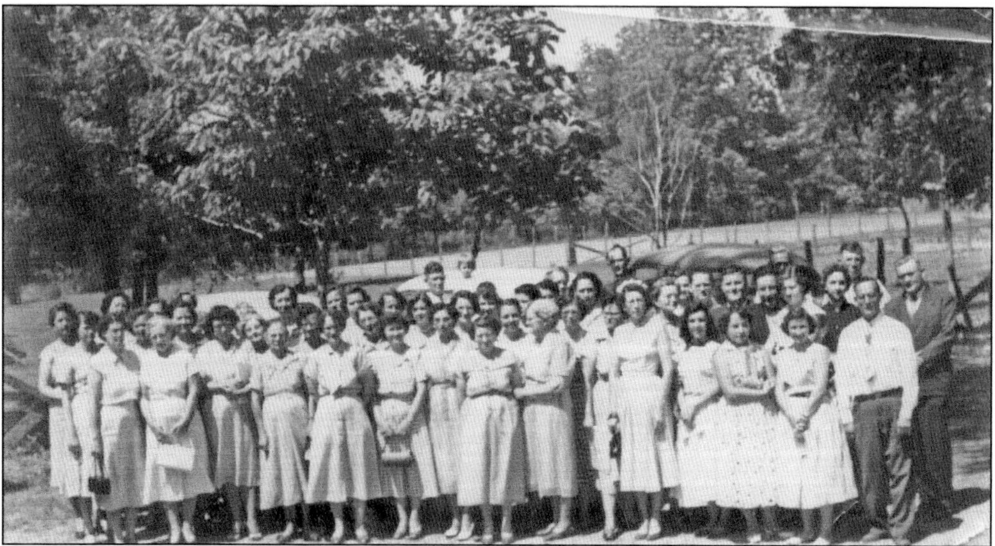

Calvary Baptist Church in Bayou Chicot was the first Baptist church established west of the Mississippi River, and it remains an important center of the community today. Shown here are participants in a Training Union Improvement Clinic in the late 1950s. Baptist Training Unions offered instruction to members of all ages in the history and beliefs of the Baptist Church. (Courtesy of Merlyn Yielding.)

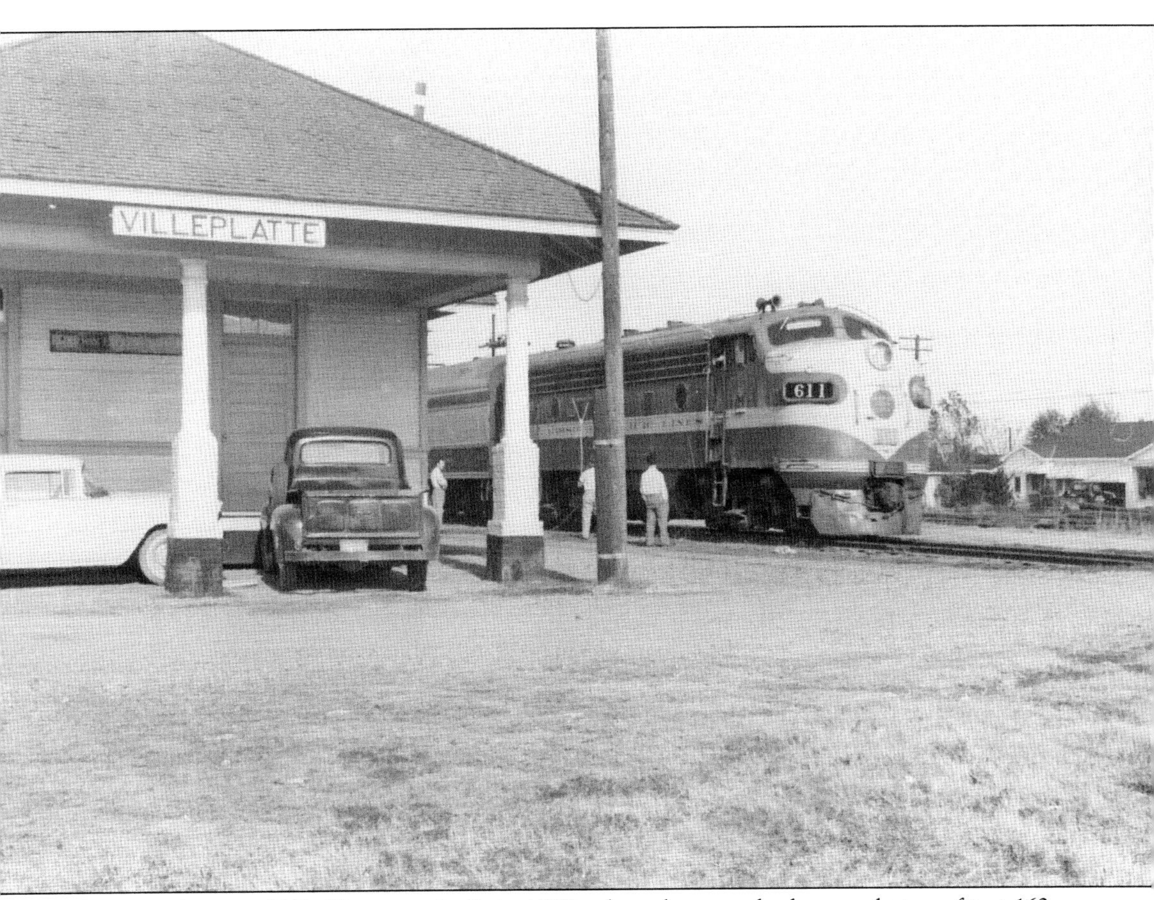

The train depot in Ville Platte was built in 1908, when the town had a population of just 163. The Texas & Pacific Railroad offered daily passenger service to Bunkie, leaving in the morning, and to Eunice in the evening. From those points, travelers could catch other trains to Alexandria, New Orleans, or Houston. The Texas & Pacific discontinued passenger service in 1931. More important, the railroad provided transportation for agricultural products, particularly cotton, to wider markets. The Texas & Pacific was acquired by the Missouri Pacific Railroad, which is now part of the Union Pacific Railroad. (Courtesy of *Ville Platte Gazette*.)

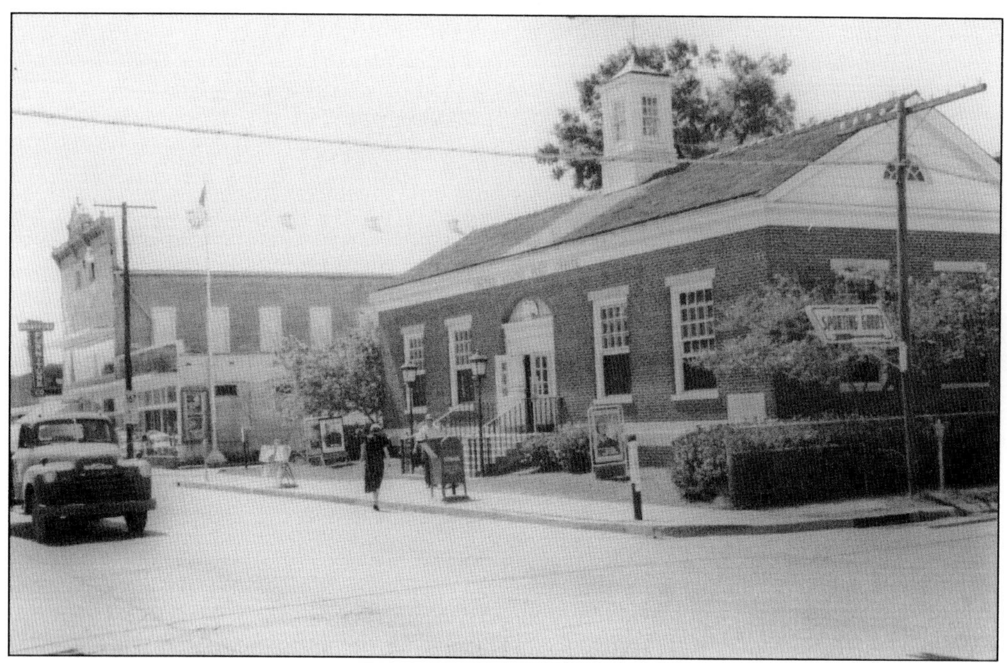

This building on Main and South Coreil Streets in Ville Platte has served several important functions in its time. First built as the post office in 1937, it was later used as the city hall, then was occupied by the chamber of commerce. Most recently, it has housed the Evangeline Parish Library's main branch. (Courtesy of *Ville Platte Gazette*.)

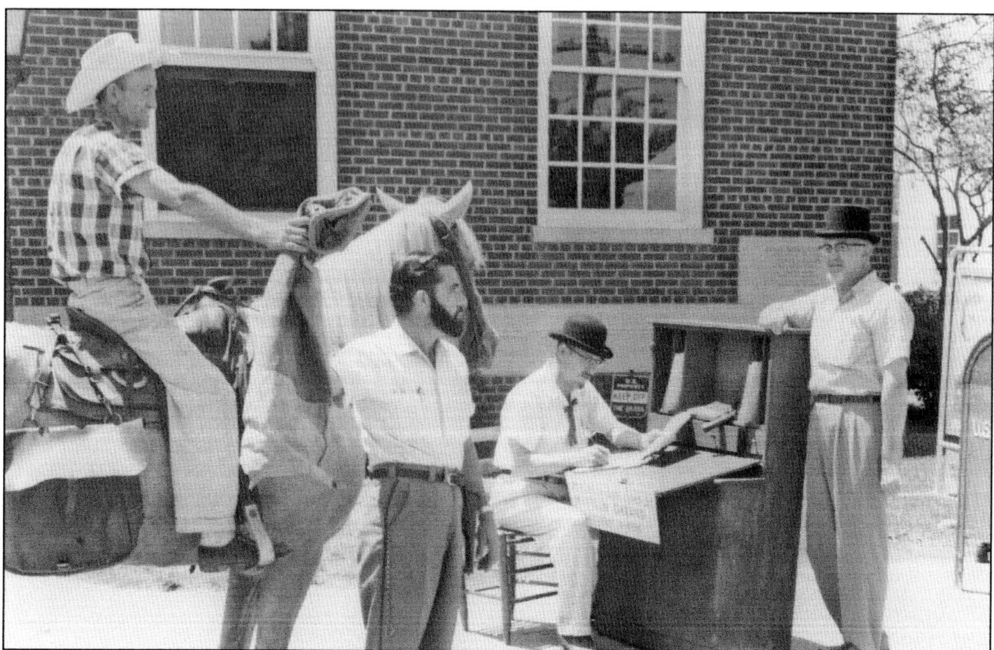

As part of Ville Platte's centennial celebration in 1958, some of Les Braves Barbes reenacted a postal delivery from 1858, when mail was carried by horseback. The sign on the desk indicates that it was used for post office business by Marcellin Garand, the founder of Ville Platte, who was also the postmaster in 1858. (Courtesy of Kathleen Deville Godchaux and Pam McGee.)

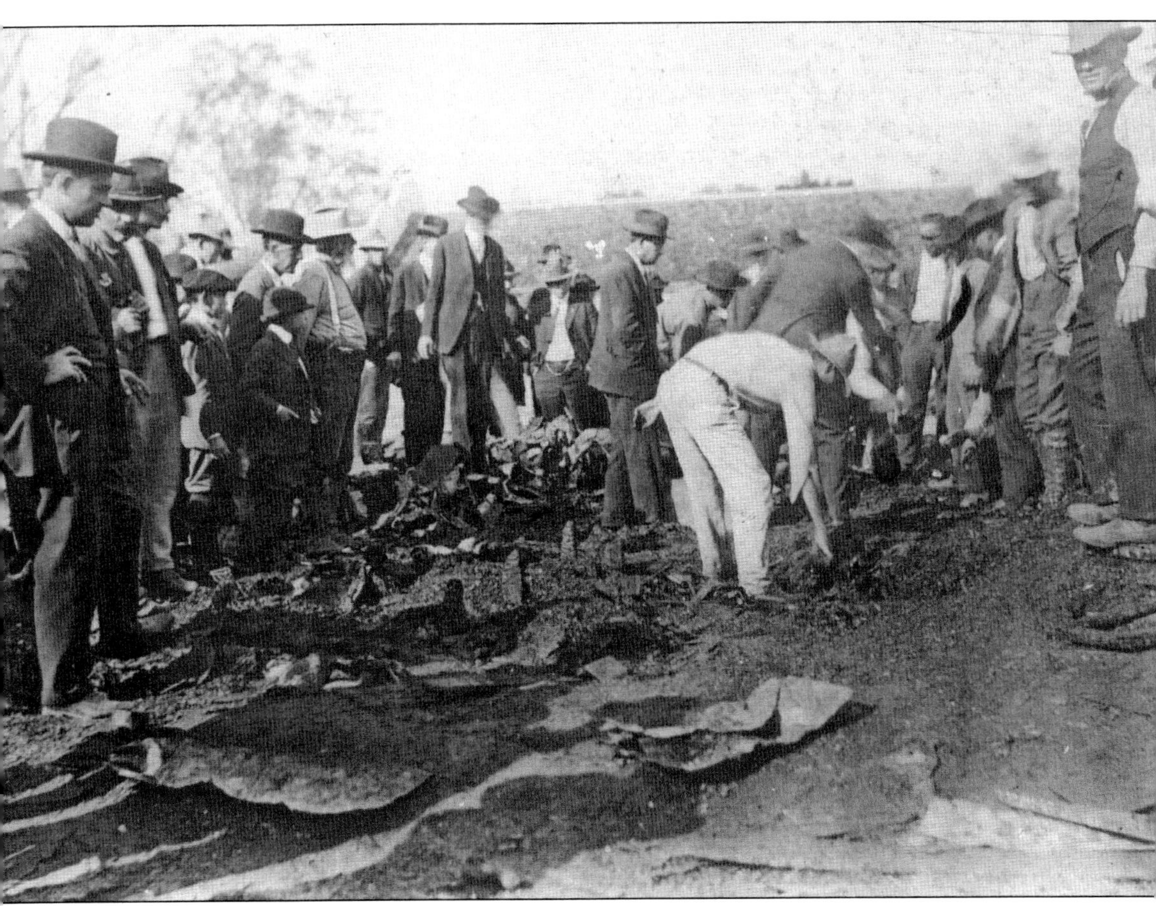

On the evening of November 22, 1919, about 150 men, women, and children were attending a fais-do-do in Goose Phillips's dancehall above Ardoin's picture show in Ville Platte when a fire broke out in Duffy Martin's coffeehouse next door. The fire spread quickly through the wooden structures. When the flames reached the dancehall, the panic-stricken crowd tried to flee down the narrow staircase, only to be trapped at the bottom, where the door opened inward. Imagine the horror on both sides of that door, as rescuers could touch those inside but could not get them out. Stories were told of babies being passed overhead and out the door, and of individuals being rescued by the superhuman efforts of their loved ones. Sadly, many could have saved themselves if they had turned around and gone out the windows of the dancehall, but in their panic, all they could think of was the staircase. The blaze claimed the lives of 28 people. Here, townspeople examine the ruins the next day, still in shock from the tragedy. (Courtesy of Joyce Coreil.)

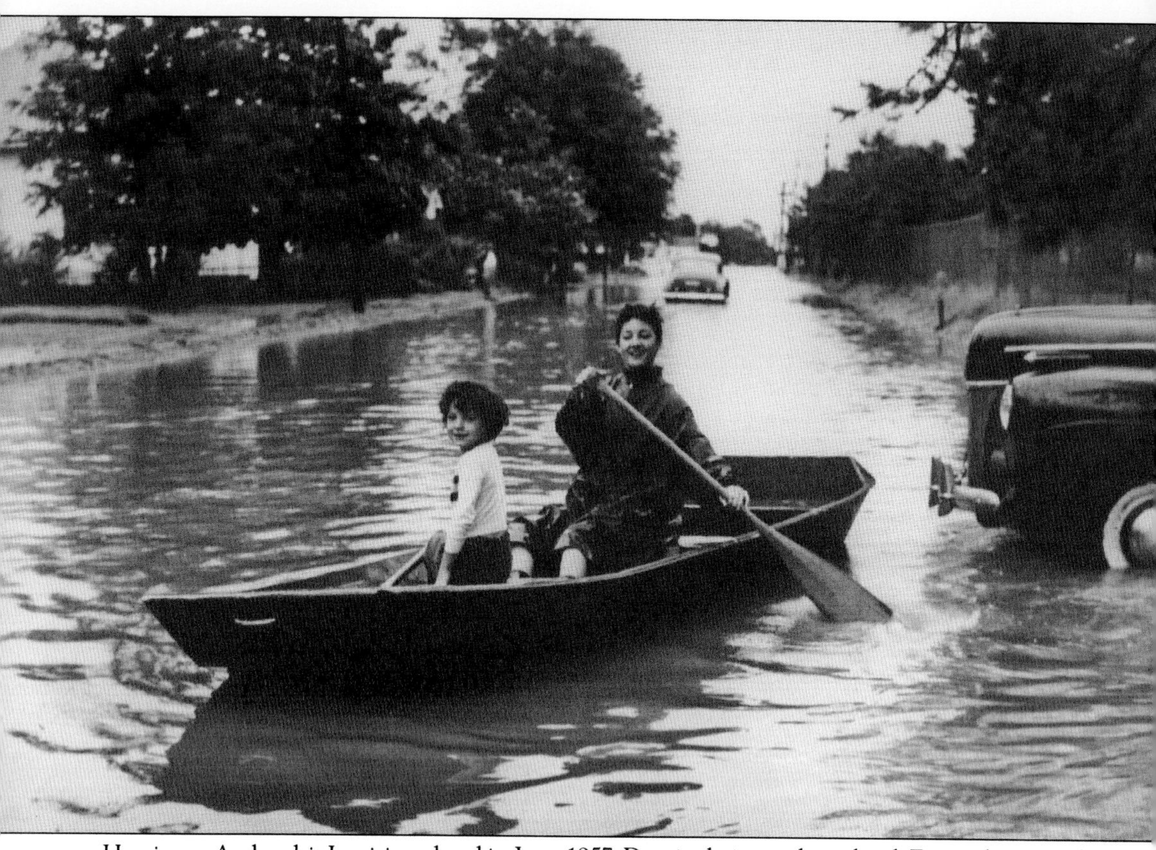

Hurricane Audrey hit Louisiana hard in June 1957. Despite being miles inland, Evangeline Parish was affected, too. The hurricane dumped 10.63 inches of rain on Basile and knocked out power in Ville Platte for two weeks. Ville Platte received enough rainfall to make boats an attractive option for getting around, as these two residents demonstrate. (Courtesy of Ville Platte City Hall.)

Two

People

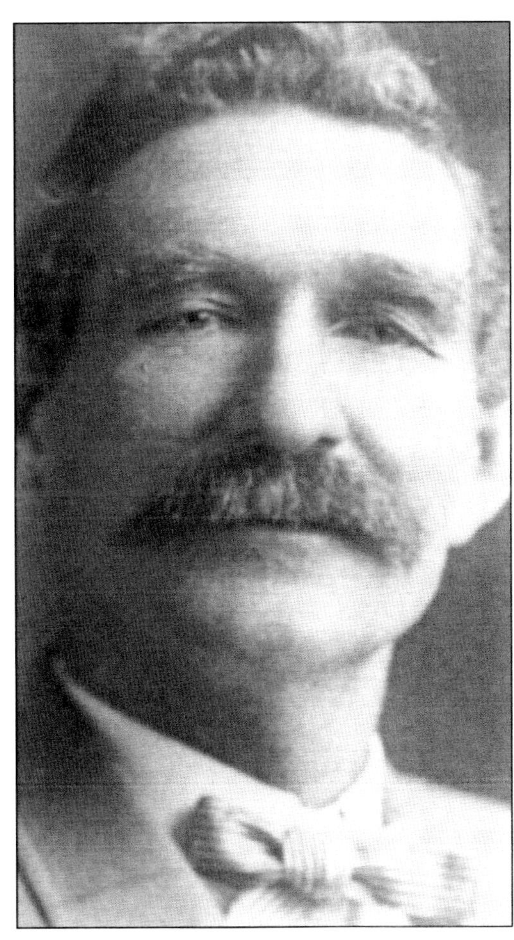

The father of Evangeline Parish, Paulin L. Fontenot, was born in 1864, the son of Jean Batiste Larose Fontenot. A farmer, merchant, and civic leader, he served 12 years on the St. Landry School Board before being elected to the state legislature. His first act as legislator was to introduce a bill to create Evangeline Parish. He later served as its first sheriff. (Courtesy of Evangeline Parish Sheriff's Department.)

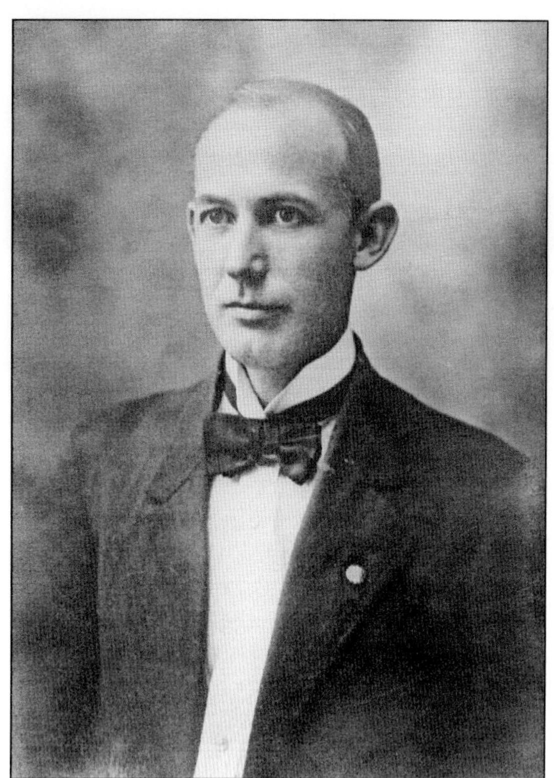

E.E. Ortego was the father of public education in Evangeline Parish. He was principal of the Evangeline Academy from 1892 to 1914 and was active in the movement to create Evangeline Parish. He became the first superintendent of schools in 1910, serving until June 1921. Under his leadership the number of schools, teachers, and students grew, and the first brick school buildings were constructed. (Courtesy of Evangeline Parish School Board.)

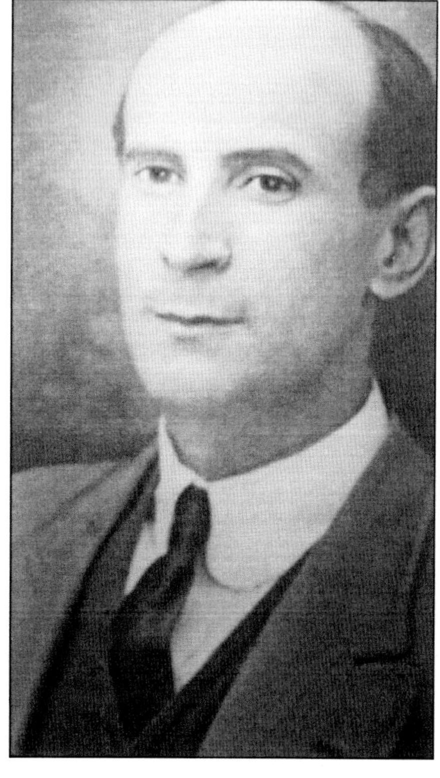

Olivrel E. "O.E." Guillory was a merchant in Ville Platte in 1908 when he became involved in the movement to create Evangeline Parish. Along with Paulin Fontenot, William Clark, and Rene DeRouen, he campaigned tirelessly on the issue. As a result of his influence, he was named the parish's first clerk of court. As a young man he fought in the Spanish-American War. (Courtesy of Evangeline Parish Clerk of Court.)

Marcellin Garand is considered the founder of Ville Platte. A former adjutant major in the French army under Napoleon, he settled here in 1824. Garand obtained two lots on the road between Opelousas and Alexandria, on what is now the south side of Ville Platte's Main Street. There he operated a store, post office, and tavern. (Courtesy of Ville Platte City Hall.)

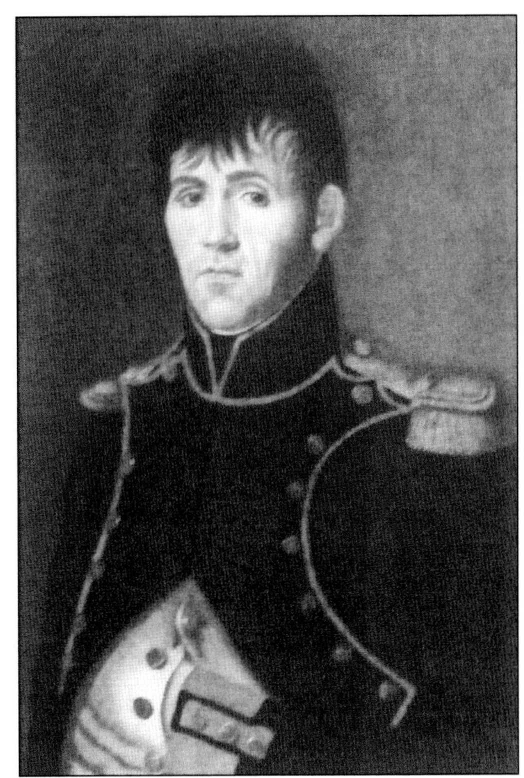

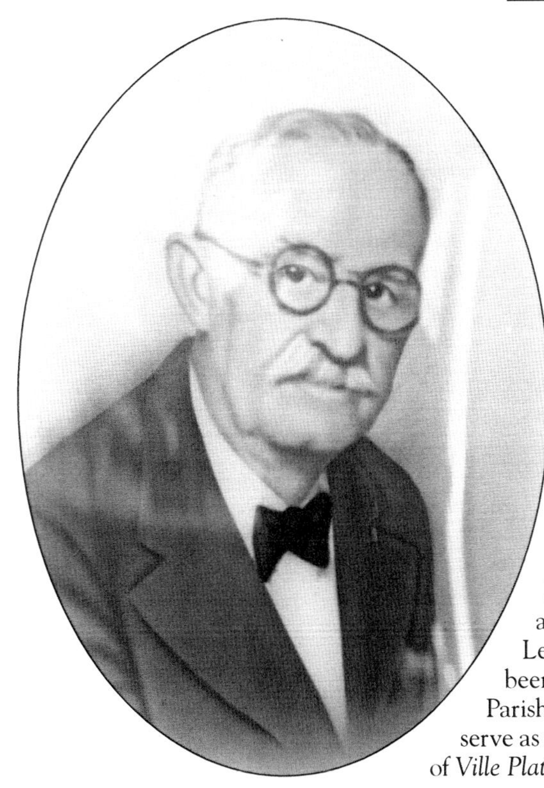

Until the charter was amended in 1912, Ville Platte did not have a mayor. It was governed by a council of five members. The first mayor was Leon Demourelle, a local businessman who had been active in the campaign to create Evangeline Parish. He served two terms as mayor and went on to serve as assistant clerk of court for 22 years. (Courtesy of *Ville Platte Gazette*.)

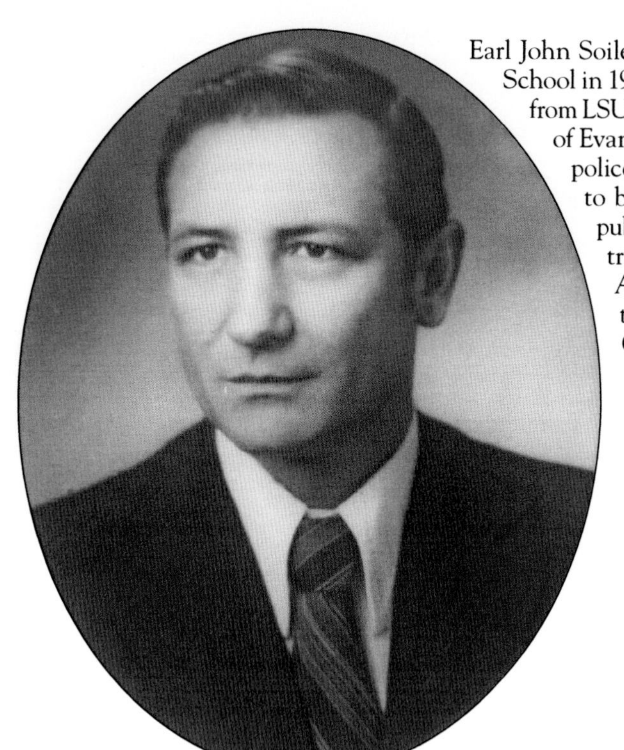

Earl John Soileau graduated from Ville Platte High School in 1950 and received a degree in education from LSU. He served as assistant superintendent of Evangeline Parish schools and was on the police jury from 1968 to 1980. He worked to build the new courthouse and other public buildings, the industrial park, the trade school, Crooked Creek Recreation Area, and drainage projects throughout the parish. (Courtesy of *Ville Platte Gazette*.)

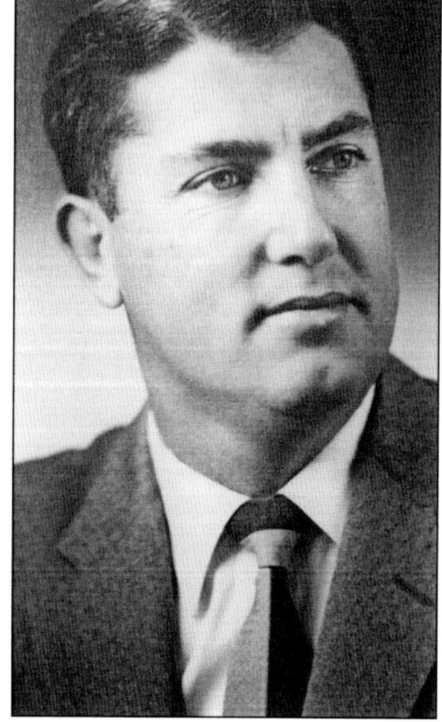

After graduating from Ville Platte High School, Walter Lee served in the US Navy for five years during World War II, mostly on the West Coast and in the South Pacific. In 1955, he was elected clerk of court of Evangeline Parish and remained in office until 2011. In 2009, he was inducted into the Louisiana Political Museum & Hall of Fame in Winnfield, Louisiana. (Courtesy of *Ville Platte Gazette*.)

George L. Fontenot served one term as mayor of Ville Platte (1929–1933). He received his law degree from Louisiana State University and served overseas during World War I. During his administration, Ville Platte's Main Street was paved for the first time. The state highway department paid for the center eighteen feet, while property owners were assessed for the remaining six feet to the sidewalks. (Courtesy of *Ville Platte Gazette*.)

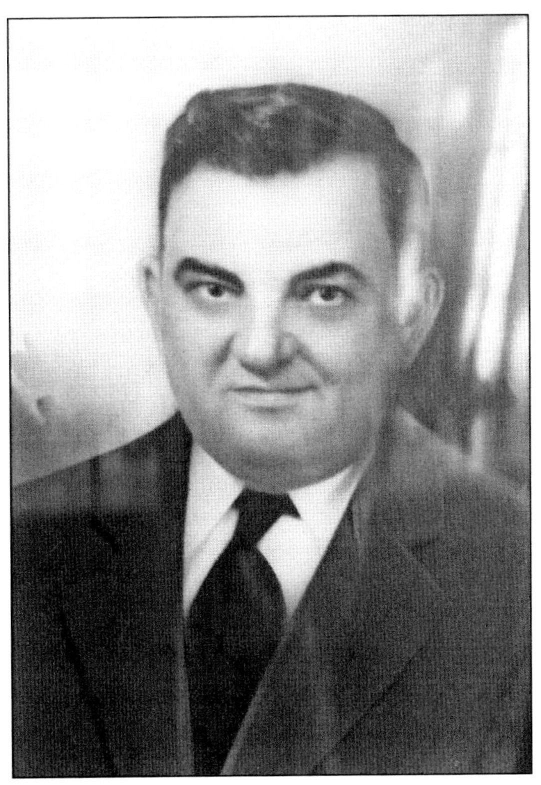

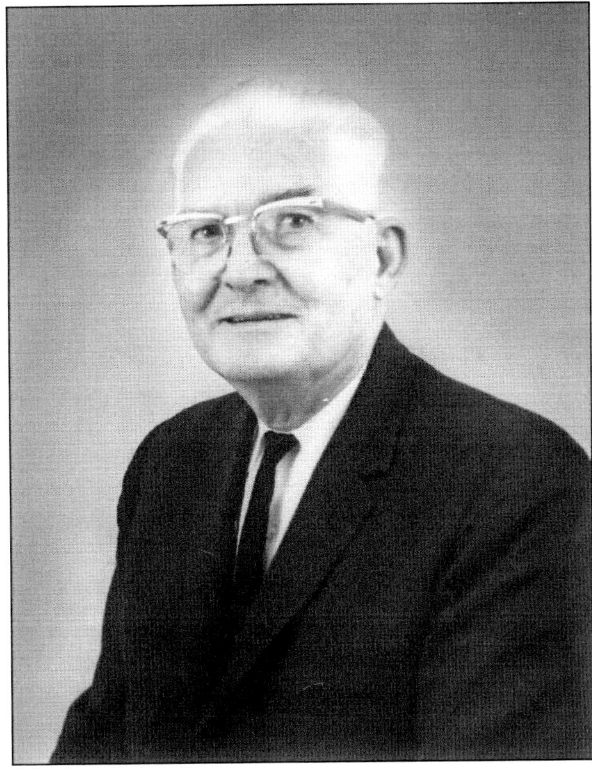

After he retired from his career as an accountant, J. Edwin Elliott served as mayor of Pine Prairie from 1961 to 1972. The street that runs in front of the town hall and Prairie Manor Nursing Home was named in his honor. (Courtesy of Pine Prairie Village Hall.)

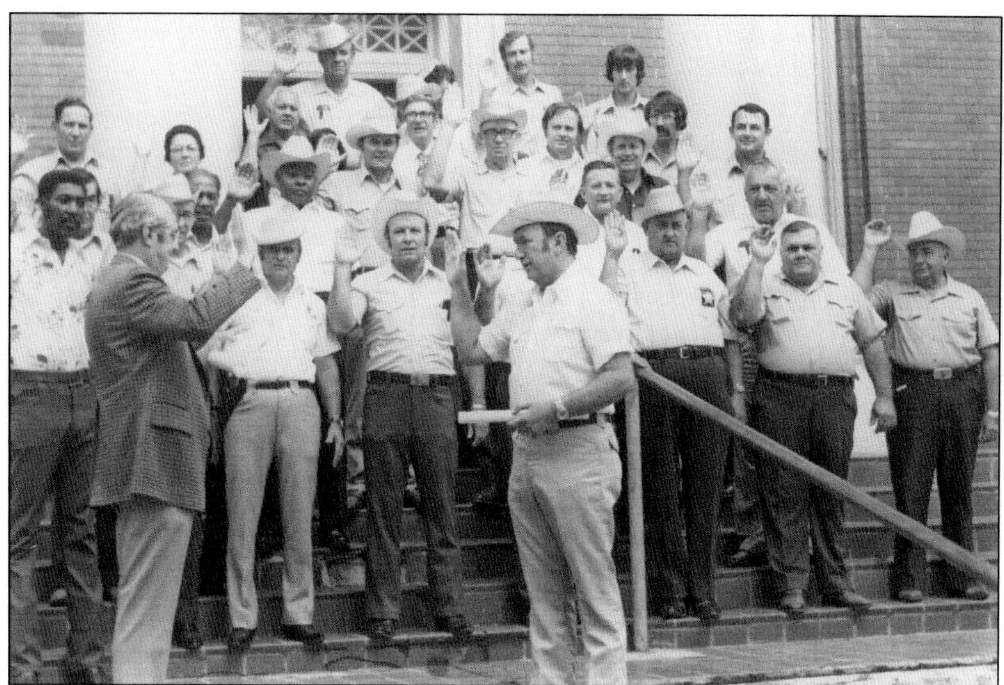

Elin Pitre (foreground, right) served as sheriff of Evangeline Parish from 1964 to 1980. Here, he and his deputies are being sworn in by Judge Burton Foret (foreground, left) on the steps of the old courthouse. The deputies include (first row) Jasper Manuel, fourth from left; Aaron Fuselier, third from right; and Wendy Johnson, far right; (second row) Carlton Jack, third from left; (third row) Ena Fontenot, second from left; and Floyd Soileau, second from right; (fourth row) L.D. Verette, to the right of the pillar; and Ken Webb, second from right. (Courtesy of *Ville Platte Gazette*.)

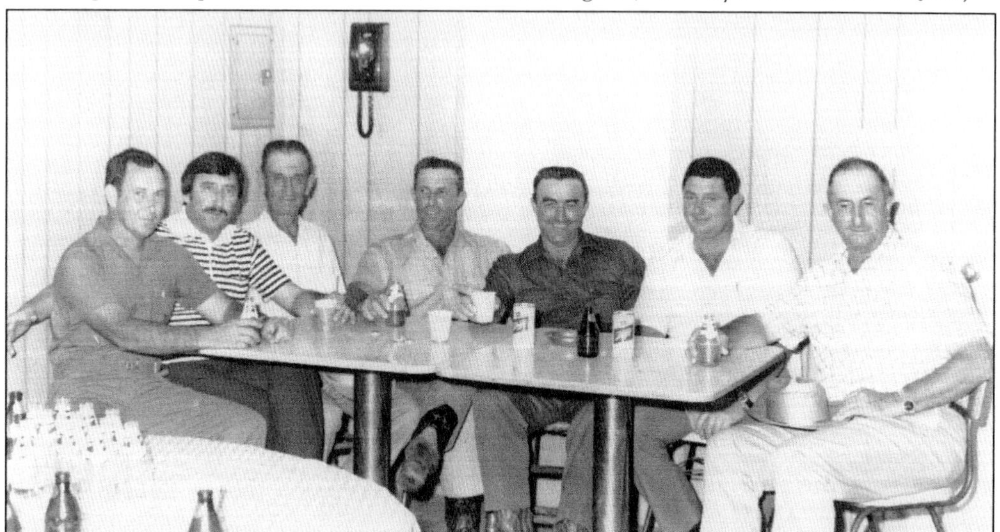

Gerald and Hassa Fontenot hosted political suppers in their outdoor kitchen in Belaire Cove in the 1970s. The events offered their favorite candidates an opportunity to meet with their neighbors. Pictured here are, from left to right, D.L. Fontenot, B.J. Fontenot, Hammick Lafleur, Jessie Lee Chapman, Andrew Chapman, L.J. Chapman, and Mayo Chapman. (Courtesy of *Ville Platte Gazette*.)

Floyd R. Soileau began working as a deputy for Sheriff Elin Pitre in 1964. After completing law enforcement training at Louisiana State University in Eunice, he served as chief deputy and later as chief detective under Sheriffs Pitre and Ramson K. Vidrine. He was elected sheriff in 1983 and remained in office until 1990. (Courtesy of Evangeline Parish Sheriff's Office.)

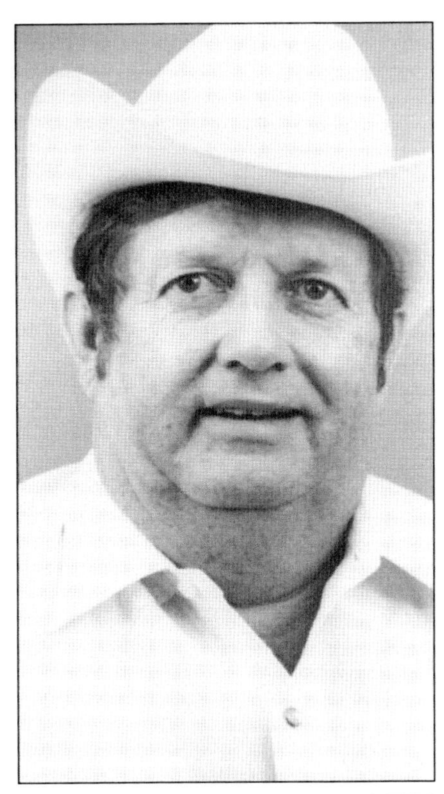

In 1954, *Gazette* publisher Jules Ashlock contacted Marcellin Garand's family in France and arranged for them to donate his portrait to the city. It was formally unveiled during the Cotton Festival. Shown here are, from left to right, Councilman Ellus Foret, Councilman Dr. Reed Fontenot, Mayor Harvey Lebas, Ashlock, Councilman Leroy Veillon, and Councilman Benny Fontenot. Today the portrait hangs in the city council chamber in city hall. (Courtesy of Pam McGee.)

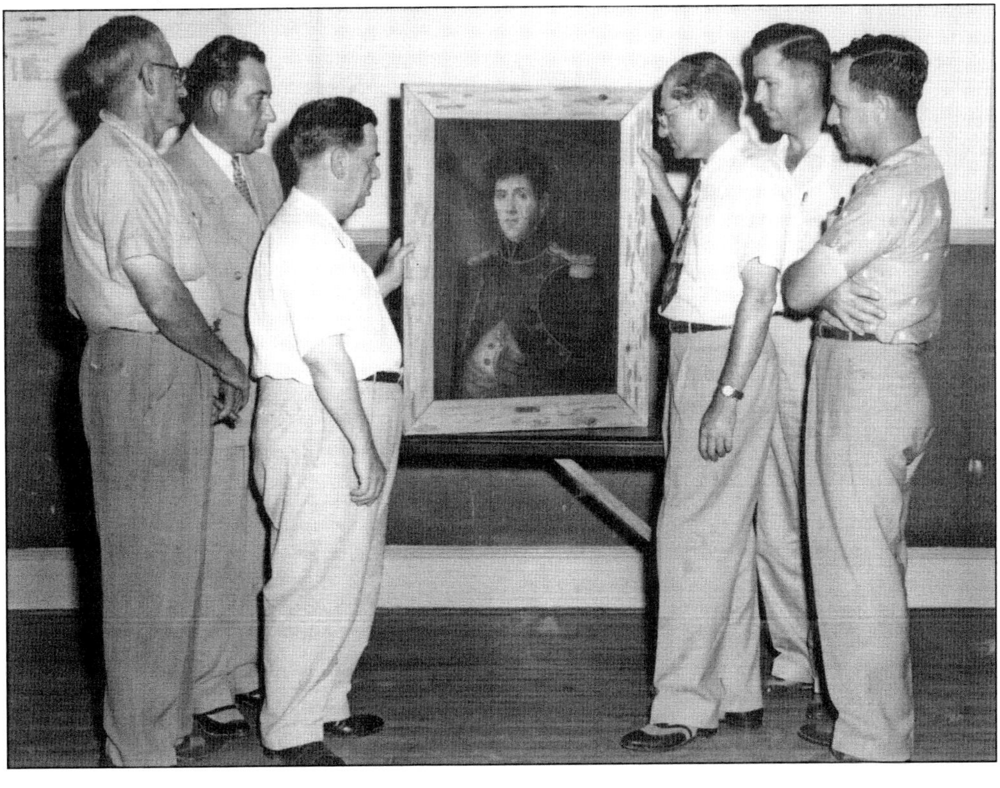

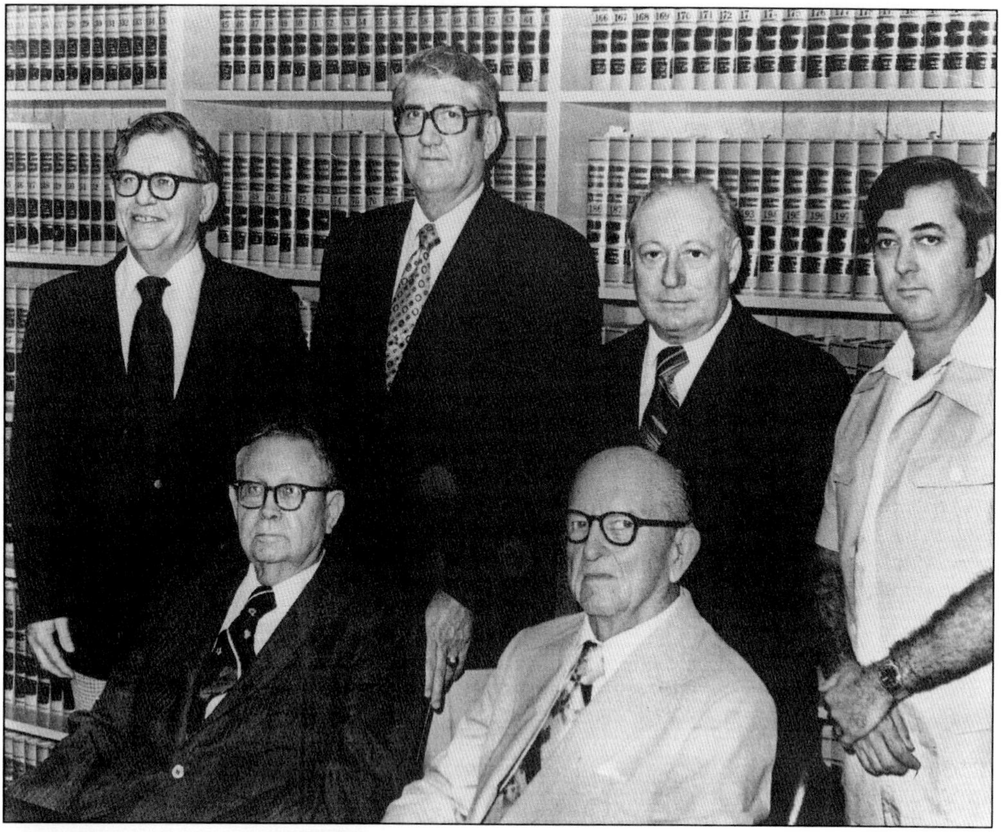

A group of Evangeline Parish jurists gathered with retired Louisiana Supreme Court chief justice J.B. Fournet around 1977. Shown here are, from left to right, (seated) J. Cleveland Frugé, Third Circuit Court of Appeals; and Fournet; (standing) Albert Tate Jr., associate justice of the Louisiana Supreme Court; J. Burton Foret, Third Circuit Court of Appeals; and Joseph E. Coreil and Wendel Fuselier, Ville Platte City Court. (Courtesy of Wendel Fuselier.)

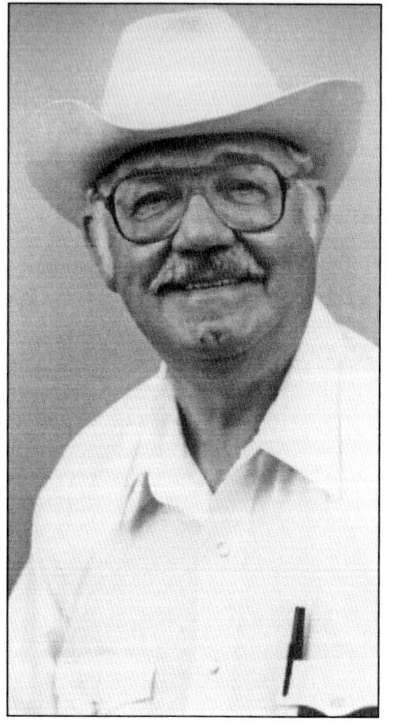

Ramson K. Vidrine wore many hats during his life: physician, politician, and law enforcement official. He grew up in Point Blue, graduated from Tulane Medical School, and practiced medicine in Ville Platte. He served as state senator, state health inspector, and Evangeline Parish coroner before being elected sheriff in 1980. He served one term before his life ended at age 53. (Courtesy of Evangeline Parish Sheriff's Office.)

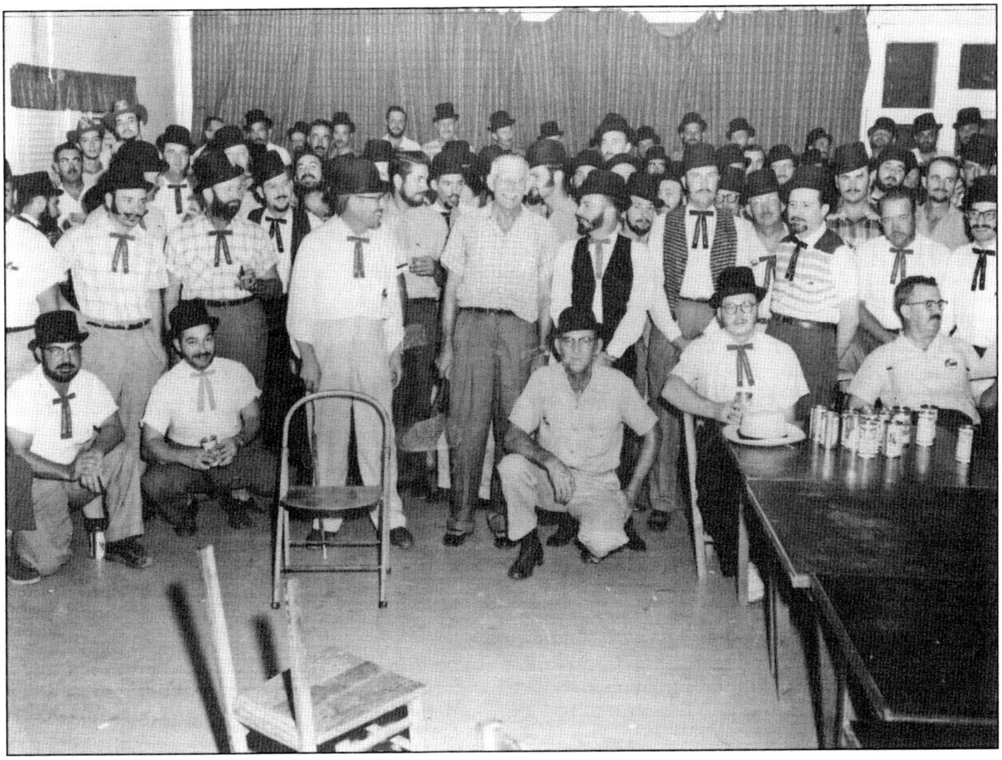

In 1958, Ville Platte celebrated the centennial of its incorporation. As part of the festivities, over 200 men grew beards. Calling themselves "Les Braves Barbes" and sporting bowler hats and bow ties in addition to their facial hair, they made frequent public appearances to promote centennial events. This group includes many prominent citizens of Ville Platte, but they cannot easily be identified behind all the hair! (Courtesy of Pam McGee.)

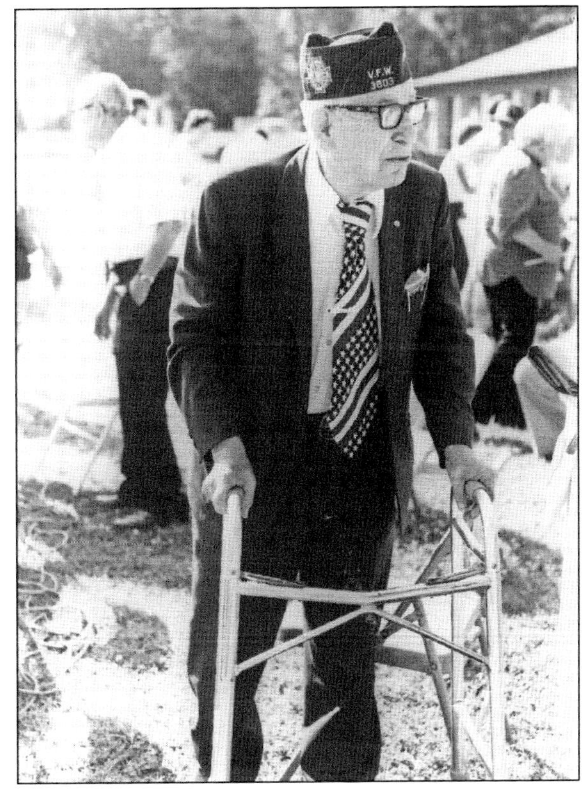

Dallas Deville was drafted into military service during World War II. He served in the Army Postal Service, spending 18 months in the European theater of operations. After his discharge, he taught school, then worked for the US Postal Service for 33 years. Extremely active in veterans' affairs, he is shown here enjoying the Veterans Day parade in 1983. (Courtesy of Kathleen Deville Godchaux.)

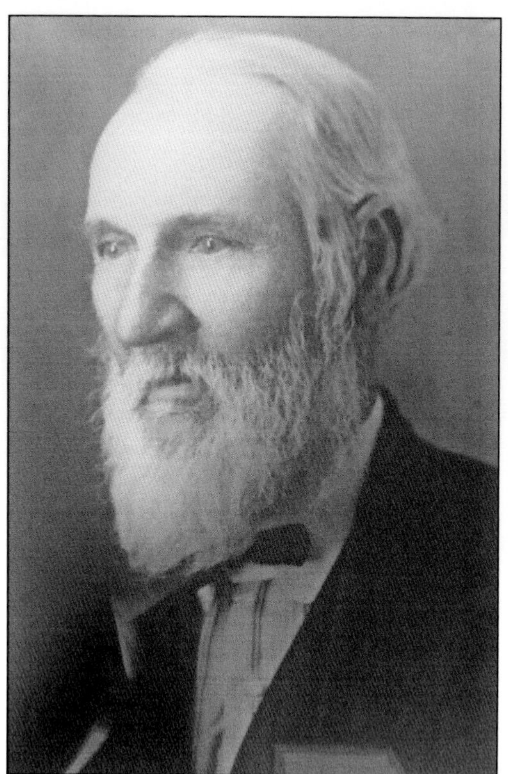

Alcin Vidrine was born on October 21, 1845, on his father's plantation. At the age of 16, he enlisted at Ville Platte in the Big Cane Rifles, Company K of the 16th Louisiana Regiment. He participated in the Battle of Shiloh, one of the bloodiest battles in American history. Vidrine was captured twice and taken for dead, but he survived and returned home after the Civil War. (Courtesy of Kathleen Deville Godchaux.)

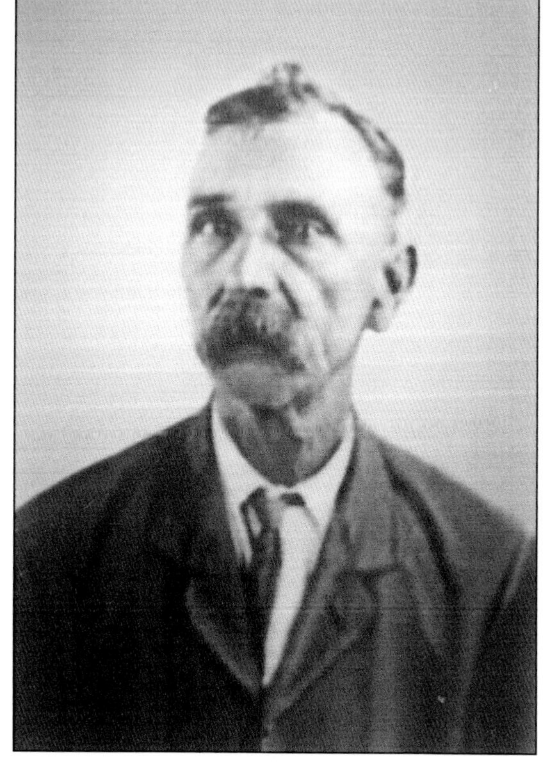

Pierre Azelien Manuel of Belaire Cove was 22 when he enlisted in the 6th Louisiana Infantry in 1862. He fought under Stonewall Jackson and was taken prisoner in 1863. Manuel spent the remainder of the Civil War in Federal prisons before being released on May 5, 1865. According to descendants, he was sent to New Orleans and had to make his own way home from there. (Courtesy of Rollins G. Fontenot.)

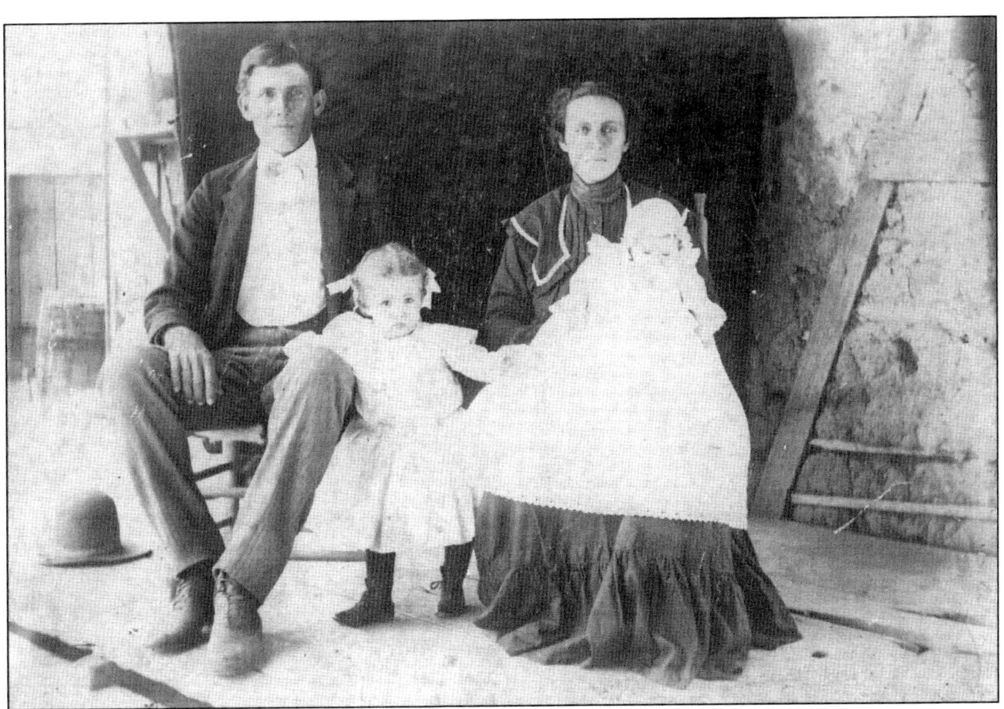

Dubuisson and Florentine Johnson Brunet pose with their daughters Edna (center) and Corinne about 1905. The Brunets farmed near Chataignier for many years, but moved to Lake Charles during the Depression. The wall behind them is bousillage, a mixture of mud and moss over sticks. It was a common building material in south Louisiana, especially on the prairies, where wood was scarce. (Courtesy of Deen Fontenot.)

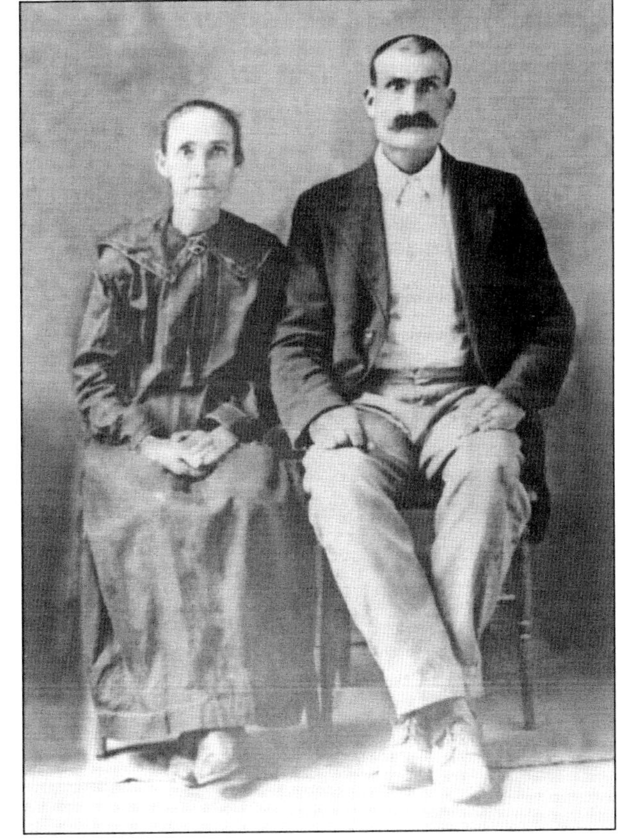

Omer G. Fontenot and Bertha Manuel were married on January 6, 1891, and raised 13 children. Both were from the Belaire Cove area, where they lived out their lives and where many of their descendants remain today. Homer's parents were Theodate Fontenot and Hortence Reed; Bertha's parents were Azelien Manuel, a Civil War veteran, and Alphonsia Soileau. (Courtesy of Rollins G. Fontenot.)

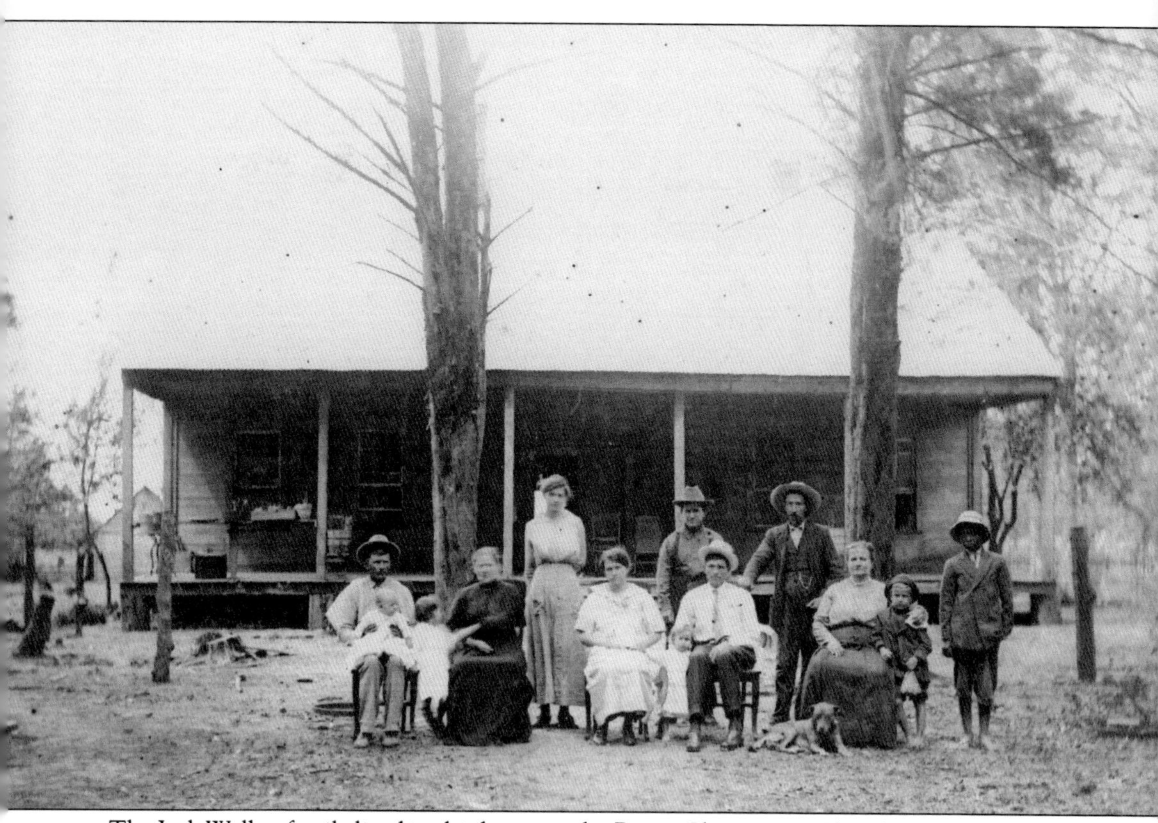

The Jack Walker family lived in this house in the Bayou Chicot area. This photograph must have been taken in the late 1800s, for in 1900 a small room was added to the left side of the house. It was the oldest house in Chicot for many years, standing for over two centuries before it was torn down. Bayou Chicot was the center of English-speaking settlement in Evangeline Parish. The earliest inhabitants came from the Eastern Seaboard shortly after the American Revolution. They were farmers, loggers, and tradesmen. The settlement had closer ties to Rapides Post (present-day Alexandria) to the north, rather than to Opelousas, the parish seat of St. Landry. Over time, though, it became integrated into the fabric of Evangeline Parish. (Courtesy of Jackie Jones.)

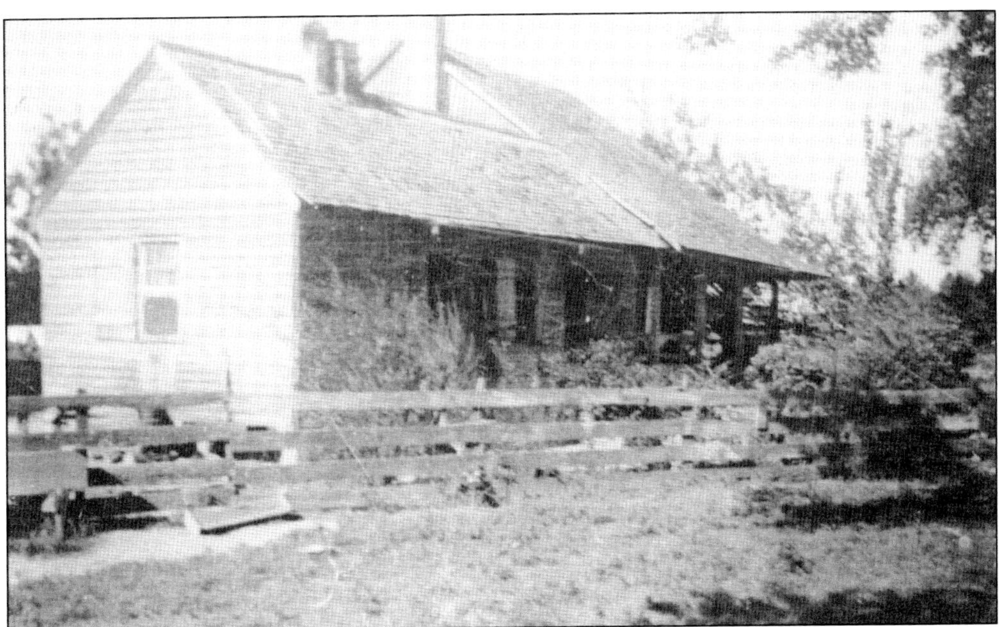

This house in Belaire Cove belonged to Alfred Young and his wife, Ernestine Belaire Fontenot. The family name originally was Lejeune, but an officious census-taker Anglicized it. Alfred, who was born in 1866, farmed about 500 acres, raised cattle, and kept a store. He also served on the Evangeline Parish Police Jury and on the board of the Evangeline Bank. (Courtesy of Warren Lafleur and Elvin Soileau.)

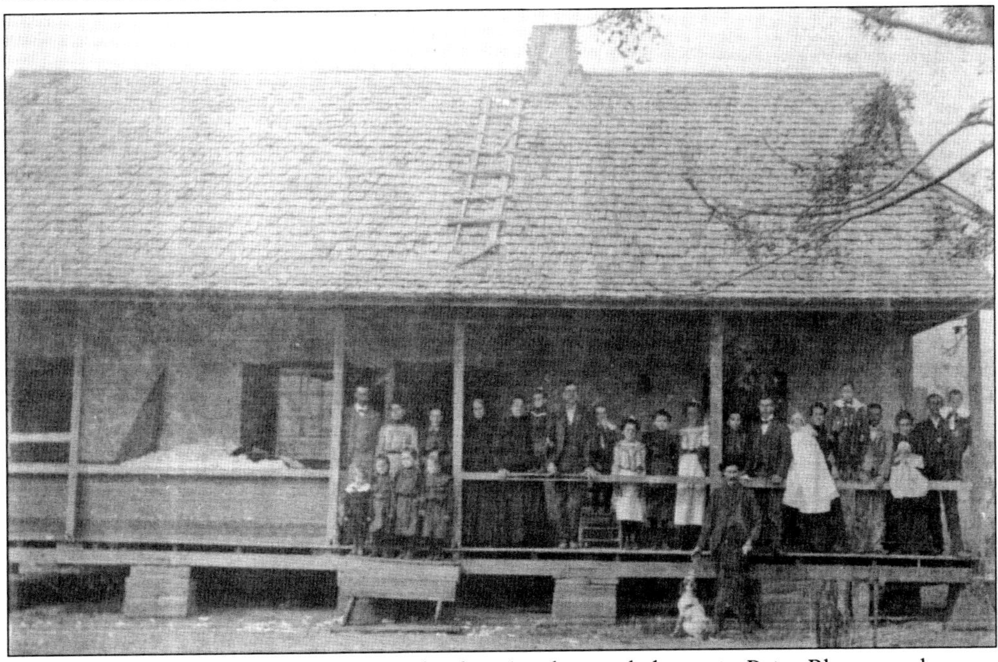

An extended family gathers on the porch of an Acadian-style home in Point Blue near the turn of the last century, possibly after a christening. Note the pile of cotton on the porch. Cotton was damp in the morning, and had to dry before it could be baled. Sometimes it would be spread on the roof, and material would be put on the cotton to help it dry. (Courtesy of J.D. Soileau.)

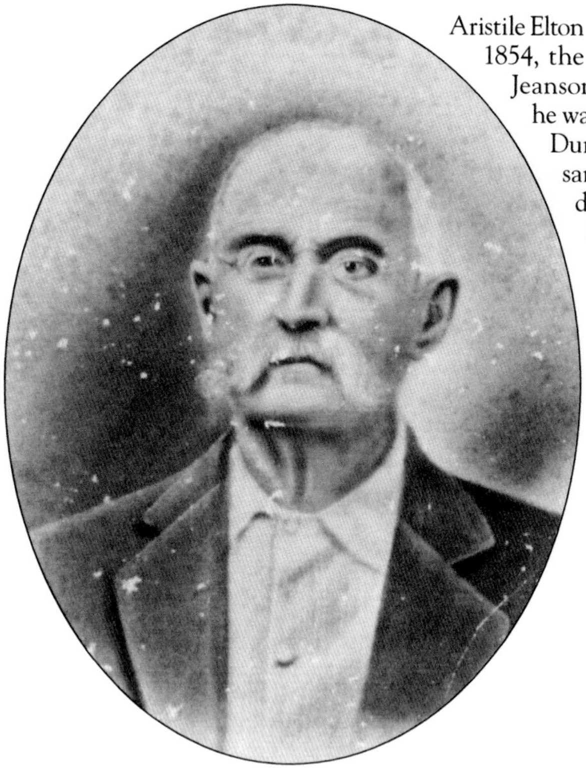

Aristile Elton Buller was born in Pine Prairie in January 1854, the son of Arcadius Buller and Adelaide Jeansonne. Like many of his contemporaries, he was a farmer. Both he and his wife, Martha Durio, claimed to be descended from the same royal house of France. Aristile Buller died on April 15, 1928, in Ville Platte. (Courtesy of Lynn Landreneau.)

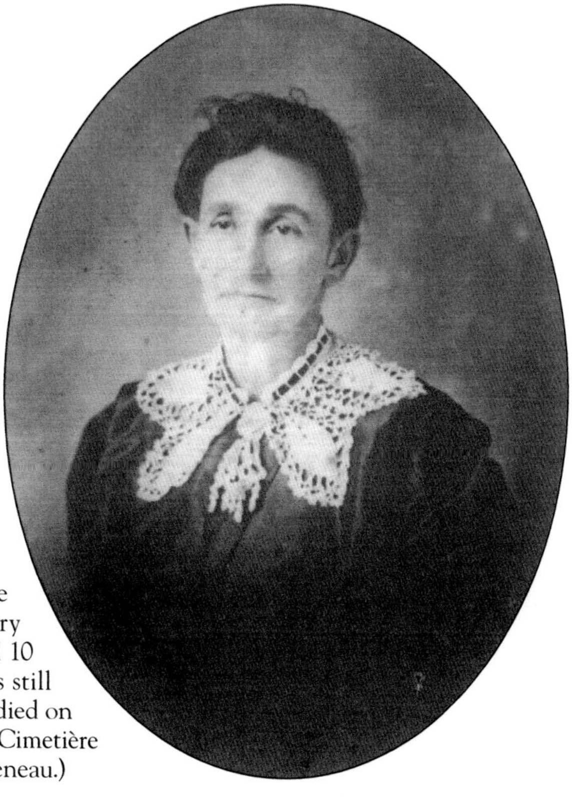

Martha Durio was born on November 11, 1867, in Glenmora, Louisiana, to Simon B. Durio and Alexandrie Deville. She married Aristile Elton Buller on January 25, 1887, in Ville Platte. The couple had 10 children, and many of their descendants still live in Evangeline Parish today. Martha died on August 19, 1939, and is buried in Le Vieux Cimetière in Ville Platte. (Courtesy of Lynn Landreneau.)

Marie Louise Pucheu was the wife of Joseph Maurice Coreil, the mayor of Ville Platte during World War I. They had eight children. One of their sons was Emile "Melo" Coreil, a Ville Platte city judge from the 13th Judicial Court. He never went to law school, and was the last judge to pass the bar exam without doing so. (Courtesy of Lynn Landreneau.)

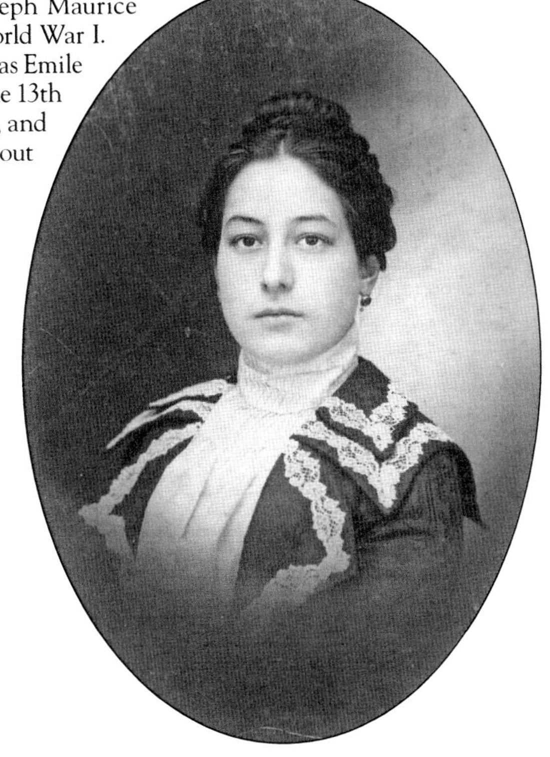

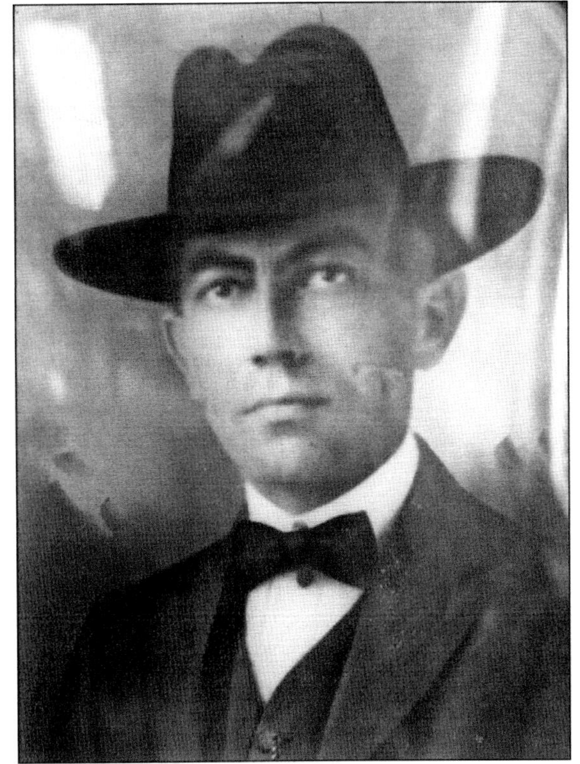

Joseph Maurice Coreil served as mayor of Ville Platte from 1915 to 1920. He was the son of Marius Barthelemy Coreil, a French immigrant who acquired a large fortune raising cattle on the prairies of southwest Louisiana. Joseph also raised cattle, and at various times operated a meat market, a general store, and a restaurant. He died in 1937 and is buried with his wife in le Vieux Cimetière. (Courtesy of Lynn Landreneau.)

Alfred Young (left) and Gustave Fontenot were residents of Belaire Cove. Located between Ville Platte and Washington, Louisiana, Belaire Cove was settled by the family of Joseph Fontenot and Marie Jeanne Brignac. Joseph's *dit* name, or nickname, was Belaire, and his branch of the Fontenot family is known as the Belaire Fontenots. (Courtesy of Warren Lafleur and Elvin Soileau.)

Elodie Young (right) was born on December 27, 1847. She married Francois Belaire Fontenot, one of the Belaire Fontenots, on December 1, 1863. They were first cousins. Their daughter Ernestine (left) was born on September 6, 1873, and she married Hebrard Soileau on December 6, 1887, when she was just 14. This photograph was taken about 1910. (Courtesy of Warren Lafleur and Elvin Soileau.)

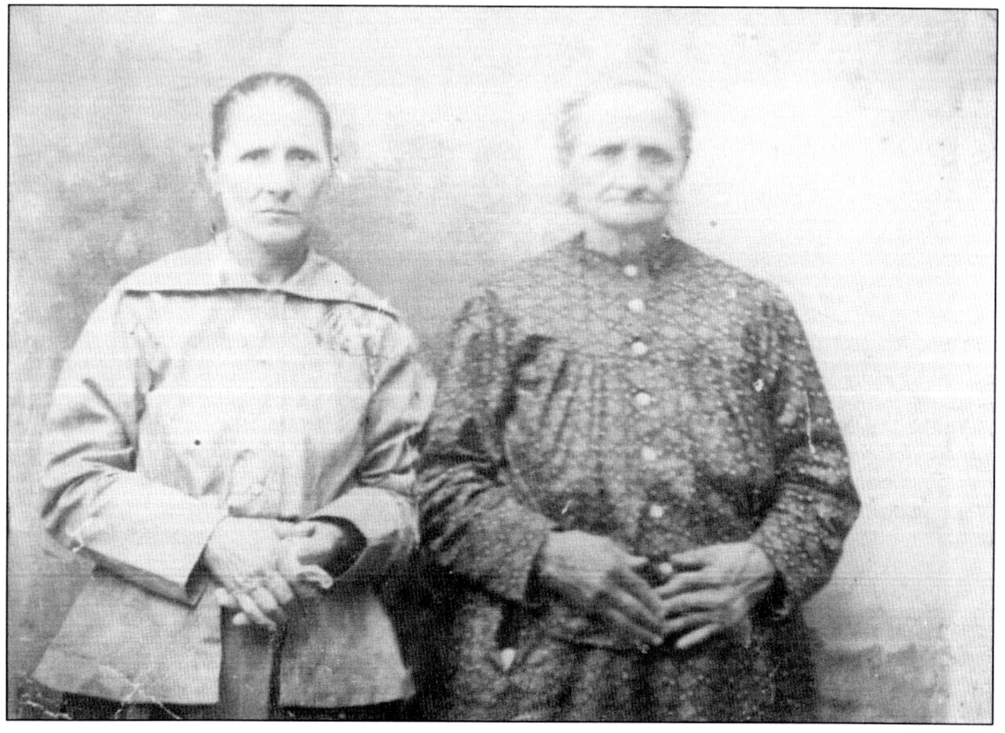

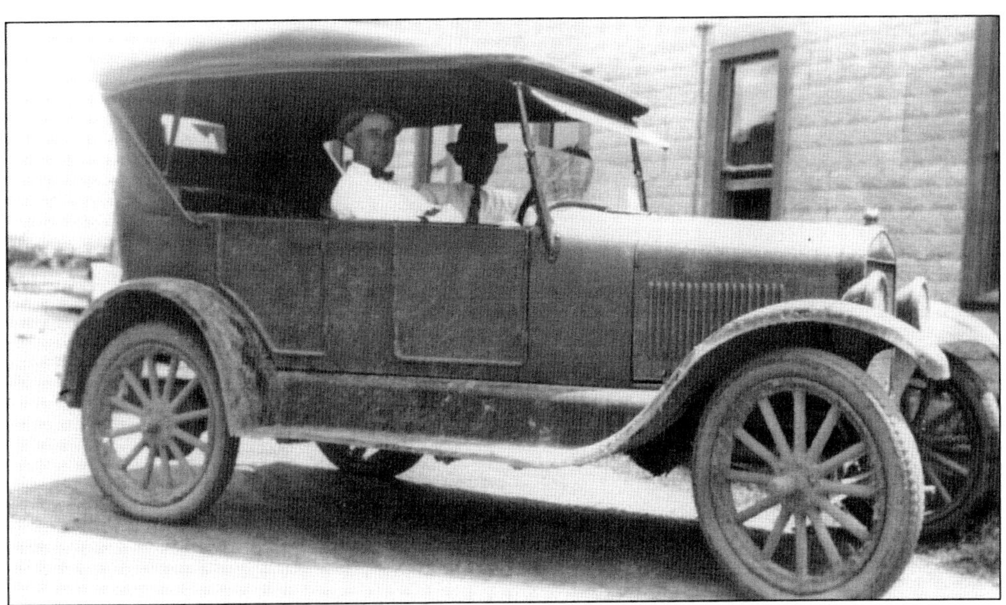

John "La Glace" Guillory (left), owner of an icehouse, was a familiar sight around Ville Platte in the early decades of the 20th century. In the days before refrigerators, kitchens had iceboxes, zinc-lined cabinets insulated with cork or sawdust and holding a block of ice to cool the foods stored inside. The iceman delivered fresh blocks as needed. The driver is unidentified. (Courtesy of Pam McGee.)

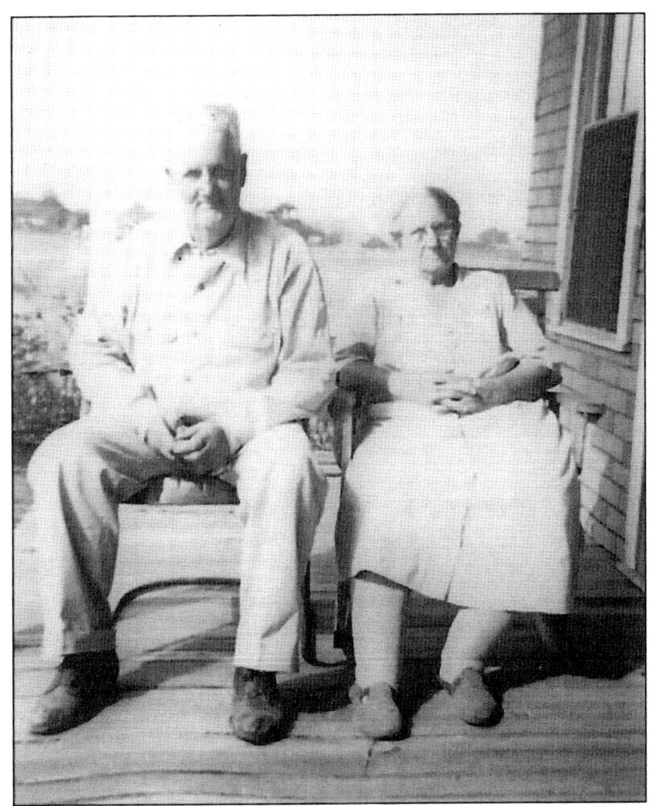

Louis Jacob Fontenot and Theosia Rozat were married on October 31, 1899, and celebrated their 50th anniversary in 1949. It was a quiet celebration at their house in Chataignier, with their nine children and their spouses, and several grandchildren. The Fontenots descended from a French colonial soldier, while the Rozats came from Mexico to Louisiana. (Courtesy of Kathryn Lebleu Guillory.)

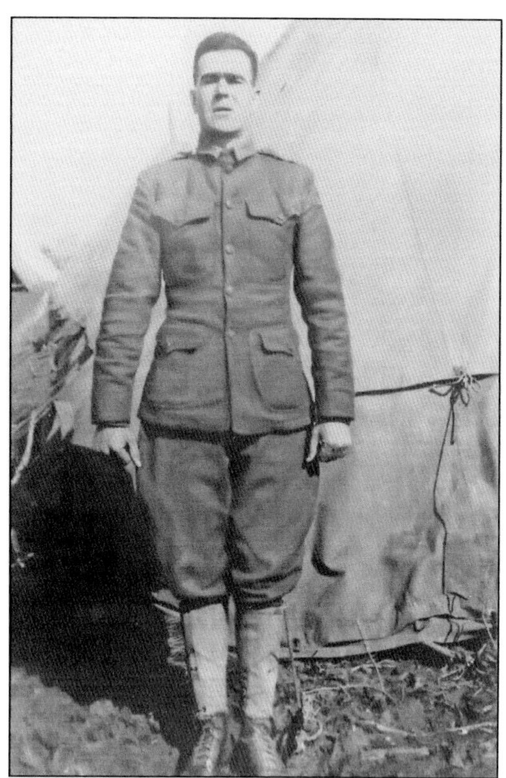

Theodore Guillory was a private in the US Army during World War I. He was mustered in on September 18, 1917, to serve "for the period of the emergency." As a member of the 54th Guard Company of the Army Service Corps, and later a member of Company F, 154th Infantry, he served overseas in France. He obtained his honorable discharge on September 24, 1919. (Courtesy of Kathryn Lebleu Guillory.)

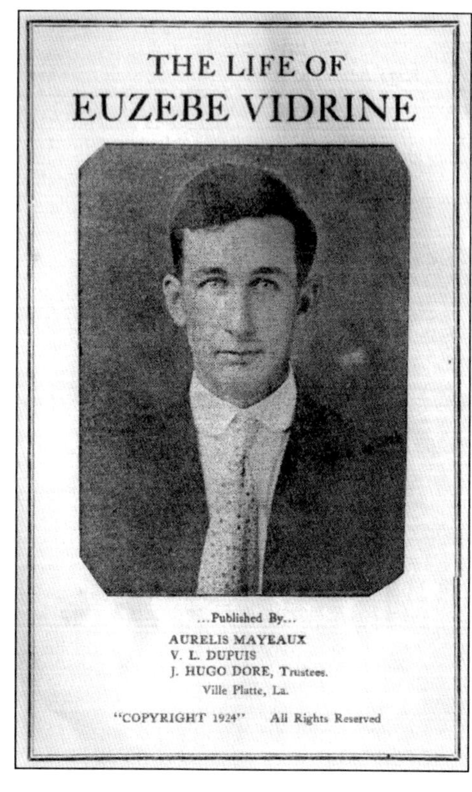

THE LIFE OF
EUZEBE VIDRINE

...Published By...
AURELIS MAYEAUX
V. L. DUPUIS
J. HUGO DORE, Trustees.
Ville Platte, La.

"COPYRIGHT 1924" All Rights Reserved

When he was arrested for killing Robert Wiggins, Euzebe Vidrine confessed to four more murders. Sentenced to hang, he requested a delay to write the story of his life. This little book took him a month to write. Before his execution, he posed for photographs and gave a rambling address on the evils of whiskey and gambling and how life had been unfair. (Courtesy of Louisiana Room, Dupré Library, UL Lafayette.)

Willis and Virginia Young Fontenot of Chataignier wrote to the Sisters of Charity in New York City requesting a child. In due time, five-year-old Joseph Wolffe arrived at the Lafayette Southern Pacific depot on an orphan train. The Fontenots picked him up on May 27, 1907, and later formally adopted him. Today, his little suit is prominently displayed in the Orphan Train Museum in Opelousas. (Courtesy of Sister Helen Fontenot.)

Guillaume Ardoin was the son of Simeon "Mayon" Ardoin, who owned a small store in Ville Platte. About the time Evangeline Parish was formed, Guillaume took over his father's store and renamed it G. Ardoin. Guillaume is shown here with his wife, Lezo Brignac. The couple had no children of their own, but adopted Helen Klein, an orphan train rider from New York. (Courtesy of Kathleen Eastin Soileau.)

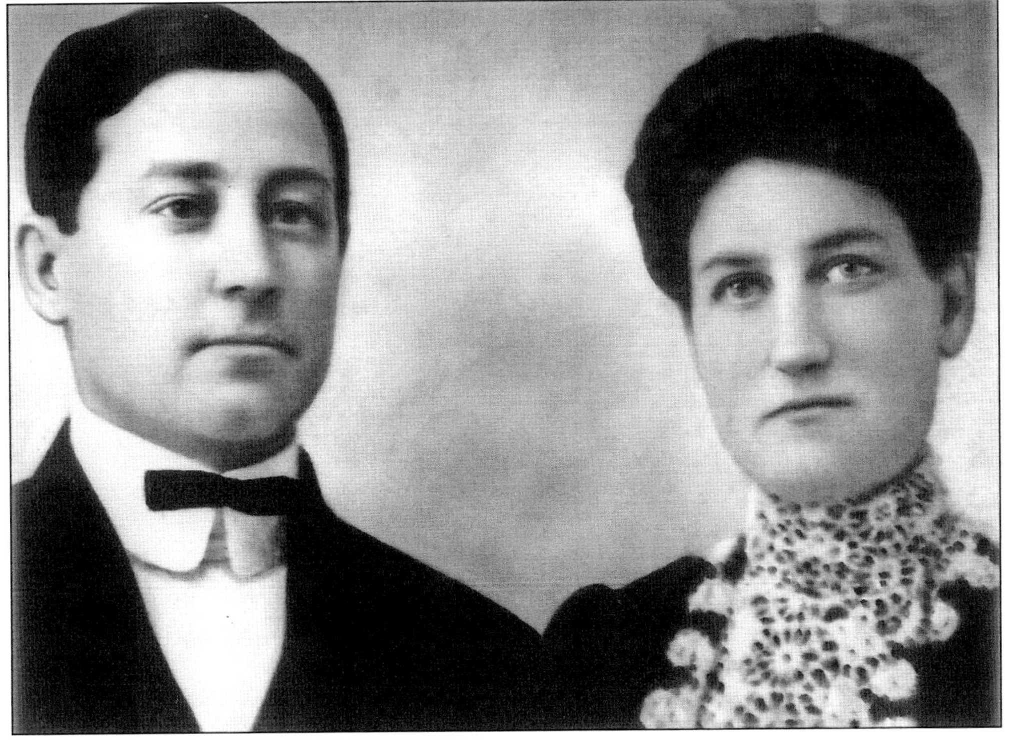

Clabert Duos owned the Service Gin Company, which operated cotton gins in Ville Platte, Basile, and Plaisance. His partner was Audley J. Soileau. Both men were active supporters in the early days of the Cotton Festival, and Duos served as Colonel Cotton in 1963. The award is given to a person who has contributed to the community through farming, business, or civic leadership. (Courtesy of Mitzi Duos Cochrane.)

Jules Ashlock was a world-class journalist and an avid hunter. The editor of the *Ville Platte Gazette*, Ashlock published a special edition in 1958 chronicling the history of the town's first century. His best writing, however, was in stories of outdoor adventure for national publications such as *Field and Stream*. One of his best experiences was a safari hunt in 1966. (Courtesy of Ville Platte Chamber of Commerce.)

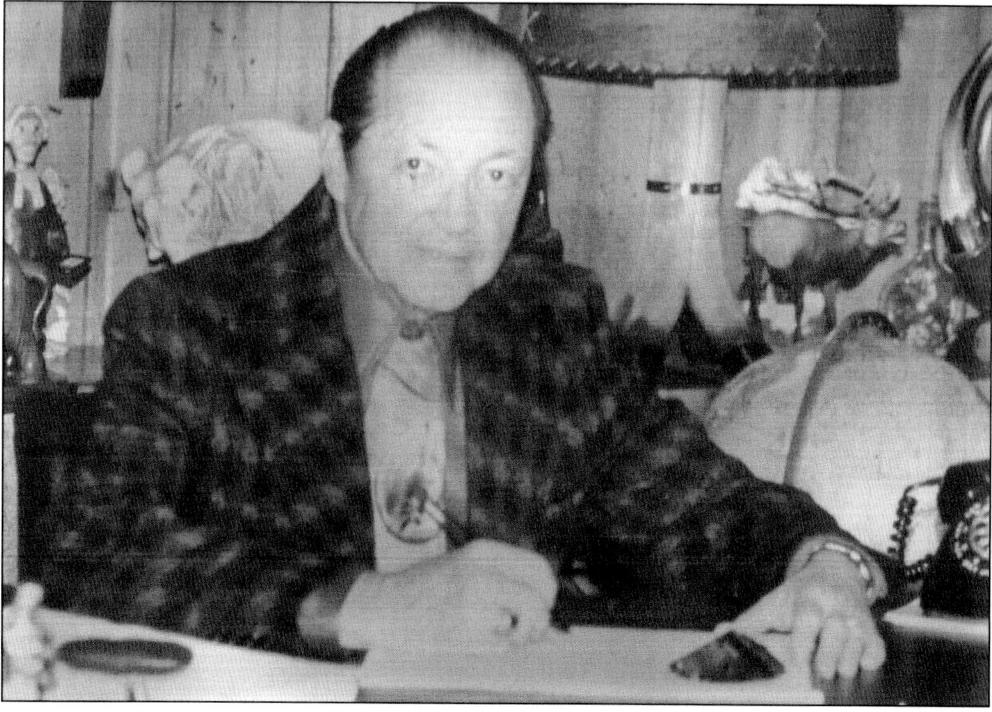

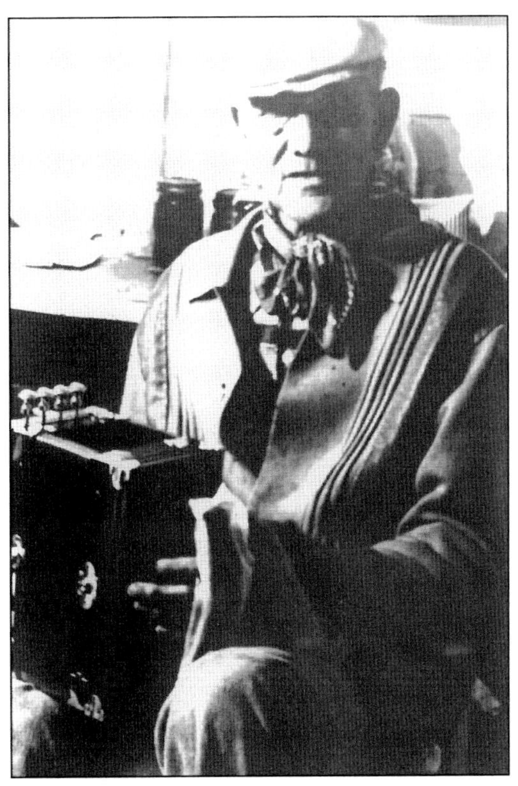

Freeman Fontenot was born in 1900 near Mamou, Louisiana. He learned traditional music from older members of the community, such as Adam Fontenot and Amédé Ardoin. He built a school for African Americans near Basile, which doubled as a dancehall on the weekends for pioneering musicians like Clifton Chenier and Bois Sec Ardoin. Thus, Fontenot served as a bridge between generations. (Courtesy of Center for Louisiana Studies, UL Lafayette.)

Dewey Balfa was born on March 20, 1927, in Mamou. A fiddler and singer, he helped create the Cajun music revival and became one of America's leading traditional musicians. During the 1960s and 1970s, he usually performed with his brothers. Shown here are, from left to right, Will Balfa, Dewey Balfa, Hadley Fontenot (another outstanding musician), Burkman Balfa, and Rodney Balfa. (Courtesy of Center for Louisiana Studies, UL Lafayette.)

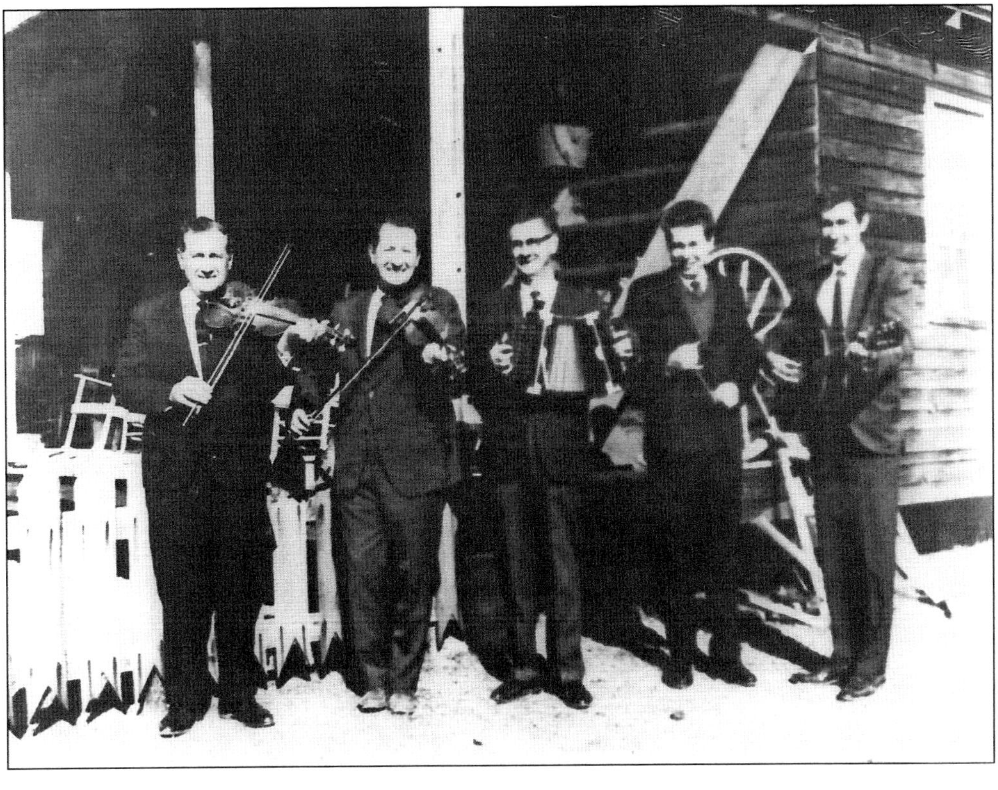

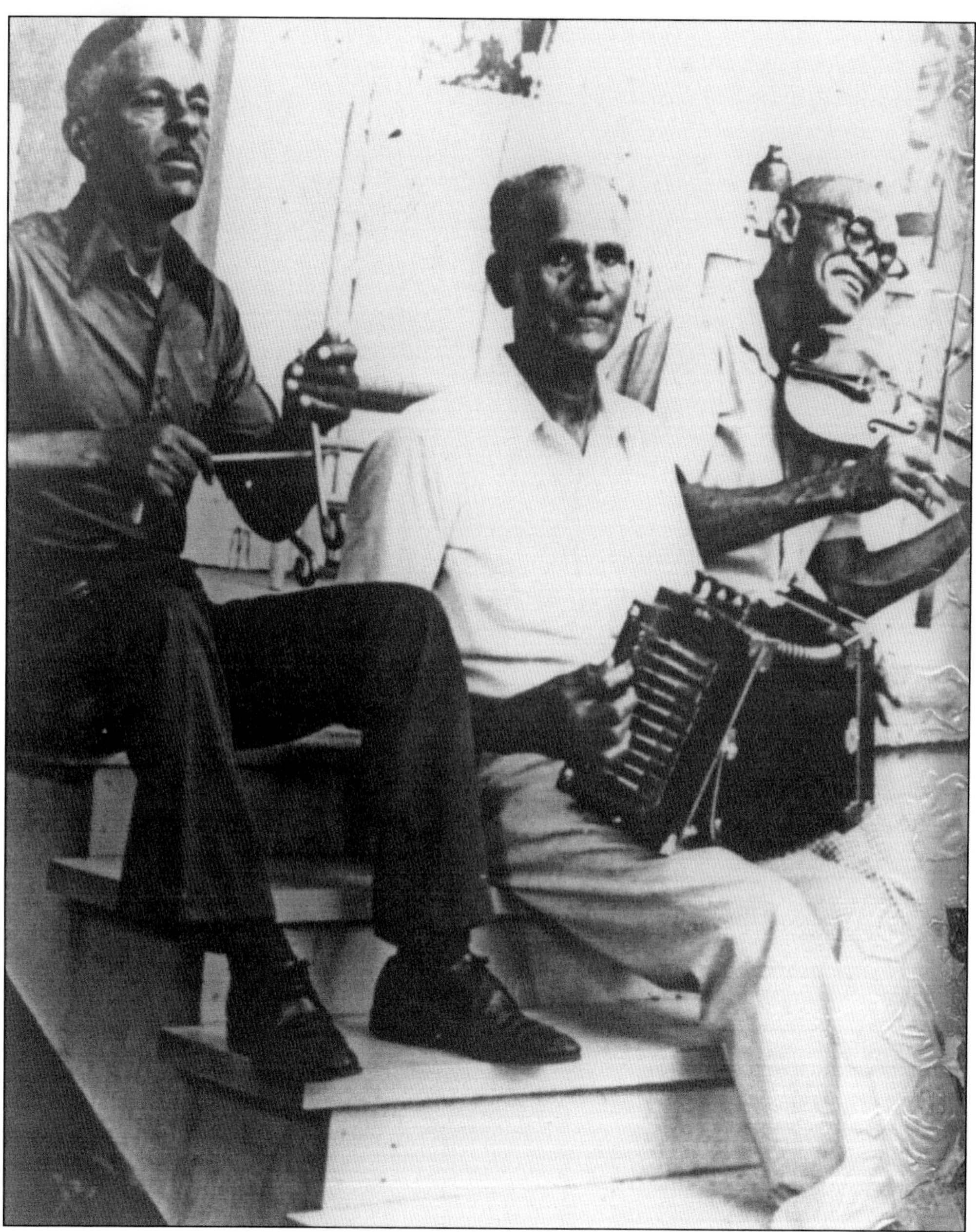

Alphonse "Bois Sec" Ardoin (left) and Canray Fontenot (right) were Creole musicians from near Basile. Ardoin played the accordion, and Fontenot played the fiddle. They learned to play traditional Creole music from older members of the community, including Bois Sec's cousin Amédé Ardoin and Canray's father, Adam Fontenot. They played for house dances, in clubs, and on local radio stations. The duo was "discovered" by the musical world when they performed at the Newport Jazz Festival in 1966. Later that same year, they recorded their first album, *Les Blues du Bayou*. For the next three decades they traveled extensively, giving concerts and performing at music festivals throughout the country. Seen here at center is Freeman Fontenot, another accordion player who played traditional Creole music. (Courtesy of Center for Louisiana Studies, UL Lafayette.)

Identical twins Ed (left) and Bee Deshotels were born in 1920 and grew up on a cotton farm near Mamou. They learned to play fiddle and guitar from their father, a talented musician, singer, and raconteur. He also taught them many of the old songs that later made up their repertoire. The brothers also performed their own compositions, created in the old style. (Courtesy of Center for Louisiana Studies, UL Lafayette.)

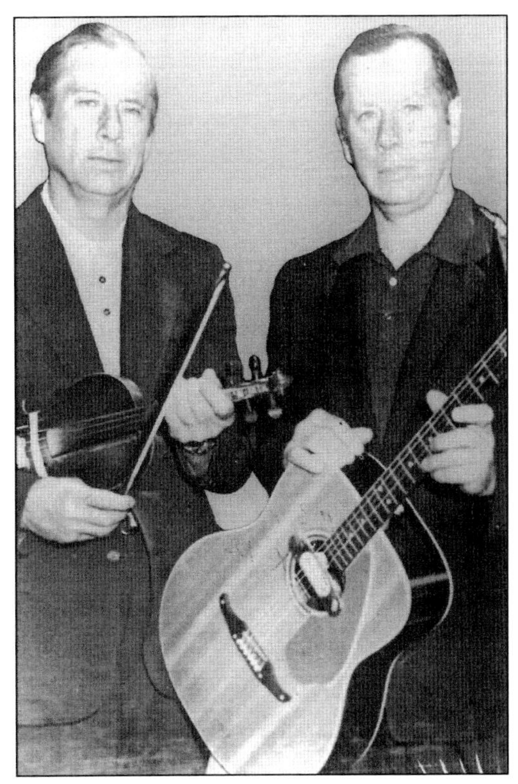

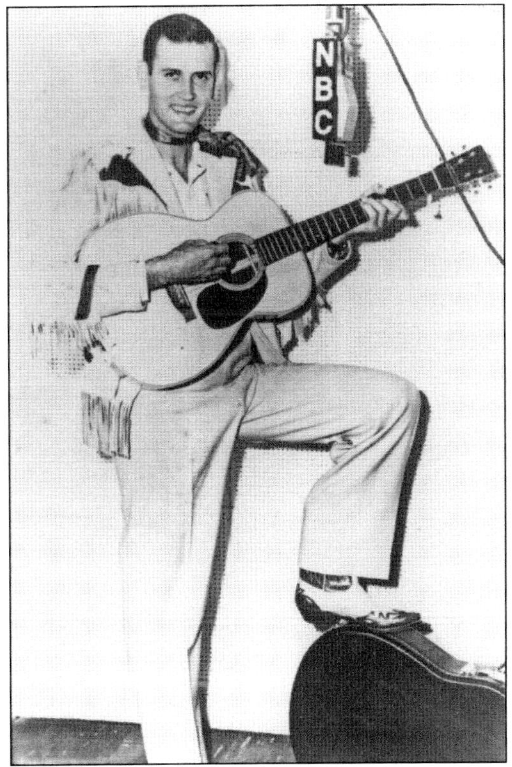

A native of Mamou, Jimmy C. Newman gained fame in the 1950s as a country music singer in Nashville, and was a regular performer on the *Louisiana Hayride* radio program out of Shreveport. As his career progressed, he added more Cajun influences to his music. He continues to tour and appears at the Grand Ole Opry today. (Courtesy of Center for Louisiana Studies, UL Lafayette.)

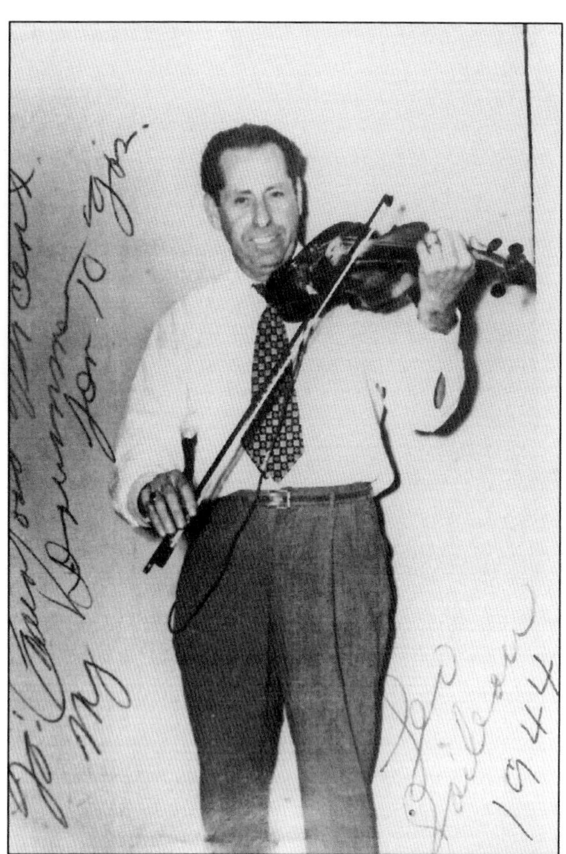

Leo Soileau was the second Cajun musician and the first Cajun fiddler to make recordings of his music, cutting his first record for RCA Victor in Atlanta in 1928. He recorded over 100 songs, from traditional Cajun tunes to Cajun versions of popular American songs. Soileau stopped playing music in the late 1940s when the accordion became more popular than the fiddle. (Courtesy of Center for Louisiana Studies, UL Lafayette.)

Leo Fontenot and the Ville Platte Playboys had a regular gig on KVPI Radio in the mid-1950s. Shown here at the radio station are, from left to right, band members Gervis Soileau, Allen Fontenot, Ronald Fontenot, Leo Fontenot, and Gaylor Soileau. At far right is radio announcer Jim Soileau. (Courtesy of Center for Louisiana Studies, UL Lafayette.)

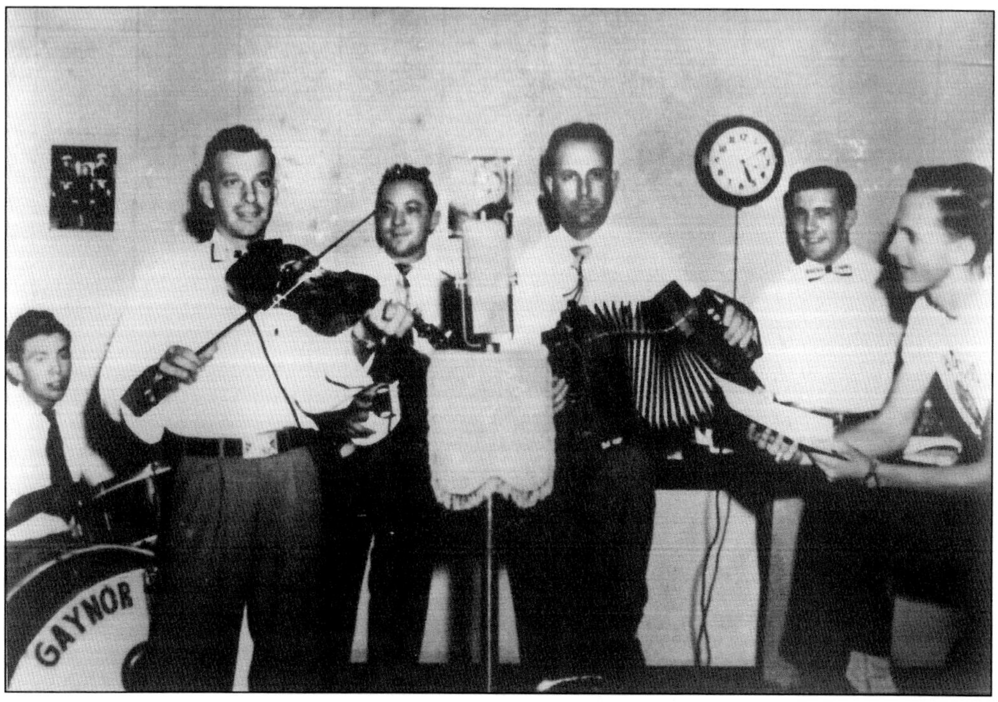

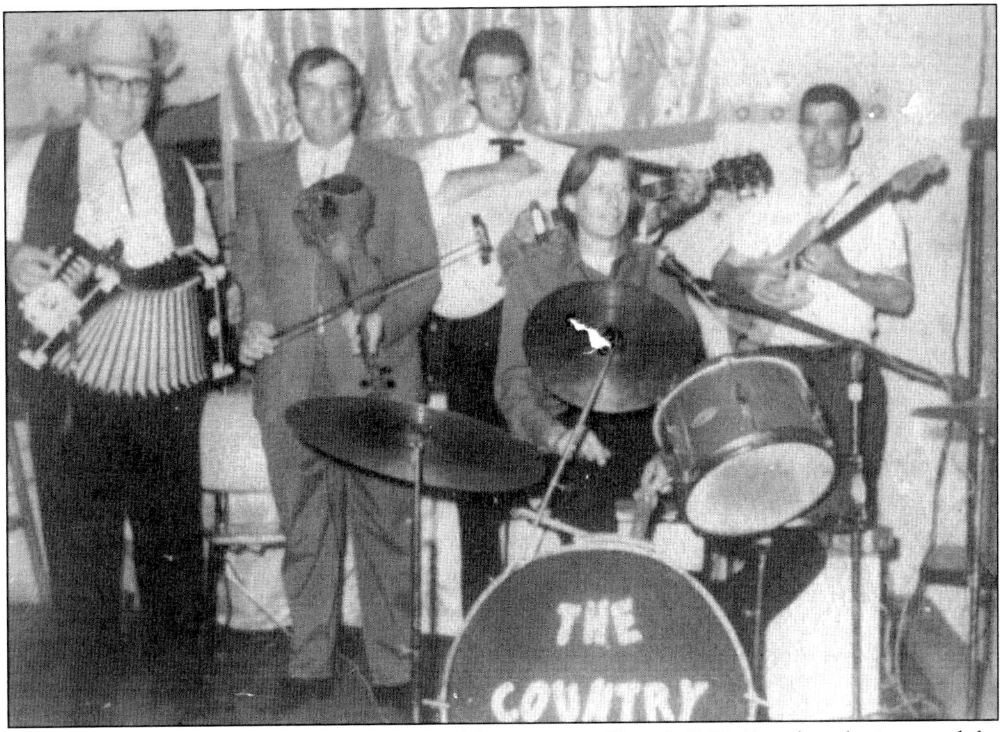

The Country Cajuns were a popular band between 1967 and 1977. Besides playing at clubs throughout Louisiana, Texas, and Tennessee, the band performed at JazzFest in New Orleans and at the Grand Ole Opry in Nashville. They also appeared in the 1975 movie *Hard Times*, starring Charles Bronson. Shown here are, from left to right, Leroy Veillon, Allen Fontenot, Clarence Vidrine, Darrell Brasseaux, and Hudren Dauzat. (Courtesy of Tim Veillon.)

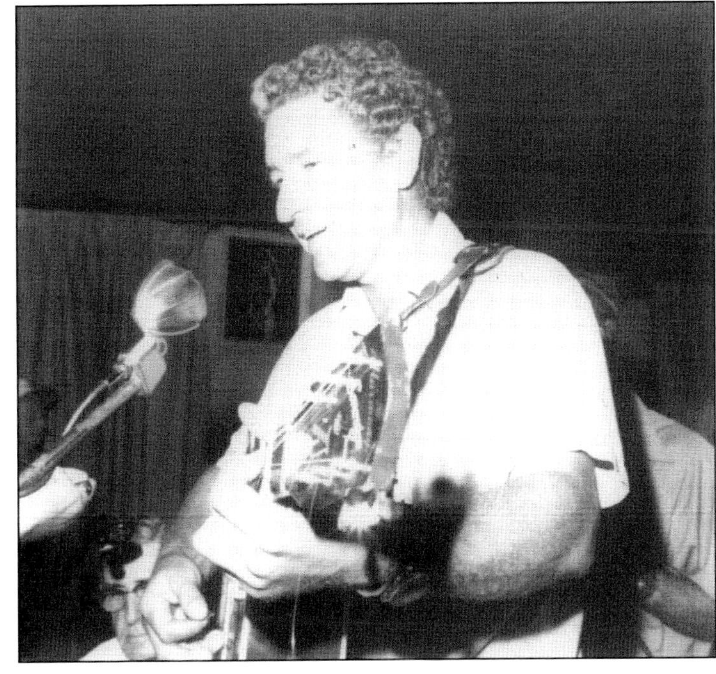

Rodney Balfa played guitar and harmonica and sang with the Balfa Brothers from the 1940s until his death. He also performed with Nathan Abshire and the New Lost City Ramblers. He and his brother Will were killed in a car accident on February 6, 1979. Rodney is shown here performing at Fred's Lounge in Mamou. (Courtesy of Center for Louisiana Studies, UL Lafayette.)

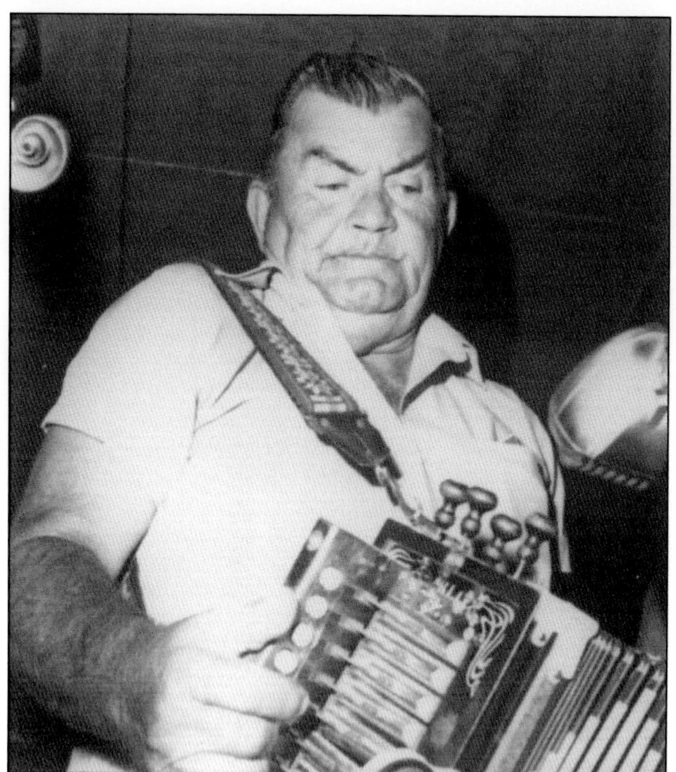

Nathan Abshire was a Cajun accordionist who made his home in Basile. A self-taught musician, he was in great demand as a performer, first at house dances, then at local dancehalls, and eventually at music festivals all over the country. In the 1930s he played with Creole musician Amédé Ardoin, who had a great influence on Abshire's music. (Courtesy of Center for Louisiana Studies, UL Lafayette.)

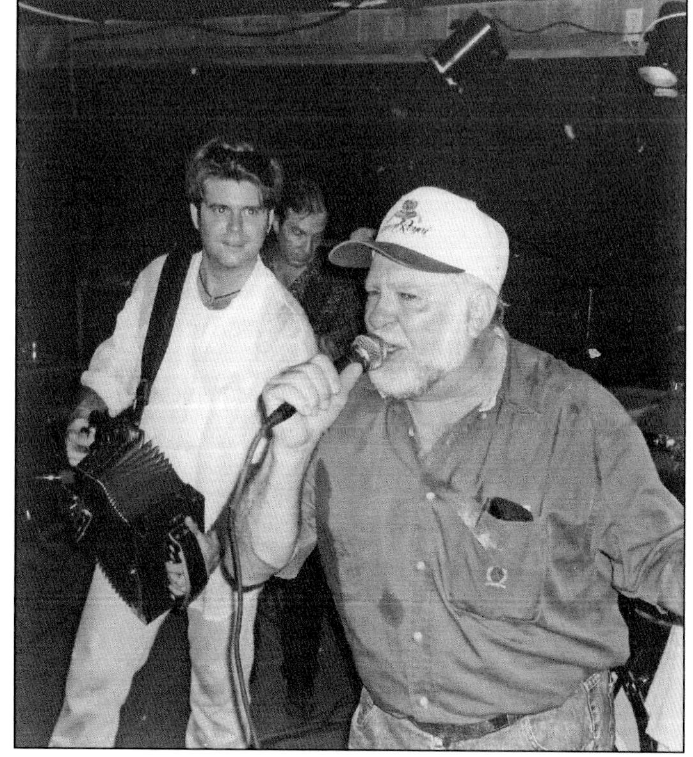

This photograph features two generations of musicians. Steve Riley, on the accordion, is a native of Mamou. He is the leader of the band Steve Riley and the Mamou Playboys, formed in 1988 and popular all over the world today. Clint West, with the microphone, is a native of Vidrine. He had a successful career singing swamp pop 50 years ago. (Courtesy of Center for Louisiana Studies, UL Lafayette.)

Floyd Soileau opened Floyd's Record Shop in 1956 in Ville Platte to supplement his income as a disc jockey for KVPI Radio. The following year, he founded Flat Town Music Company to record local musicians performing Cajun, swamp pop, and zydeco music. The store and the record company soon became so successful that Soileau gave up the DJ job. (Courtesy of Center for Louisiana Studies, UL Lafayette.)

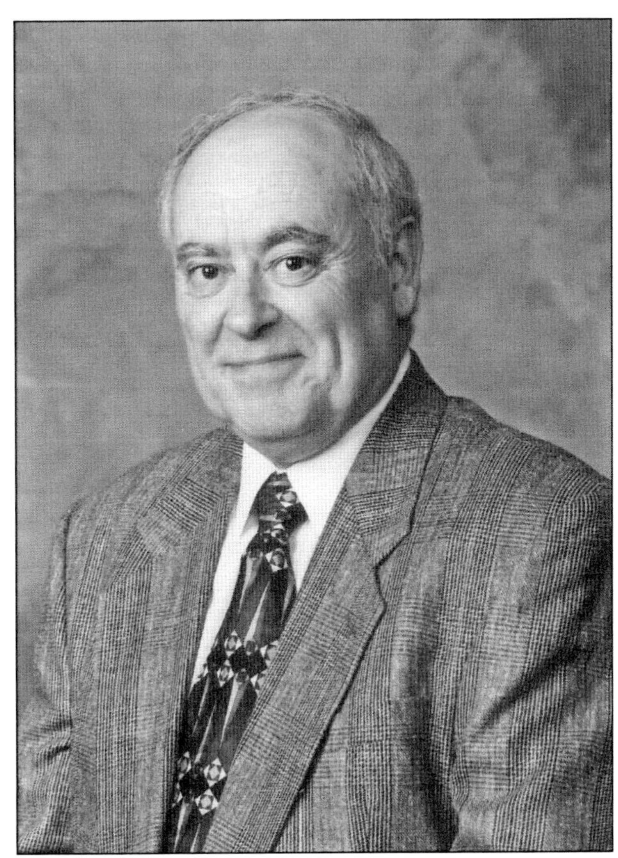

Even in 1989, small grocery stores were common in Evangeline Parish. They carried canned goods, milk and dairy products, and fresh fruits and vegetables. Many also offered fresh meat. And, like the general stores of a century ago, they often had a few chairs in the back where neighbors could visit. Shown here are, from left to right, Jessie, Mayo, and Andrew Chapman and Hassa Chapman Fontenot. (Courtesy of Jo Anna Miller.)

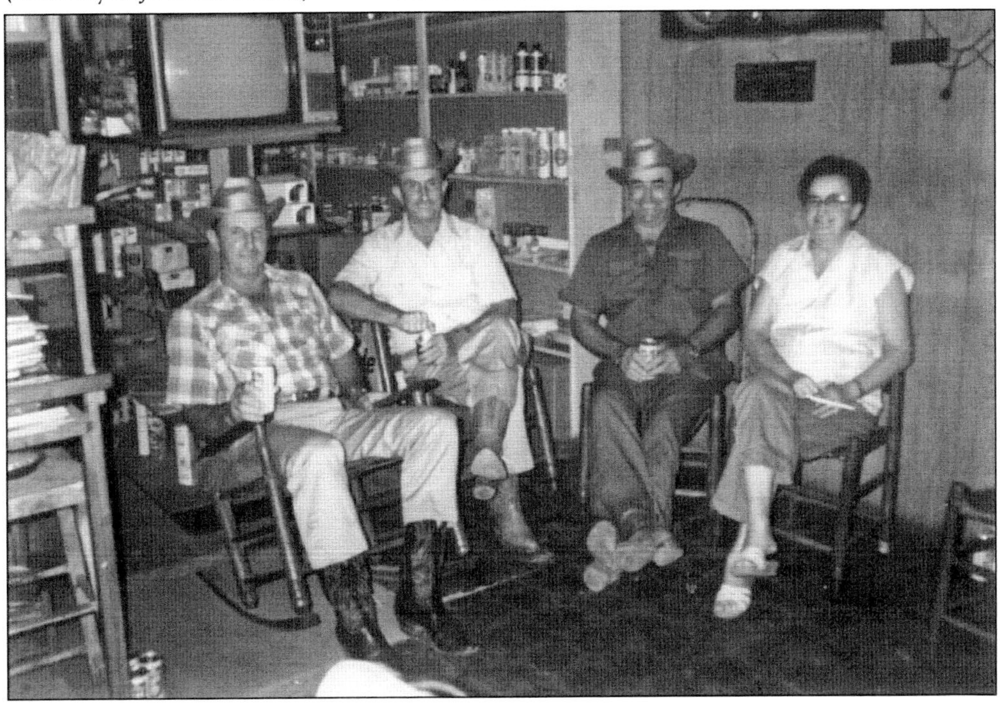

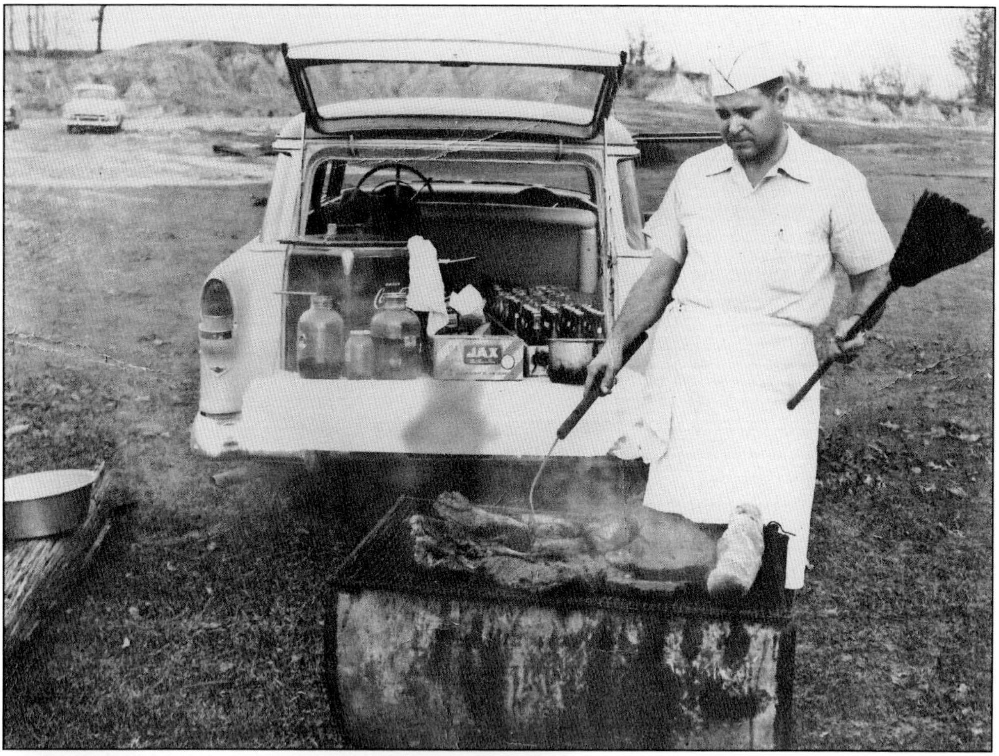

Jack Miller moved to Ville Platte in 1941, when he rented the Pig Stand restaurant and opened the American Inn. His barbecue sauce was so popular that he began to market it in 1955. By 1962 he gave up the restaurant business entirely. Active in the community, he was the chamber of commerce's first Businessman of the Year, and served as the 1981 Cotton Festival parade marshal. (Courtesy of Kermit Miller.)

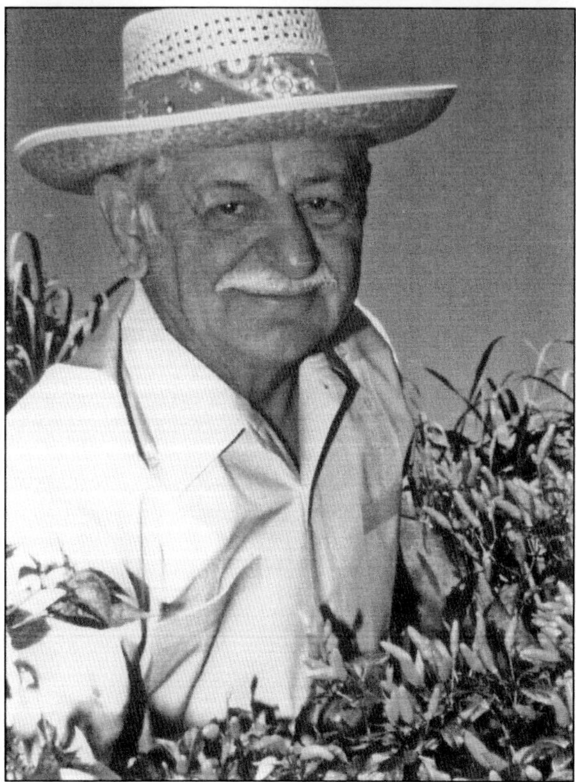

Allen Ortego began producing his popular hot sauce as a hobby in 1978. He grew his own tabasco peppers, which were picked by hand. To ensure quality, he selected the strongest pepper plants each year and saved the seeds to plant the following year. Orders came from every state and from several countries. He retired in 2000, at which time he ceased production. (Courtesy of Ville Platte City Hall.)

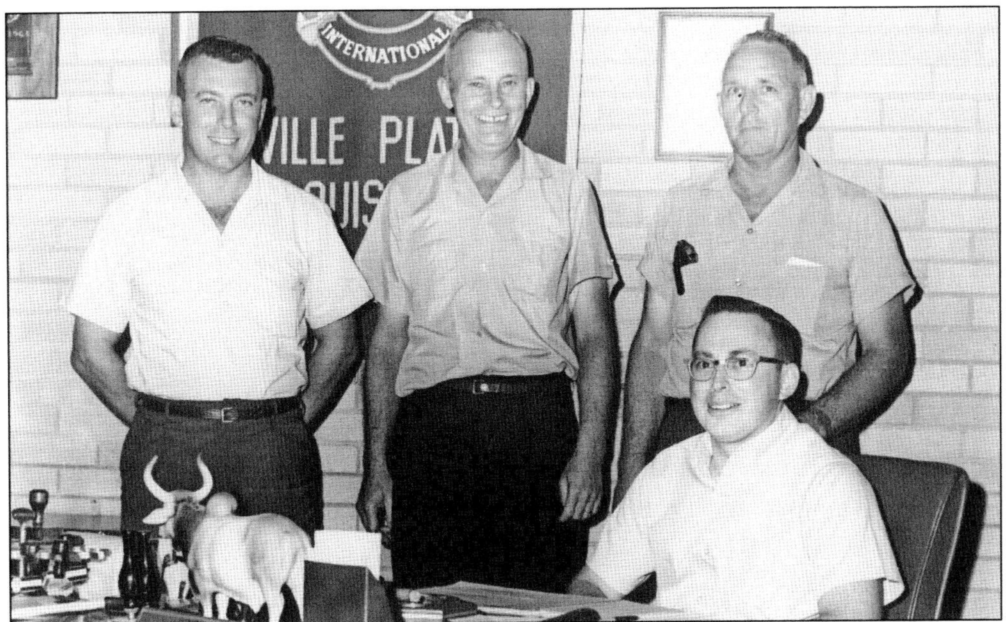

The Lions Club service organization has long been active in the Ville Platte community. Among its activities is hosting the Gumbo Festival each November, when the weather is considered cool enough for gumbo. The festival includes music and dancing as well as a gumbo cook-off. Standing from left to right are Davis Schexnayder, Cecil Pouncy, and Cliff Wagley. Dr. Jerry Veillon is seated at the desk. (Courtesy of Lynn Landreneau.)

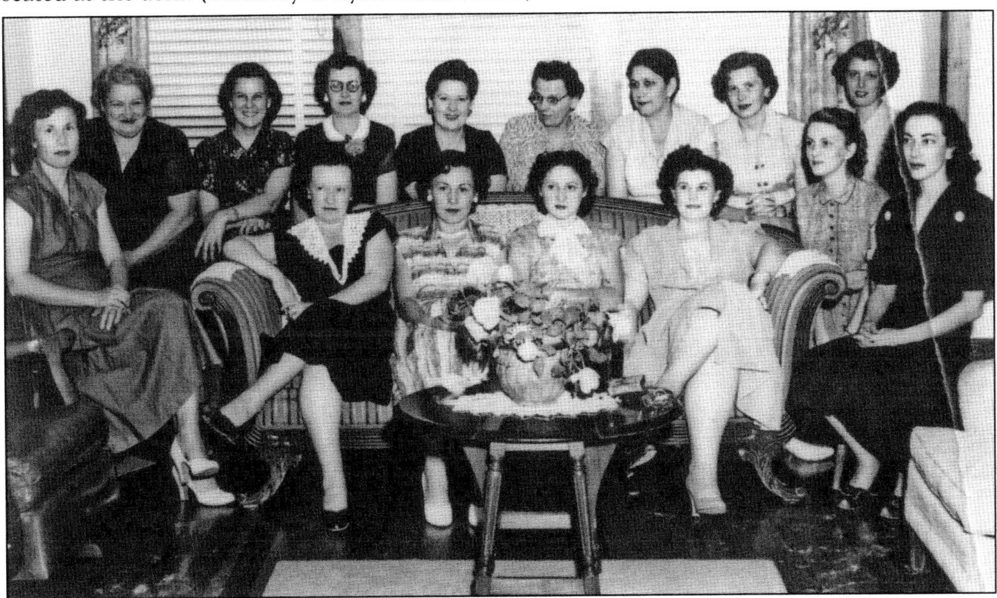

Wives of Lions Club members belonged to the Lions Auxiliary. Members shown here in 1948 are, from left to right, (first row) Mrs. Charlie Tassin, Mrs. Richard Lee, Mrs. L.O. Fusilier, and Lola Pearl Schwartzerburg; (second row) Mrs. Leroy Veillon, Mrs. Leonard Hazelton, Mrs. E.H. Elby McManus, Mrs. Linden Tatman, Mrs. Willis Knighton, Mrs. Raoul Clay, Mrs. Harvey LeBas, Mrs. Allen Savant, Mrs. Glenn Hollier, Mrs. Cecil Pouncey, and Mrs. Drouet Vidrine. (Courtesy of Lynn Landreneau.)

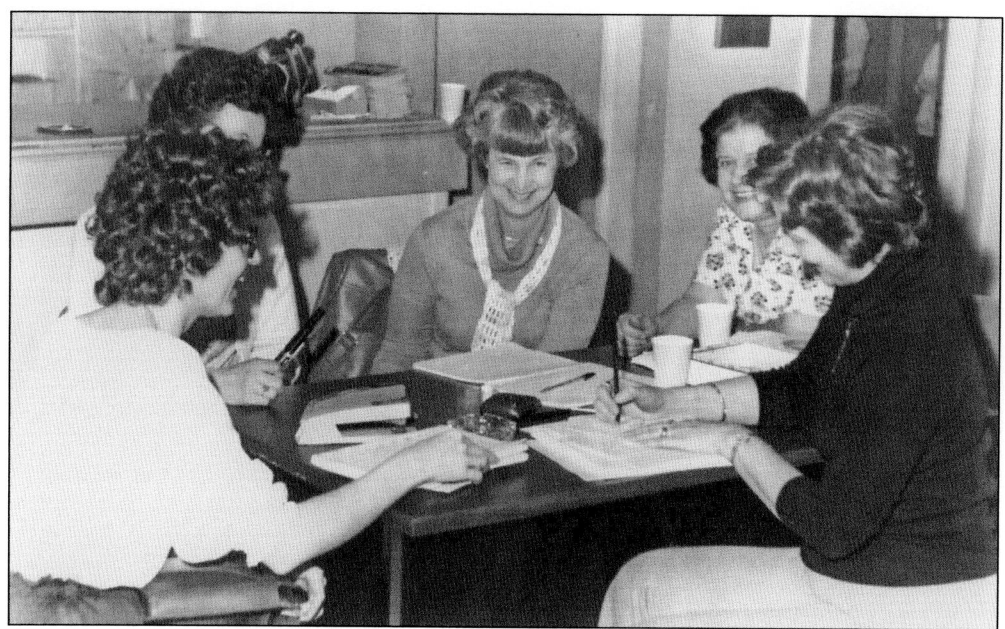

The Lions Auxiliary was formed to assist with the activities of the Lions Club community service organization. One of the auxiliary's functions was fundraising. Here, members catalog items donated for a radio auction around 1970. They are, from left to right, Sarah Webb, Dot Vidrine, Lynn Landreneau, Theresa Fontenot, and Joyce Coreil. (Courtesy of Lynn Landreneau.)

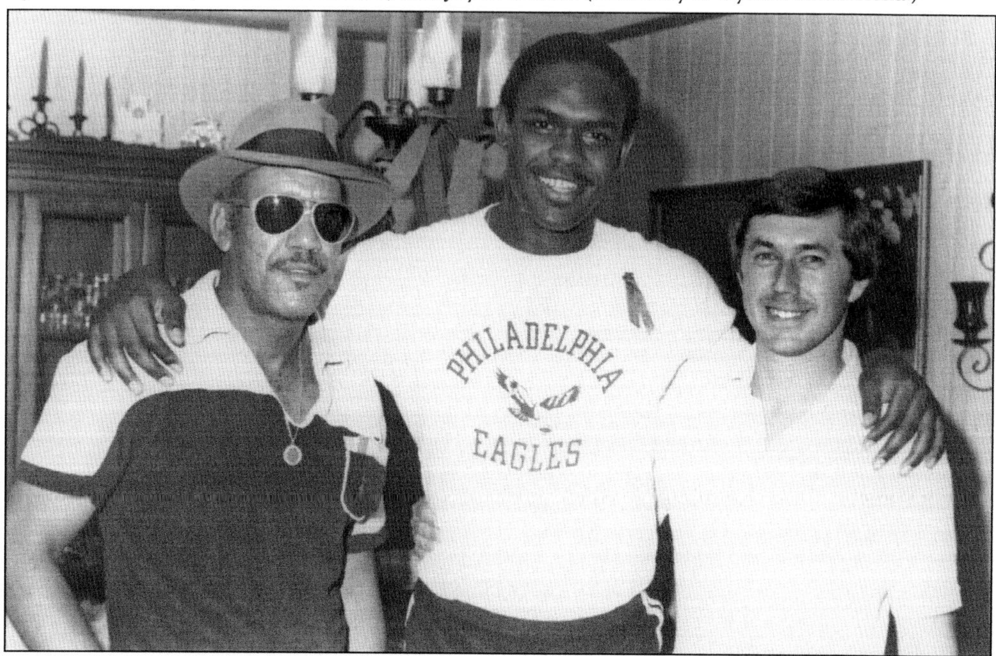

Coach Mike Frank (left) was a teacher and coach for many years at Ville Platte High School. He passed away in 2013. Greg Lafleur (center) was an outstanding football player for Ville Platte High School and Louisiana State University in the 1970s. He went on to play professionally for the St. Louis Cardinals in the 1980s. Danny Lemoine (right) was an educator and director of Charles B. Coreil Technical College in Ville Platte. (Courtesy of *Ville Platte Gazette*.)

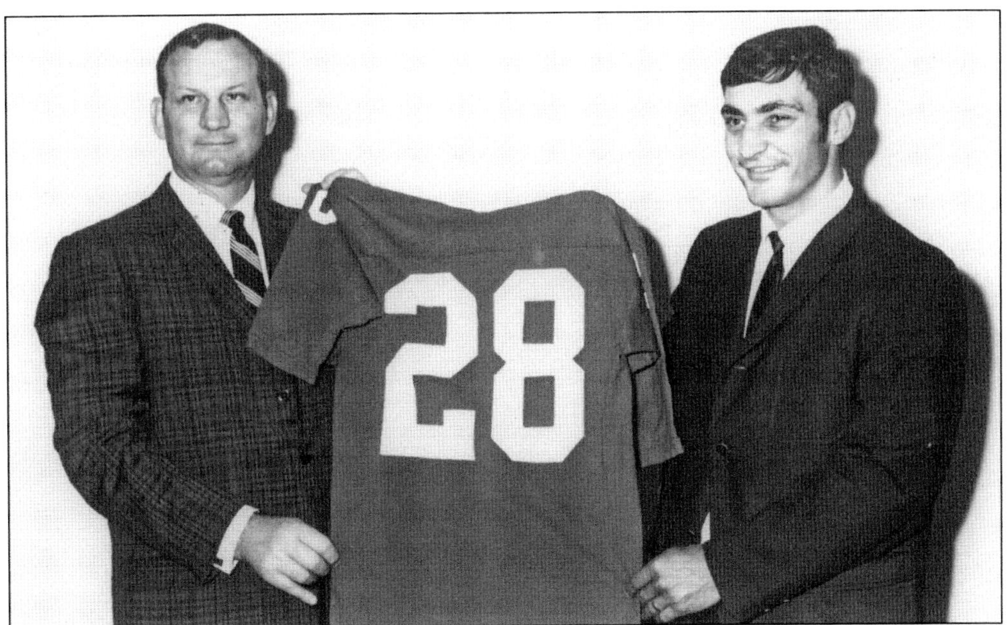

Glenn LaFleur was an outstanding football player for Ville Platte High School in the 1960s. He was a superlative running back at the University of Southwestern Louisiana from 1966 to 1969. Prevented by injuries from playing professionally, he became a high school football coach and administrator. He is shown here at right with USL coach Russ Faulkinberry in 1969, as his number was being retired after his last season. (Courtesy of Ville Platte Gazette.)

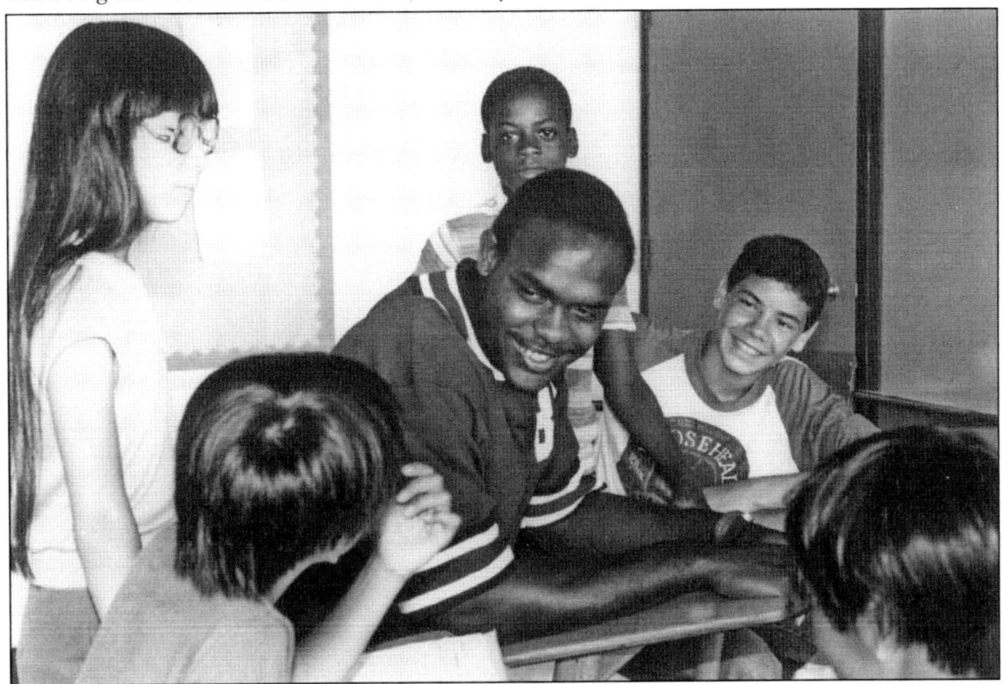

After a successful career in the National Football League, Greg Lafleur worked as an athletic administrator at several colleges. He is shown here chatting with students on one of his frequent visits home. (Courtesy of Ville Platte Gazette.)

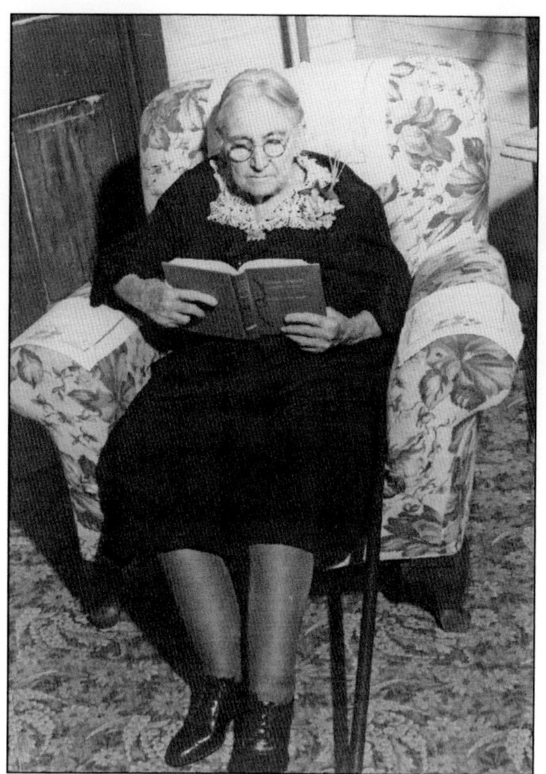

Born and raised in Bayou Chicot, Emma Scott Thompson was the mother of seven children. She loved to read and was a dedicated patron of the Evangeline Parish Library. At age 93, she read four books weekly. Her daughter Mabel Alice Thompson was a teacher in Bayou Chicot for many years and wrote newspaper articles and a book on the history of the area. (Courtesy of Evangeline Parish Library.)

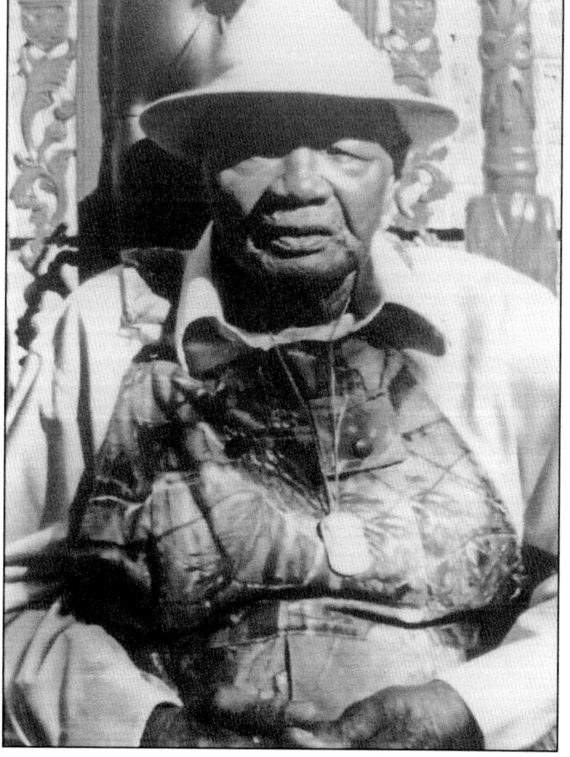

At 104 years of age, Edward "Knotoe" Thomas Jr. is the oldest living citizen in Evangeline Parish. He and his wife, Elio Deshotel, were the parents of 10 children. Knotto worked at Deville Lumber Yard and as a deputy at the courthouse. In 2011 he was given a key to the city of Ville Platte, and a street was named after him. (Courtesy of Ville Platte City Hall.)

Three

CHURCHES AND SCHOOLS

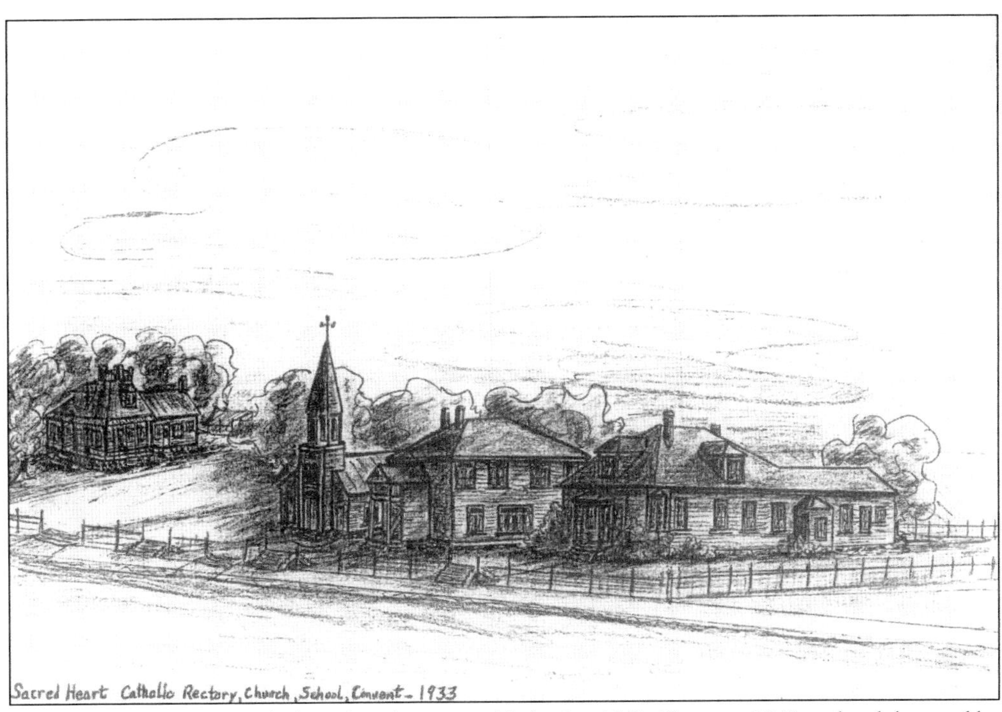

Sacred Heart of Jesus Catholic Church was established in Ville Platte in 1845 on land donated by Edouard Dardeau and Martin Rousseau. Later buildings included a rectory, school, and convent. In 1930 the new pastor, Father Maurice Bourgeois, found the buildings dilapidated and nearly abandoned. With the aid of parishioners, he made repairs and reopened the school. The church was replaced in 1938. (Artwork by Margaret Reed Fontenot.)

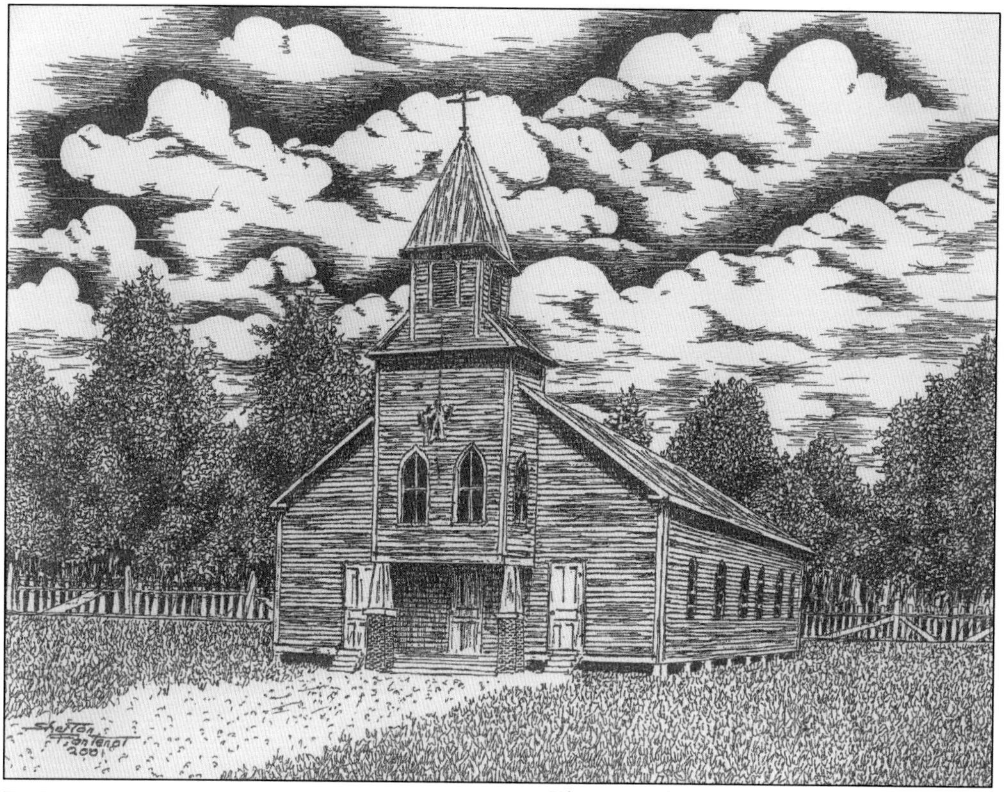

The second Catholic church to be established in what became Evangeline Parish was Our Lady of Mount Carmel in Chataignier. Archbishop Jean-Marie Odin of New Orleans established the parish in 1869, and this building was erected the following year. Father Jean Baptiste Bré was the first resident pastor. (Courtesy of Kathryn Lebleu Guillory.)

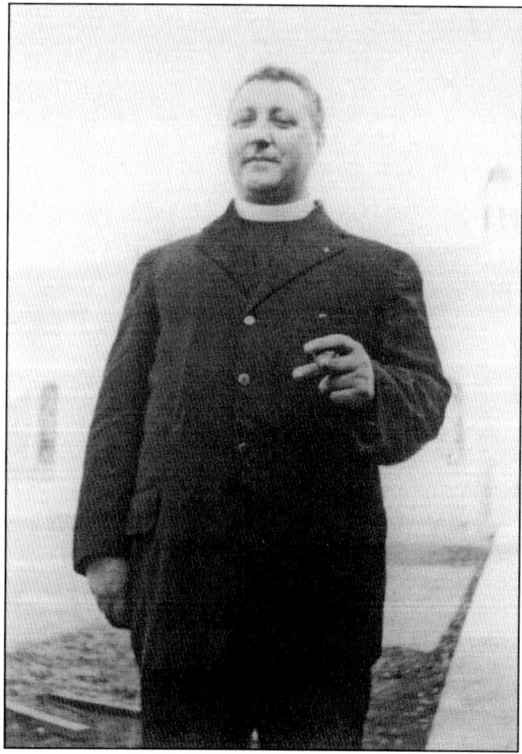

Fr. Anthony Verhoeven was one of many Dutch priests recruited by New Orleans archbishop Francis Janssens (himself a native of Holland) to serve in Louisiana. Ordained in New Orleans in 1903, Father Verhoeven served as pastor of Our Lady of Mount Carmel in Chataignier from 1908 to 1915. He died in St. Martinville in 1936 and is buried there. (Courtesy of J.D. Soileau.)

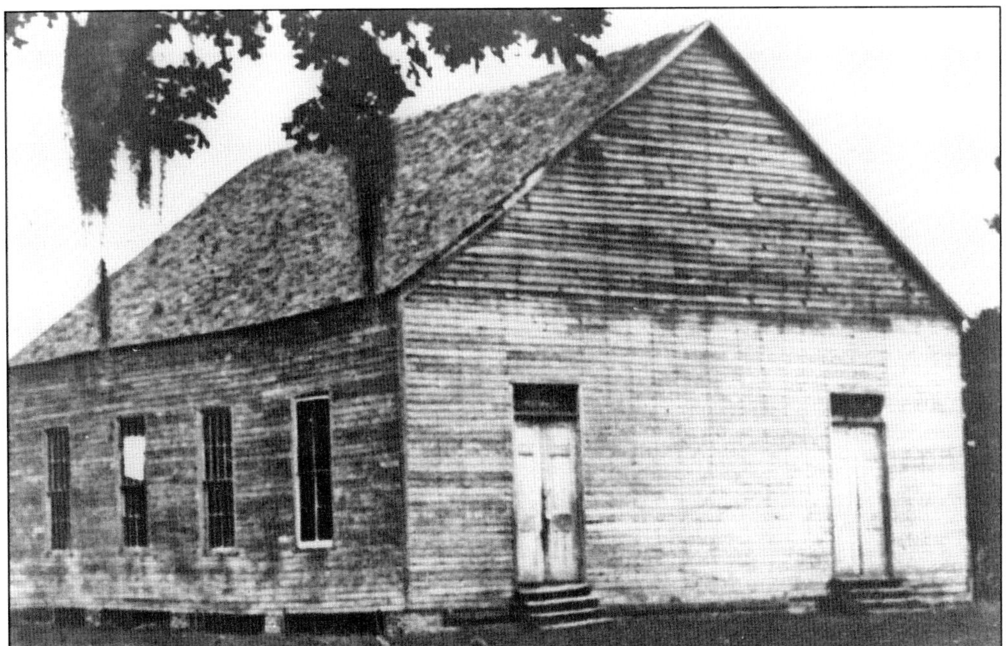

First Calvary Baptist Church was established in Bayou Chicot on November 13, 1812. The membership was composed of five men and one woman. A pair of ministers, Moses Hadley and Lawrence Scarborough, were sent from Mississippi to ordain Joseph Willis, the first preacher west of the Mississippi River. Willis constituted the church and served as its pastor for 34 years. (Courtesy of Merlyn Yielding.)

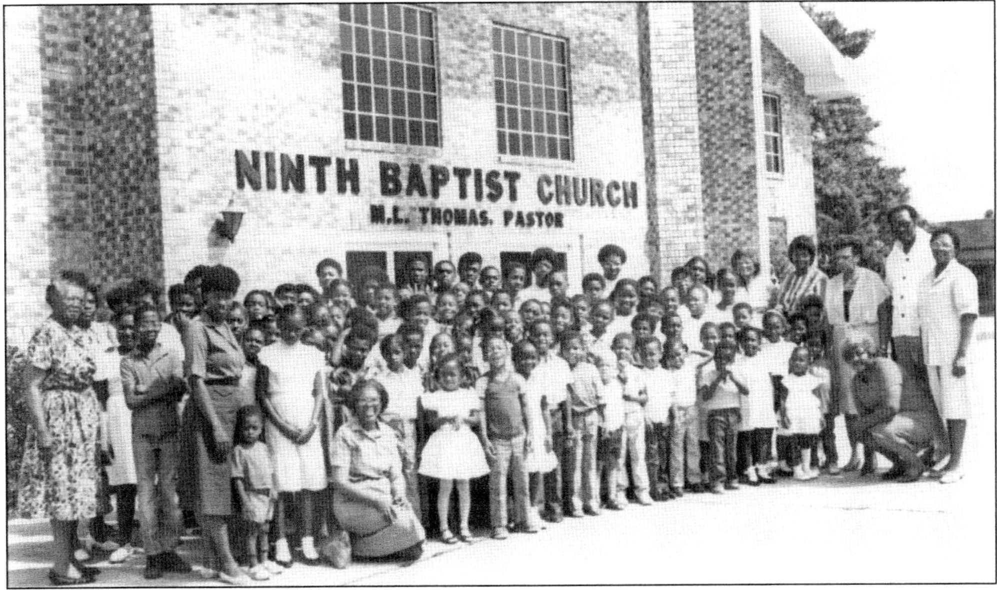

Ville Platte's Ninth Missionary Baptist Church was founded on March 1, 1873, by Rev. James Stephens of Mamou, a preacher with no formal education. The first deacons of the church were Louis Joseph, Emile Arvie, Peter Mitchell, John Joseph, Batiste Tezeno, Lastie Skinner, Francis Fontenot, Zeno Ardoin, and Octave Joseph. The church is still a vibrant part of the African American community today. (Courtesy of *Ville Platte Gazette*.)

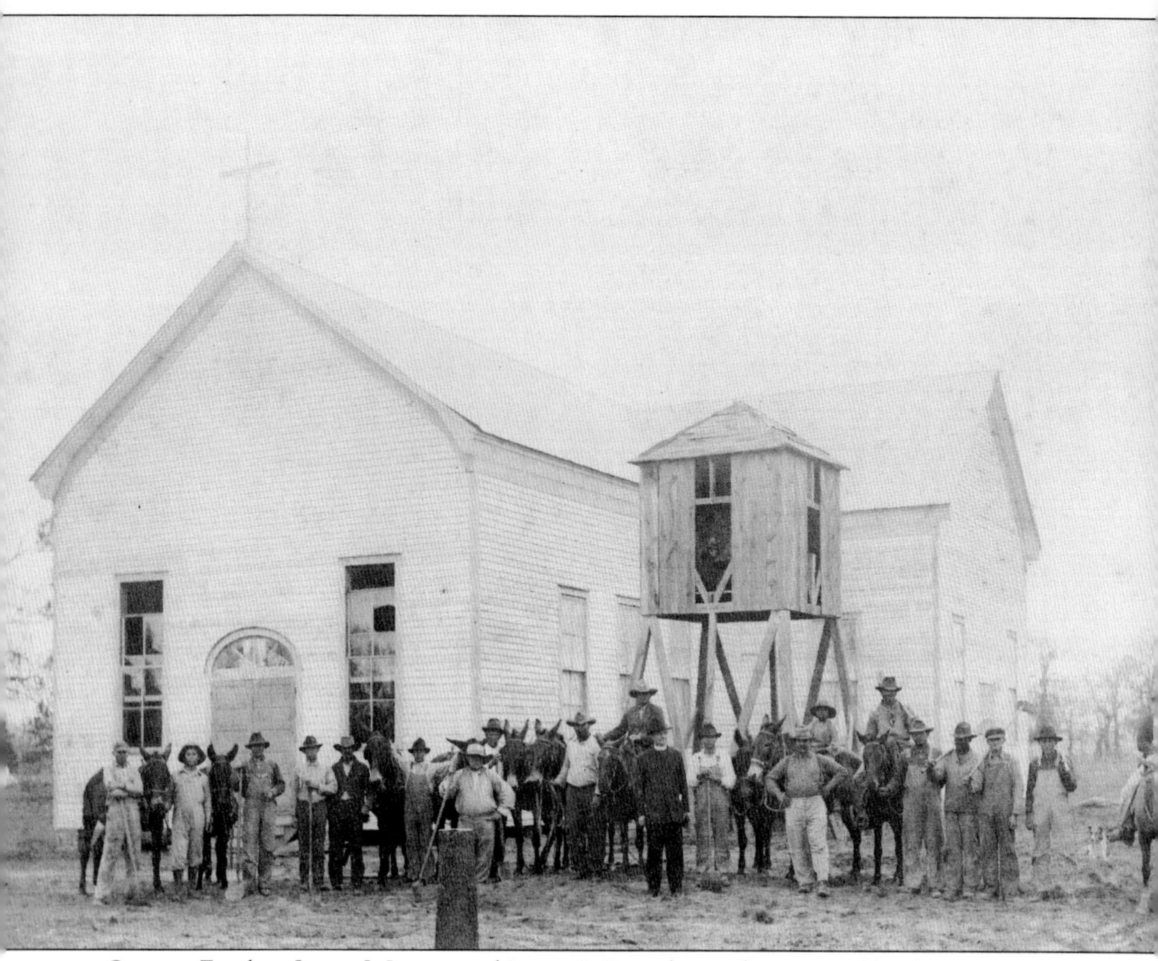

Gustave Fuselier, James J. Lewis, and Louis S. Berg donated an acre of land in Basile for St. Augustine Catholic Church in 1911. Lumber hewn from the trees on the site was used to construct this building, which seated about 500. The church burned down on April 5, 1937, and was replaced by a brick building. This photograph was taken about 1921, when the pastor was Father E.H. Derivas. The men of the congregation have gathered for a *coup de main*, literally a "stroke of the hand," a tradition in Cajun communities. People would gather for a work day to help someone who was sick to harvest his crop, or to dig a well or build a barn—any job that required more work than one person could do on his own. In return, the beneficiary would help his neighbors when they needed assistance. In this instance, the coup de main was organized to clean up the grounds around the church. (Courtesy of Diocese of Lafayette.)

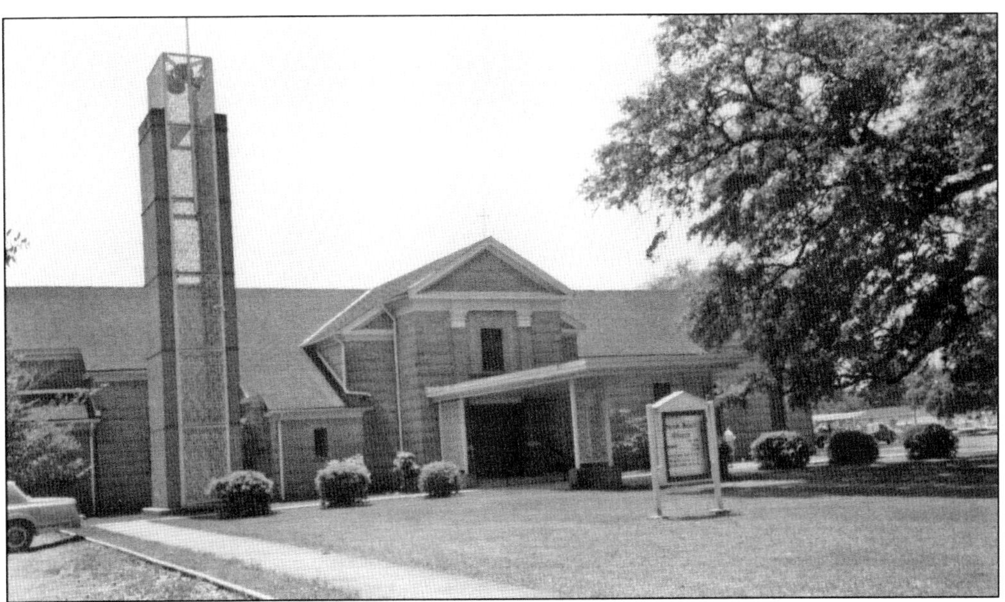

The new Sacred Heart Church was built in 1937 and was dedicated on December 8 by Lafayette bishop Jules Jeanmard. During the 1950s and 1960s, Msgr. Bourgeois realized his dream of a new convent, a new elementary school building, a completely renovated church building, and a mausoleum for the church cemetery. After 40 years of dedicated service, Msgr. Bourgeois retired and left Ville Platte in 1970. (Courtesy of Diocese of Lafayette.)

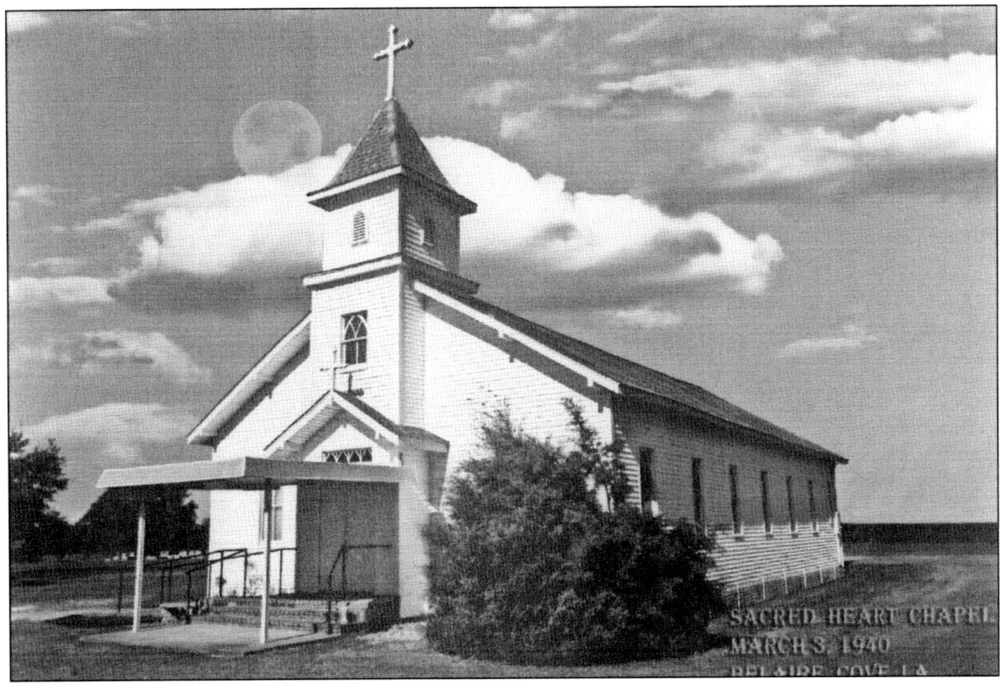

Sacred Heart of Jesus Chapel stands in Belaire Cove, a few miles from the main church in Ville Platte. The property was purchased in 1938 from Marie B. Fontenot for $150, and the building was erected two years later for $3,000. Bishop Jules B. Jeanmard of the Diocese of Lafayette officiated at the dedication and blessing of the chapel on March 30, 1940. (Courtesy of Runnie F. Matte.)

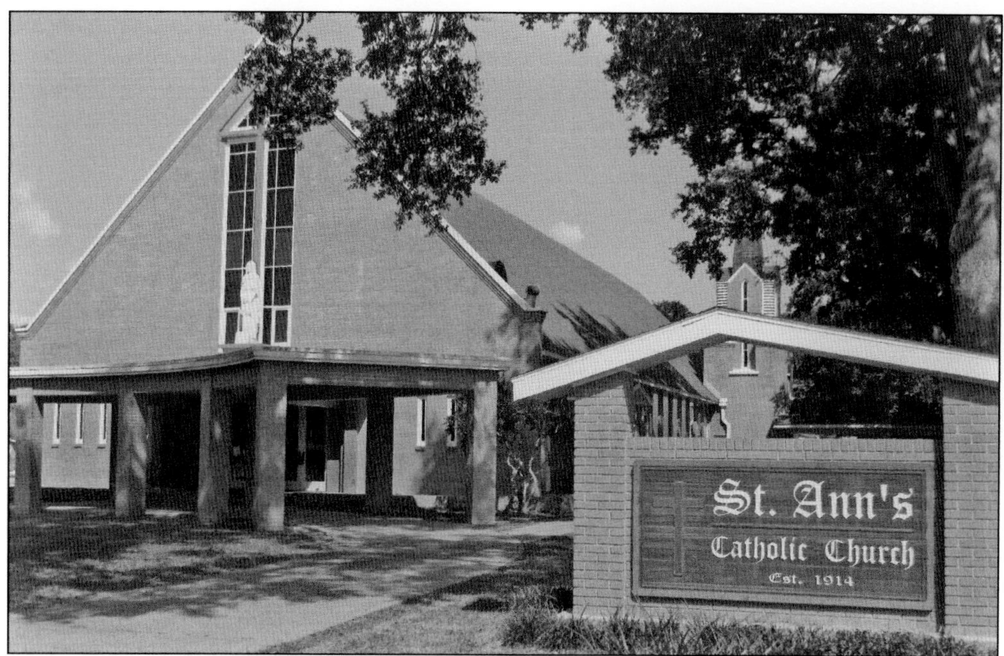

St. Ann's Catholic Church was established in 1914 to serve the many Catholic families scattered over the prairies of central Evangeline Parish. The town of Mamou had been laid out only three years earlier, but it was growing rapidly. The original church building burned down in 1936, but it was rebuilt the following year. (Courtesy of Jane Vidrine.)

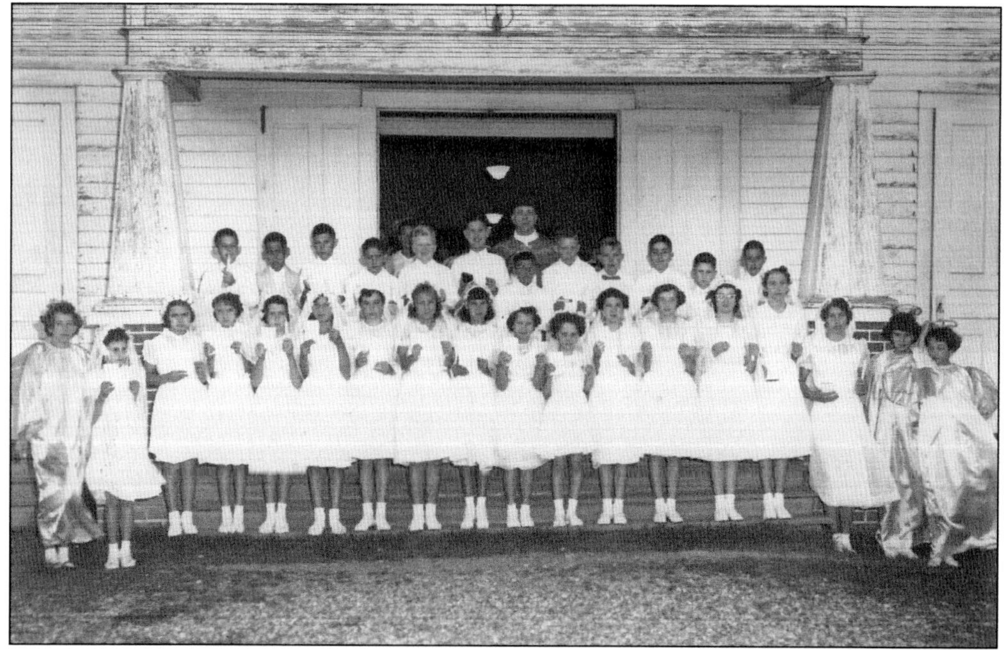

First Holy Communion is an important event for Catholics. The children dress in white, and the families often hold parties to celebrate the event. In this photograph, taken in the 1940s, a First Communion class from the Point Blue area assembles with the parish priest in front of Our Lady of Mount Carmel Church in Chataignier. (Courtesy of J.D. Soileau.)

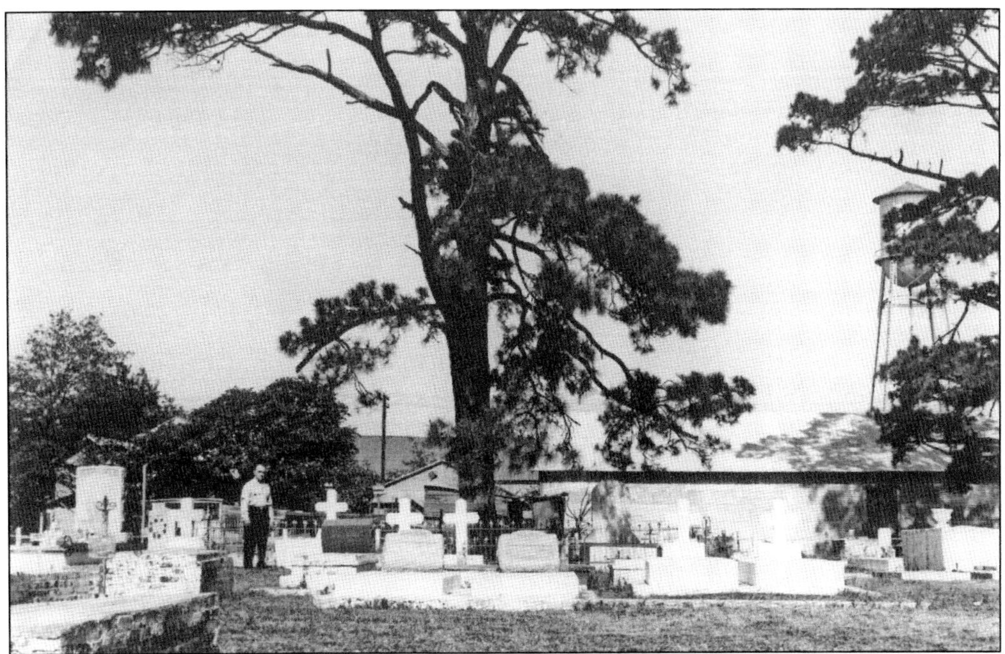

The Old Ville Platte Cemetery, or Le Vieux Cimetière, as most people call it, is located on Chataignier Road. The oldest marked graves date back to 1851, although the sign on the entrance indicates that the cemetery was founded in 1852. Marcellin Garand, the founder of Ville Platte, is buried here, as are many other early citizens. (Courtesy of *Ville Platte Gazette.*)

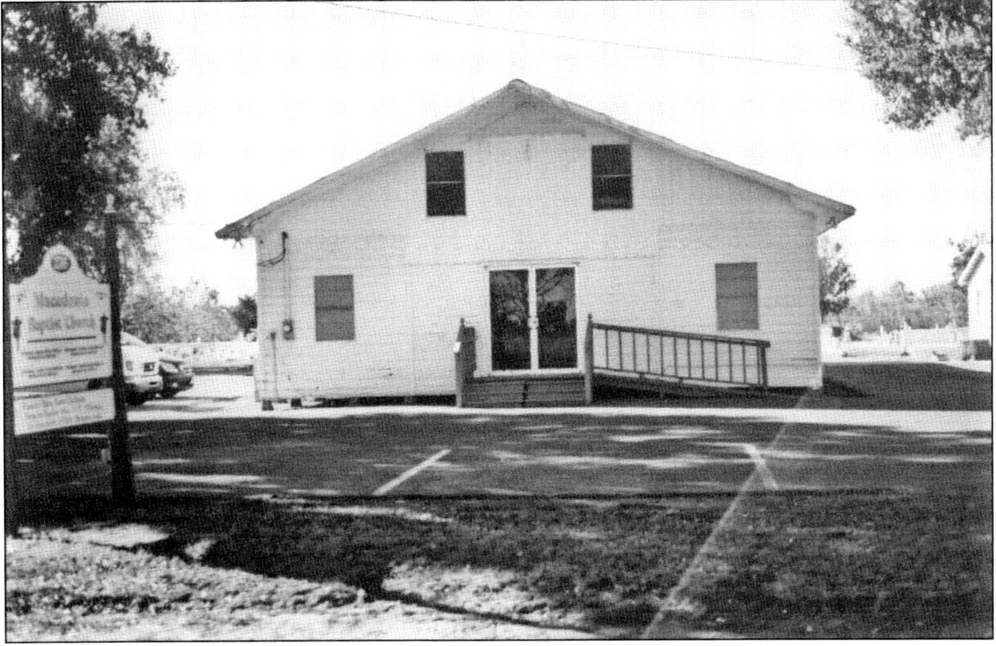

Macedonia Baptist Church has been in existence for more than 70 years, serving the African Americans of Belaire Cove. At one time the church also housed a school for grades one through four. There is a small cemetery behind the church where members of the congregation have been buried. (Courtesy of Jean Kiesel.)

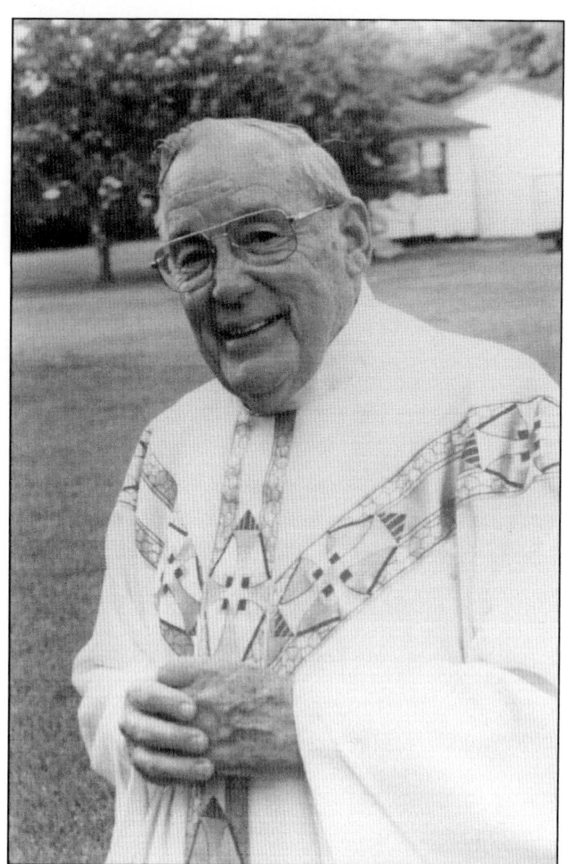

Fr. Leslie Prescott became pastor of St. Peter's Church in Pine Prairie in 1964. His bishop referred to the appointment as a "somewhat difficult mission," for at the time there was a fair amount of friction between the Catholic and Protestant communities. In his quiet, humble way, Father Prescott soothed tensions and persuaded the various factions to work together. He remained in Pine Prairie for 34 years. (Courtesy of Linda McGee.)

The Church of Our Lady, Queen of All Saints was founded in Ville Platte in 1969. Fr. Robert Sibille was the first pastor. Mass was offered in an old skating rink until 1973. This photograph shows the new pastor, Fr. Joseph Brennan, and members of the parish council breaking ground for the new church. (Courtesy of University archives and Acadiana Manuscripts Collection, Dupré Library, UL Lafayette.)

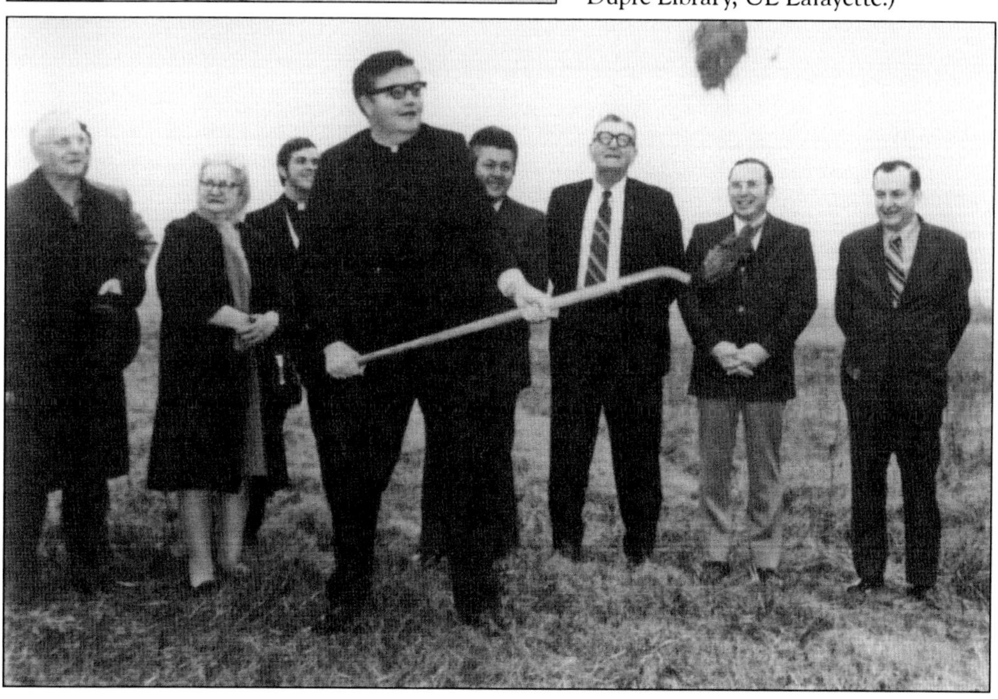

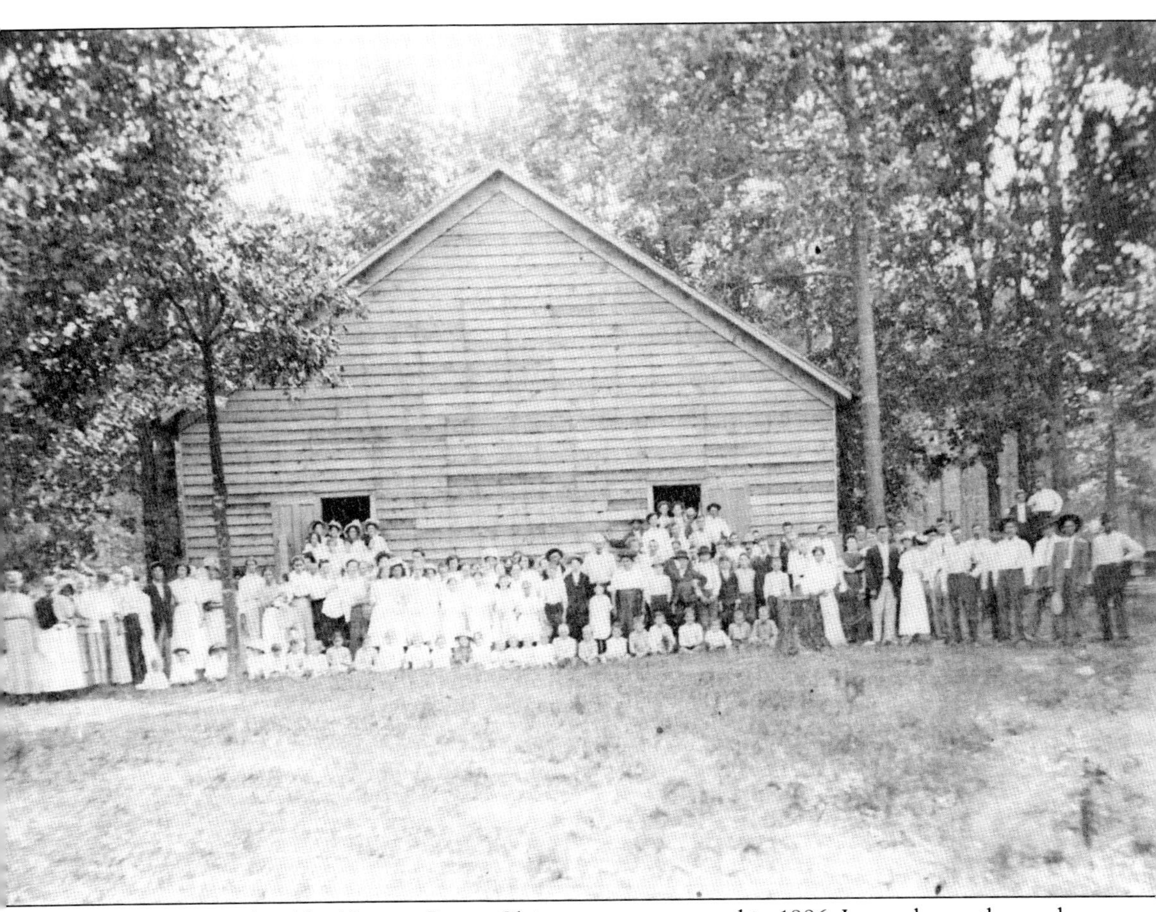

This one-room school building in Bayou Chicot was constructed in 1886. It stood near the road between Ville Platte and Alexandria, today's US Highway 167. The schoolroom was finished, with a ceiling, and had all the modern conveniences of the day: wooden desks and benches, glass windows, and even a chalkboard. Later, a second room was added to the building to house the Baptist church. There were schools in the Bayou Chicot area as early as 1814, for the early settlers valued education. The teacher was usually a young man with some education, or a clergyman. His salary, paid by parents, often came in the form of goods rather than cash. School was held in a church or a vacant house and might run for five months or so. (Courtesy of Jackie Jones.)

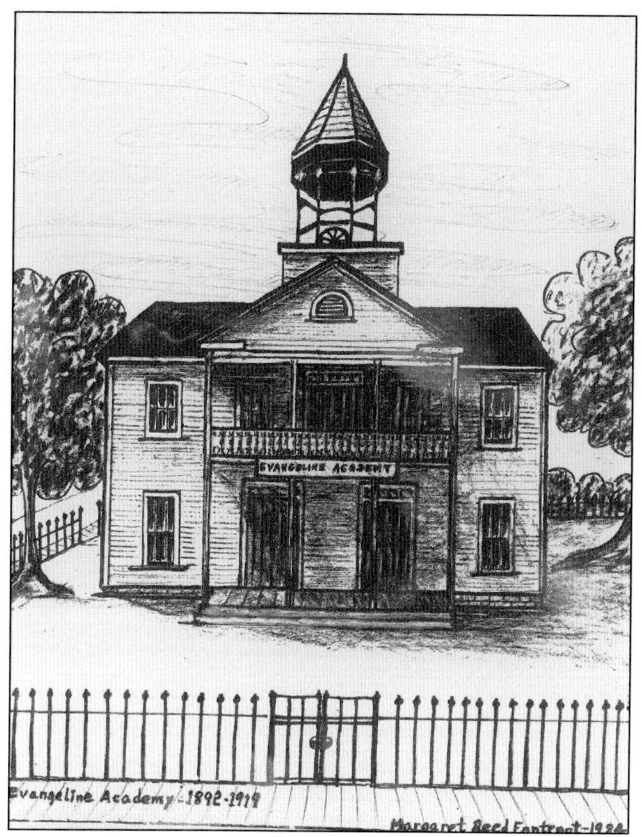

Ville Platte's first school building, on the corner of Main and South Coreil Streets, was the Evangeline Academy, which opened in 1879. George Coverdale was the first principal. E.E. Ortego, who is known as the father of Evangeline Parish education, served as principal from 1880 to 1912. The school was accredited as a high school in 1909, when five students graduated. (Artwork by Margaret Reed Fontenot.)

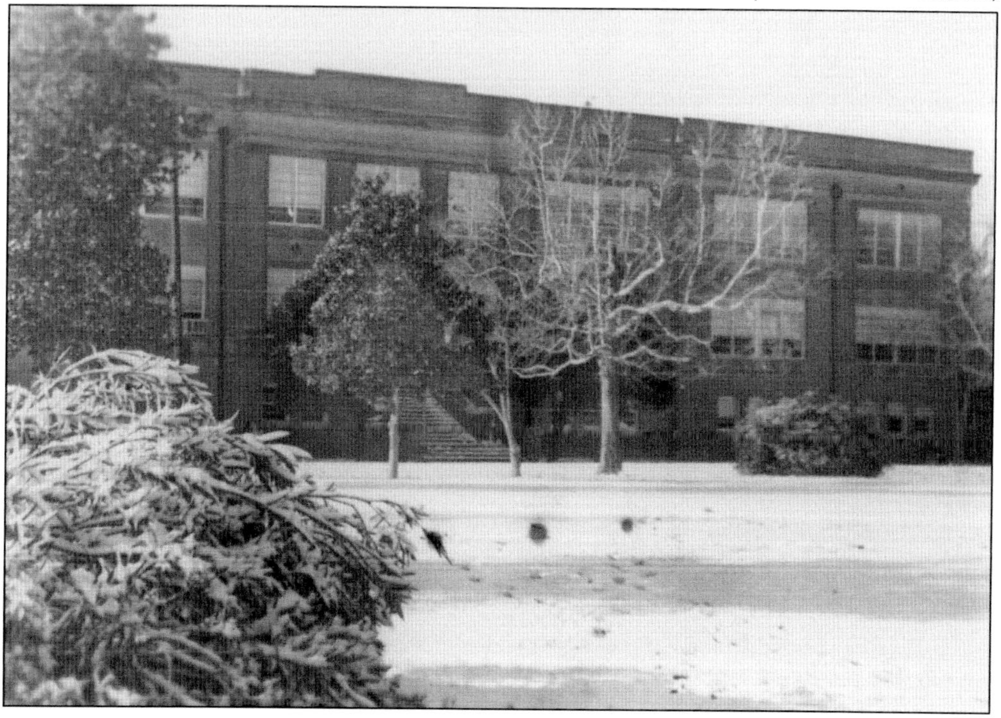

Ville Platte High School was founded in 1908. This brick building was erected in 1938 with Public Works Administration funds. The bell from the Evangeline Academy was presented to Ville Platte High by the city administration in 1958 and was mounted on the campus as a permanent memorial by the school's alumni. The school is shown here after a rare snowfall. (Courtesy of *Ville Platte Gazette*.)

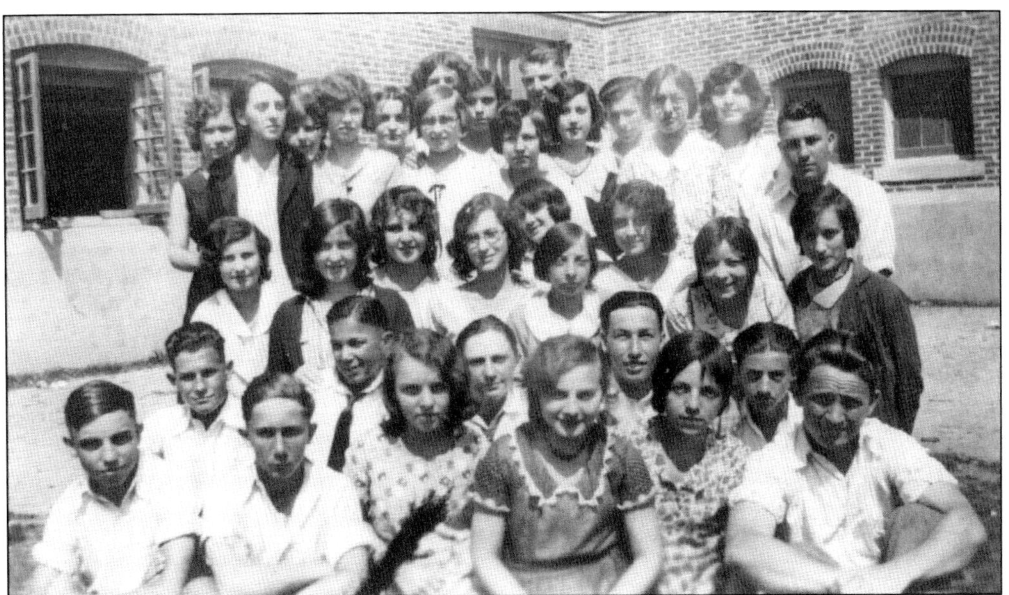

Some of the teachers in this picture of the Chataignier School in 1928–1929 have been identified. In the fourth row on the left is Mrs. Ardoin, fifth grade. On the far right is Joseph Rozas, math teacher. At top center is John Manuel, seventh grade teacher and coach, later principal of the school. Also pictured are Miss Annie Manuel, second grade; and Miss Israel, fourth grade. (Courtesy of Mike Miller.)

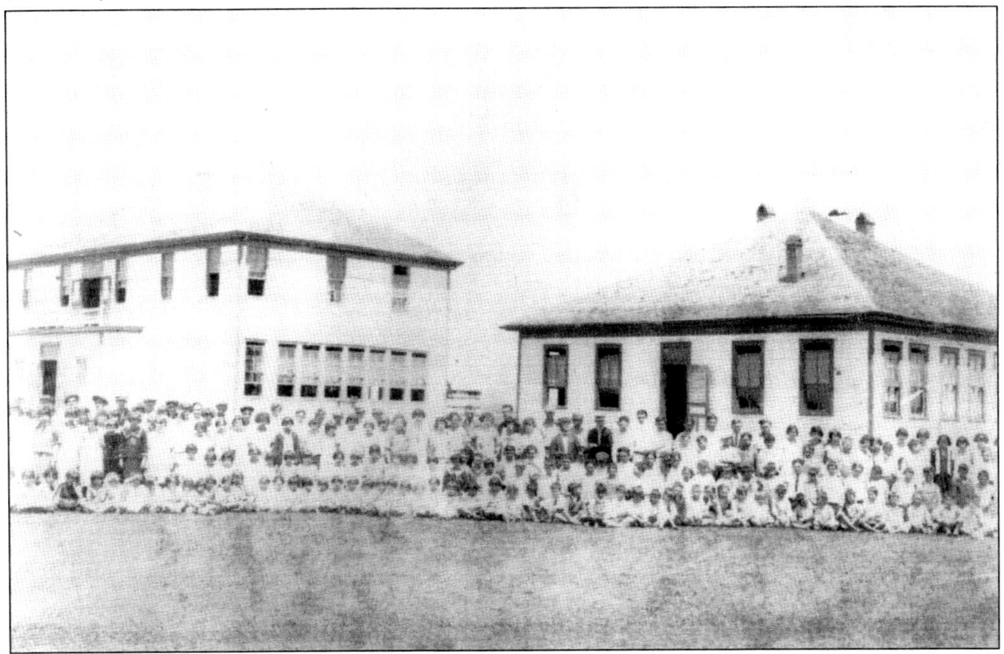

The Chataignier School included both elementary and secondary grades. The high school only went through grade 11. This photograph, taken sometime in the 1920s, shows the student body in front of the school buildings. The building on the left held the elementary school, and the one on the right contained the high school and the home economics department. (Courtesy of Rayford and Delores Chapman.)

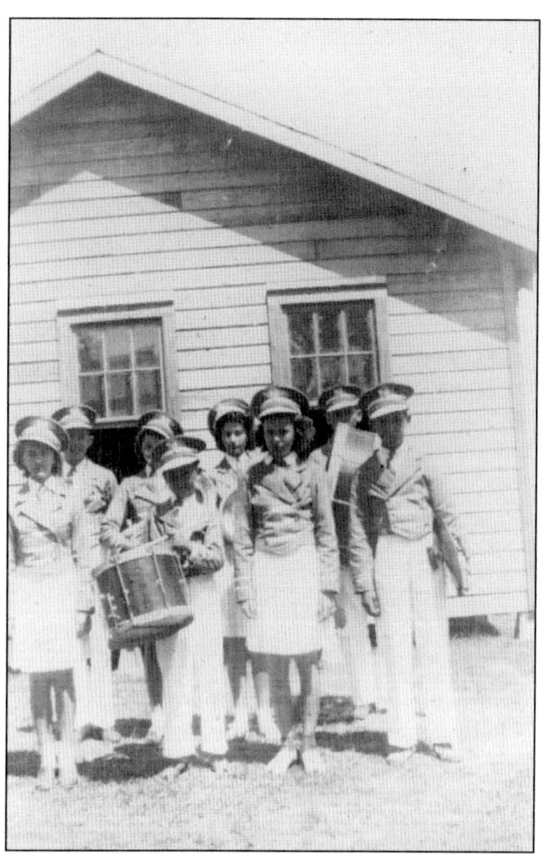

Chataignier School organized a band in the early 1940s under the direction of Miriam LeBlanc, a teacher from Reserve, Louisiana. Local citizens helped purchase the uniforms. Here, members of the percussion section pose with their instruments in their new uniforms. In addition, the band boasted eight clarinets, five saxophones, four horns, seven trumpets, and five drum majors or majorettes. (Courtesy of Allison "Sonny" Launey.)

The third-grade class of the Chataignier School gathered on the school steps for a group photograph in 1945 or 1946. The students are wearing their best clothes. The boys have collared shirts and either pants or overalls, and the girls are in their best dresses. A few of the girls even have shoes, which were decidedly optional most of the year. (Courtesy of Rayford and Delores Chapman.)

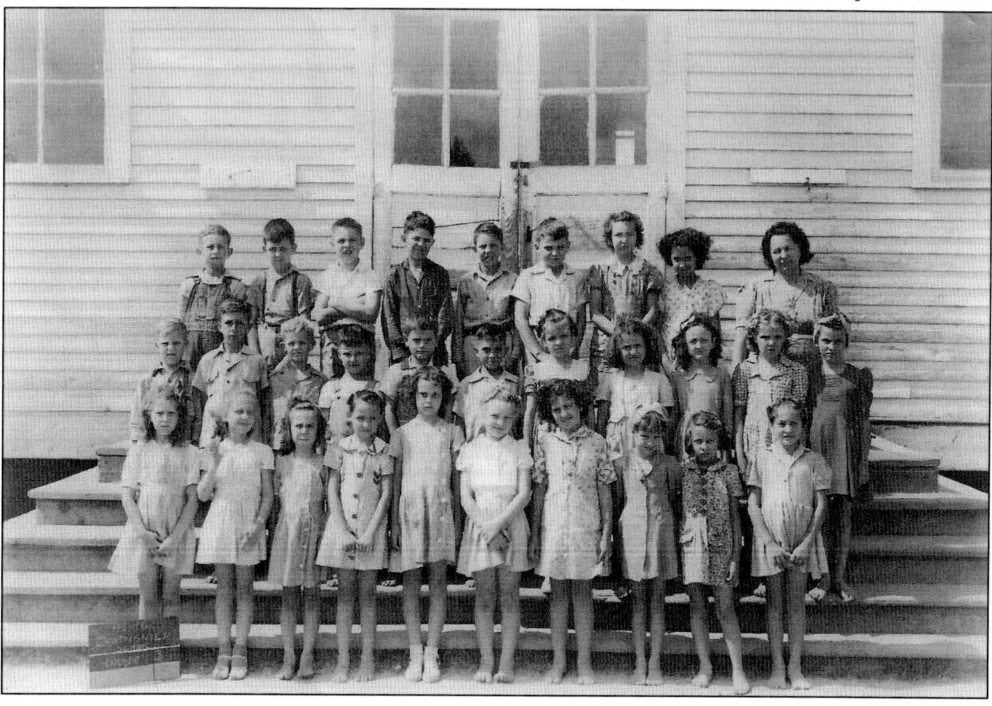

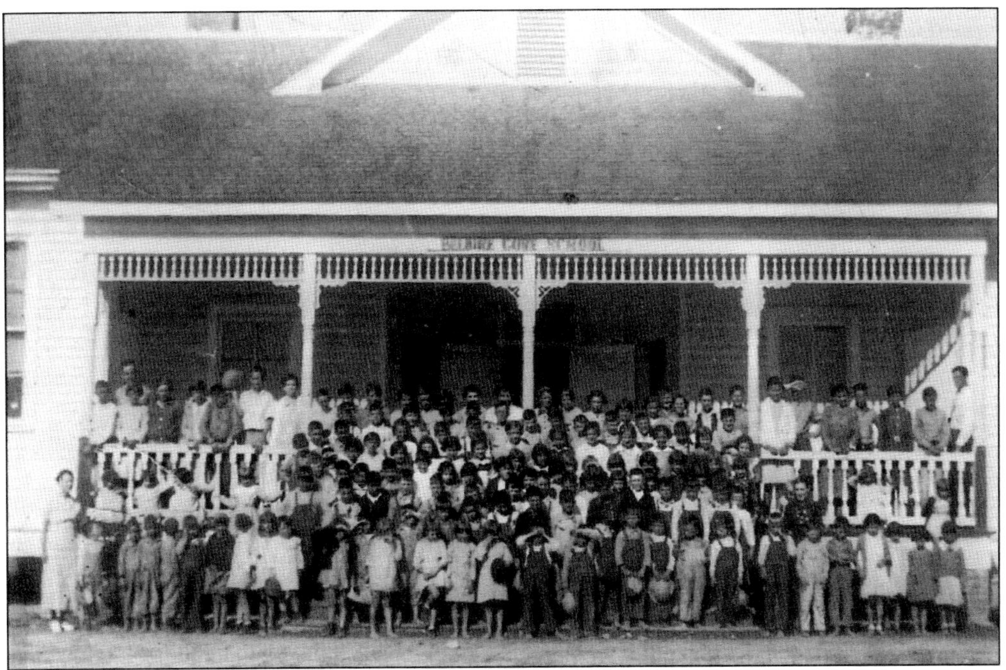

Belaire Cove School was located on Belaire Cove Road near Sacred Heart Chapel, and set back from the road. In the early 1940s, it had about 200 students in grades one through seven, led by seven or eight teachers. Children walked as much as two miles to school each day. The school closed around 1948. (Courtesy of J. Kilren Vidrine.)

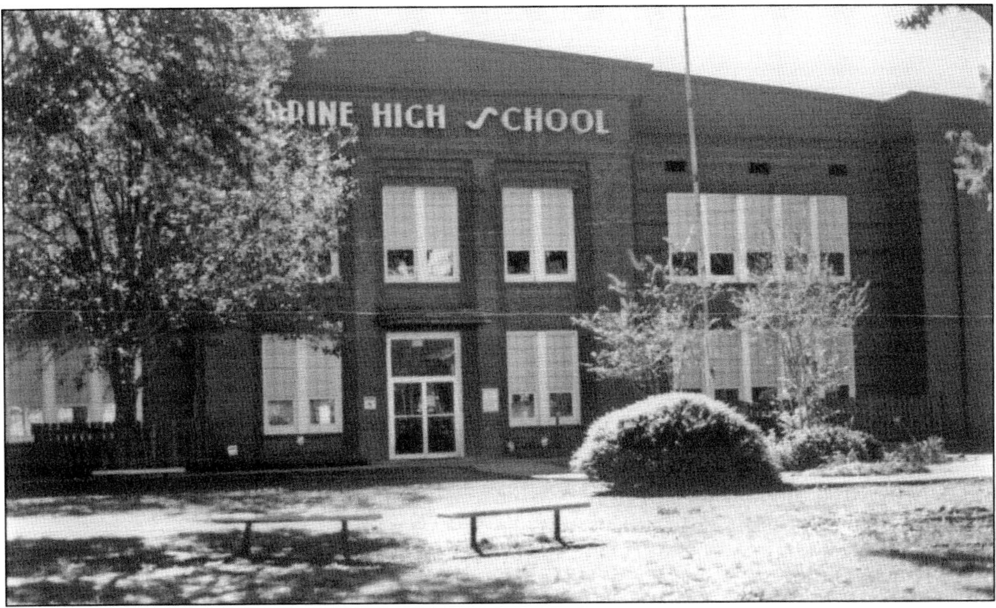

Dr. Jules Vidrine practiced in the Vidrine community for 51 years. A landowner and planter, he was interested in agricultural development. He was active in the establishment of Evangeline Parish and was the first president of the school board. He promoted higher education in the parish and established the agriculture program at Vidrine High School. The school also had the first home economics curriculum in the state. (Courtesy of Jean Kiesel.)

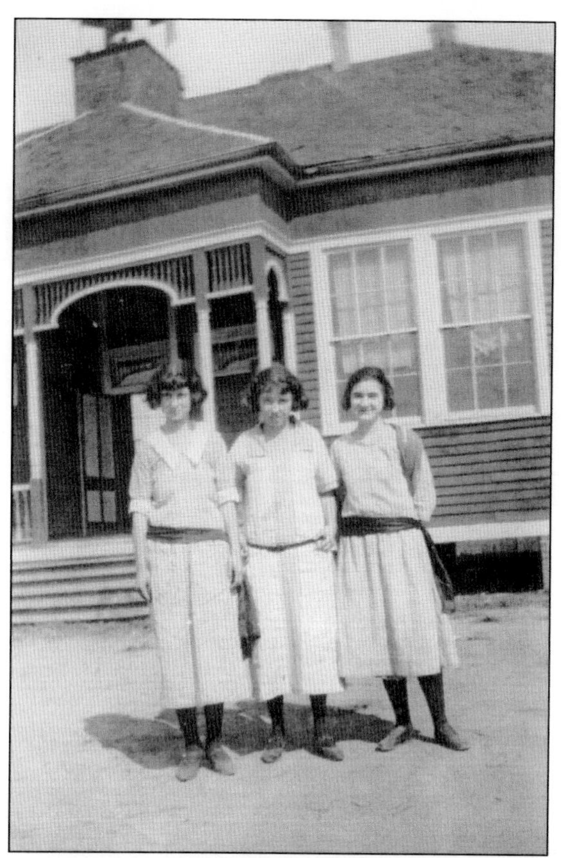

The Point Blue School was housed in this building from 1910 until the 1940s. The land for the school was acquired from Paul Perron. In the 1940s, it had over 100 students in grades one through seven, and five teachers. It was accredited by the state. The last principal was Ed Manuel. (Courtesy of J.D. Soileau.)

The Chataignier senior class of 1954–1955 gathers on the steps of the school. From left to right are (first row) Mavis Fontenot, Delores Pitre, Barbara LaFleur, Juanita Bertrand, and Jessie Ardoin; (second row) Jimmy Ardoin, Mary Hebert, Genevieve Rozas, Shirley Fruge, Ruth Ann Fontenot, Winnie Manuel, and Wilbur Rozas; (third row) Wilbert Guidry, Donald Ray Hebert, Gene Pitre, Earl Courville, Floyd Guilbeau, and Harry Lee Bertrand. Not present was Jackie Brown. (Courtesy of J.D. Soileau.)

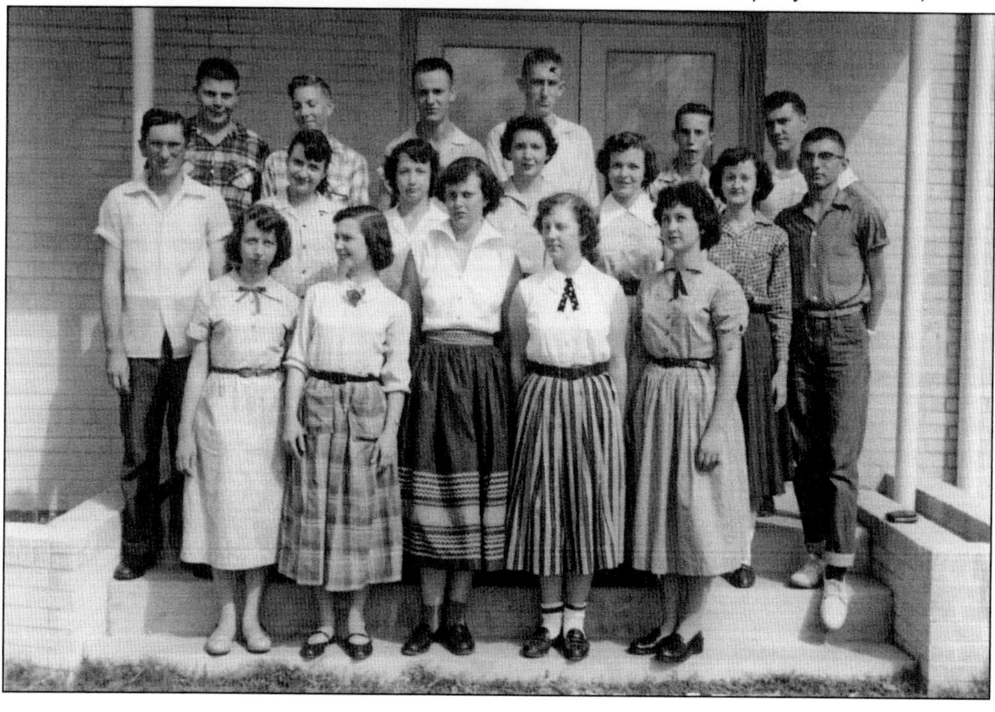

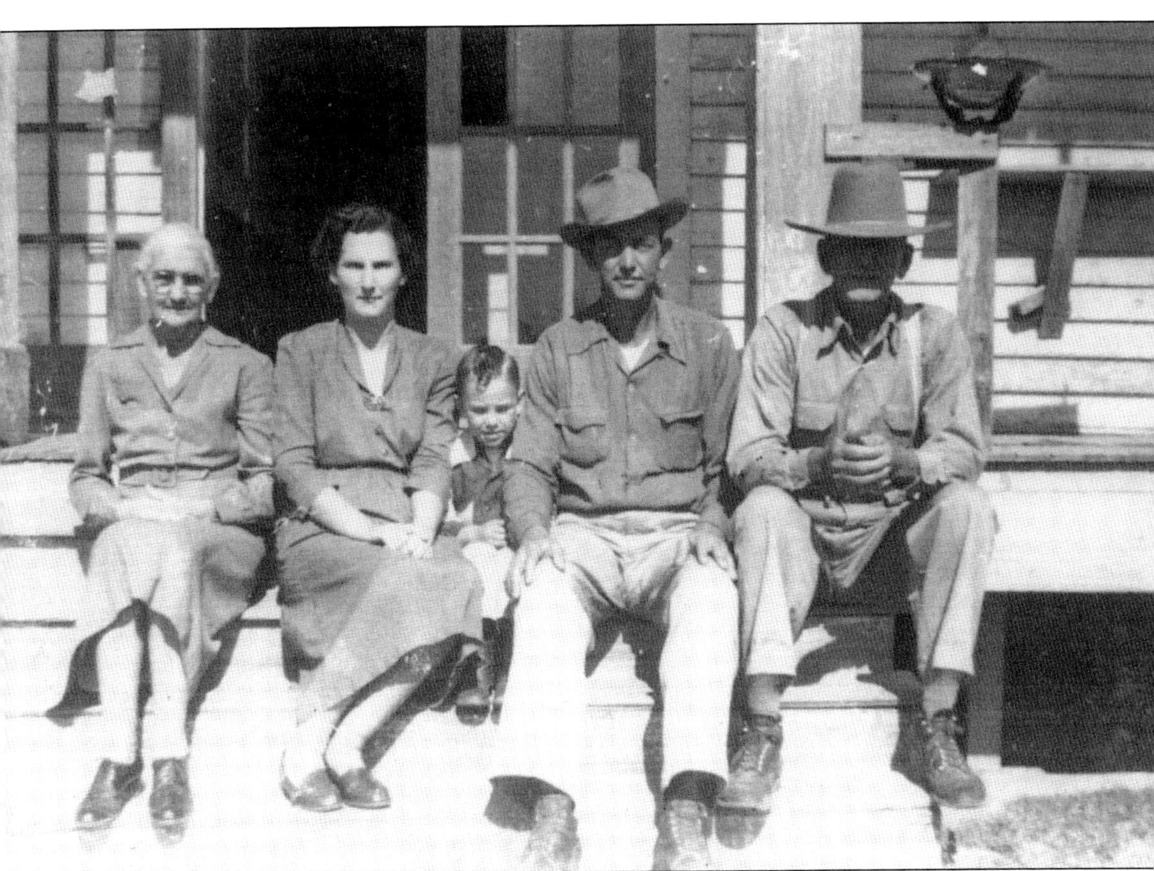

Point Blue School closed about 1944, and the students transferred to Chataignier. Later, the school building in Point Blue was converted into retirement apartments for local seniors. Here, Marius (far right) and Edmonia Fontenot (far left) visit with their son Habie Fontenot and his wife and son in 1952. (Courtesy of J.D. Soileau.)

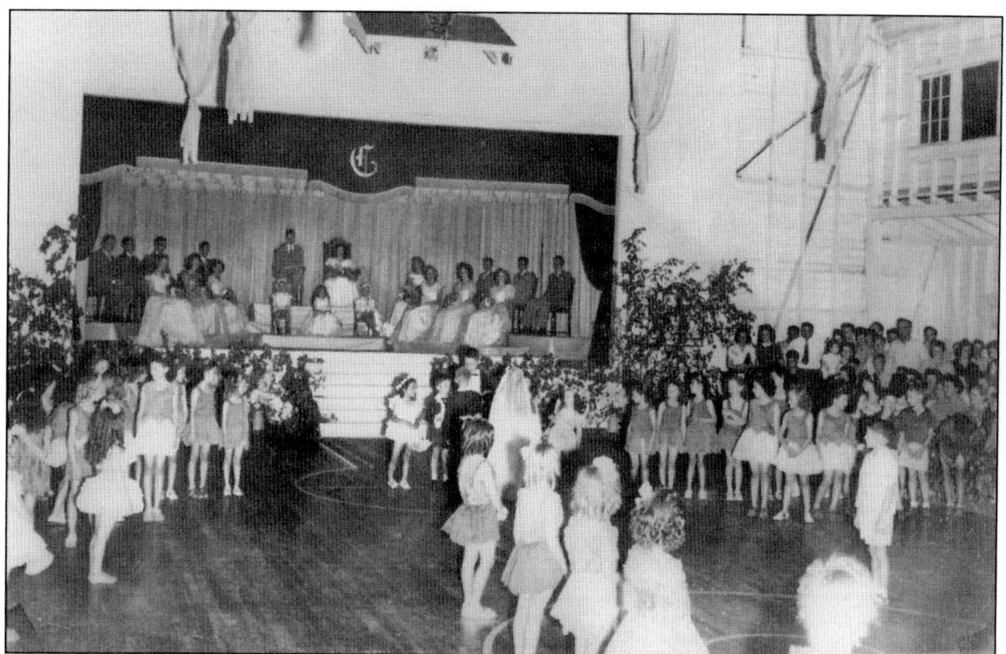

In this photograph, students are putting on a May Day pageant in the Chataignier School gymnasium in 1944 or 1945. The king and queen of May Day sit on the stage with their court. On the floor is a mock wedding, with Gwen Rozas and Clyde Vidrine as the bride and groom. The Fairy Princess is Kathryn Lebleu. Everyone else is a flower. (Courtesy of Kathryn LeBleu Guillory.)

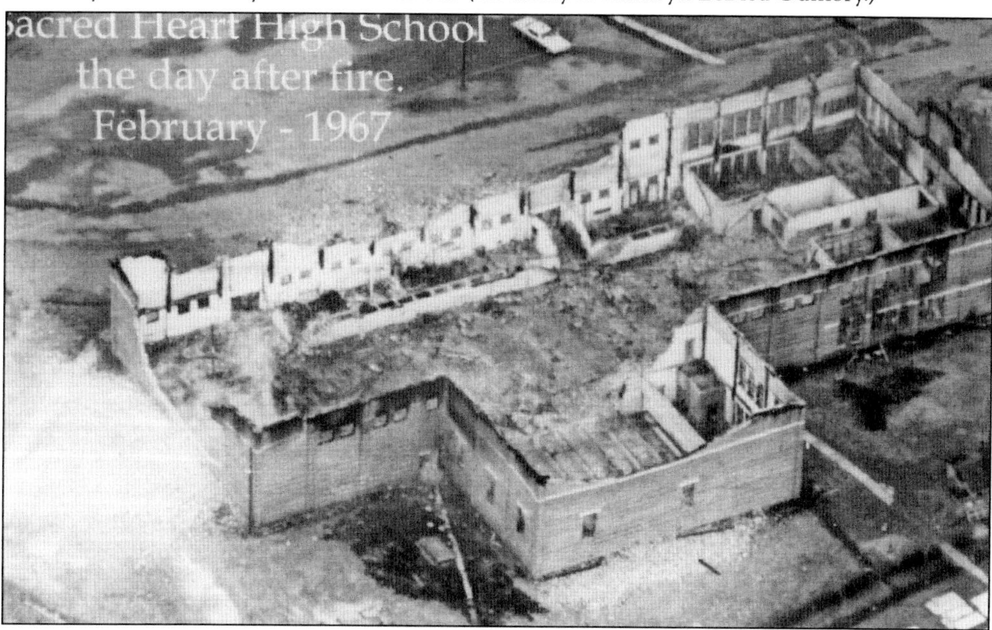

Sacred Heart High School burned down on February 16, 1968, despite the best efforts of fire departments from Ville Platte and neighboring communities. Only the shell was left, as seen here. The school was quickly rebuilt, however, and reopened 15 months later. The cross from the old building was salvaged and remounted on the entrance to the new school. (Courtesy of Nick's on Main.)

Four

AGRICULTURE

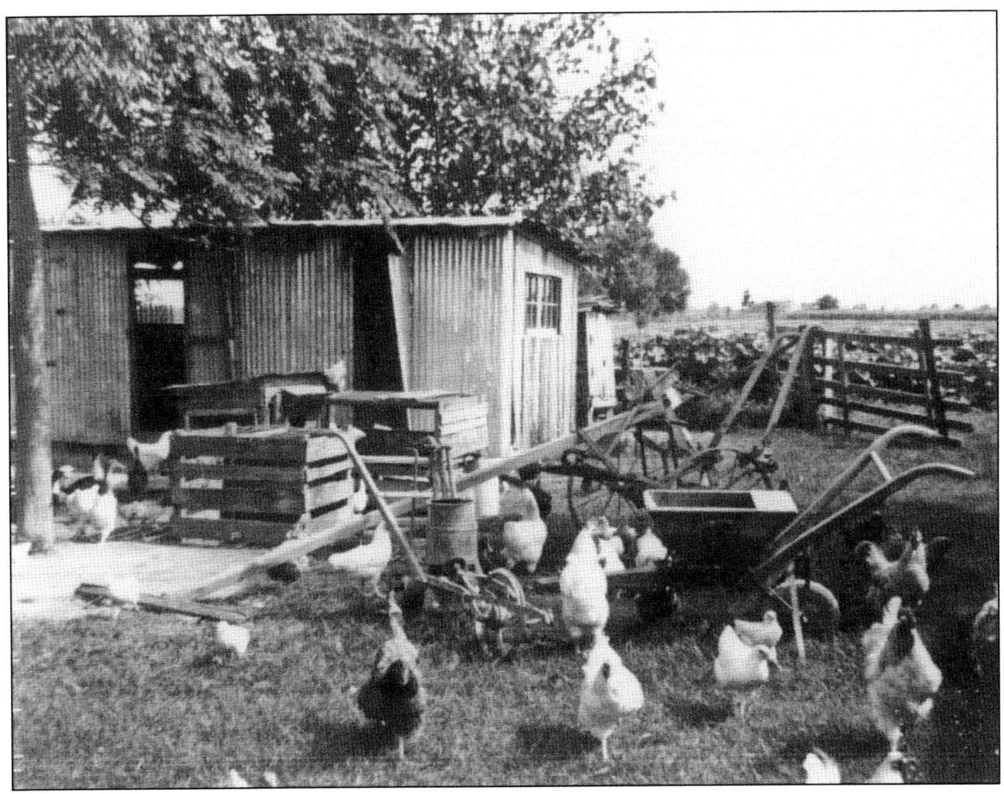

Evangeline Parish is largely rural. Typically, farmers grew a staple crop such as cotton, sweet potatoes, or rice, but families also kept livestock and maintained large gardens to help feed themselves. This farmyard in the Point Blue area includes chickens and ducks raised for eggs and meat, and assorted farm implements, including two seeders and a plow. (Courtesy of J.D. Soileau.)

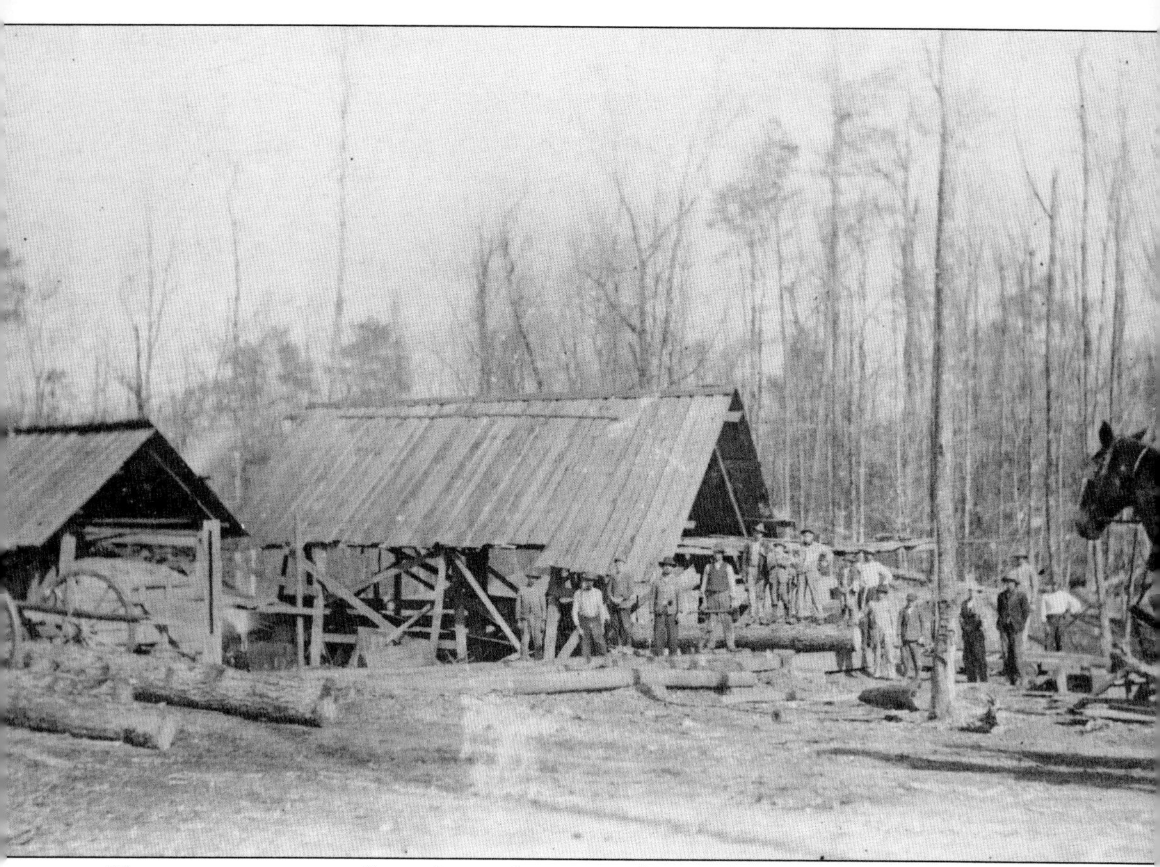

There were many sawmills in the northern part of Evangeline Parish at the turn of the 20th century. This one was owned by Guy Johnson and was located in the woods near Bayou Chicot. Trees were cut down by two men using a crosscut saw, and the logs were hauled to the sawmill by ox teams. Much of the wood cut down was pine, but there were also abundant hardwoods, such as hickory, poplar, magnolia, and red gum. The first sawmills were powered by water; later ones used steam. Sawmills employed many men from the area and were a welcome source of cash income for farmers when the crops were laid by. (Courtesy of Jackie Jones.)

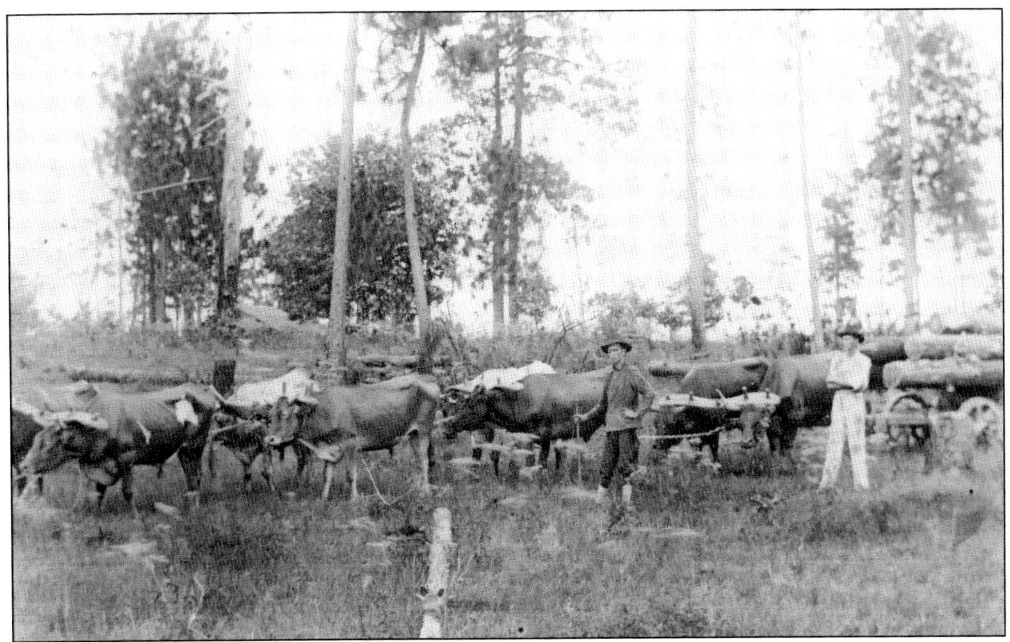

The piney woods of northern Evangeline Parish provided timber to supply a number of sawmills around Bayou Chicot. At times, there were as many as five or six sawmills operating in the area. The lumber usually was sold for construction or used for railroad ties or on oil wells. Trees were cut with crosscut saws, and the timber was hauled to the mills by ox teams. (Courtesy of Jackie Jones.)

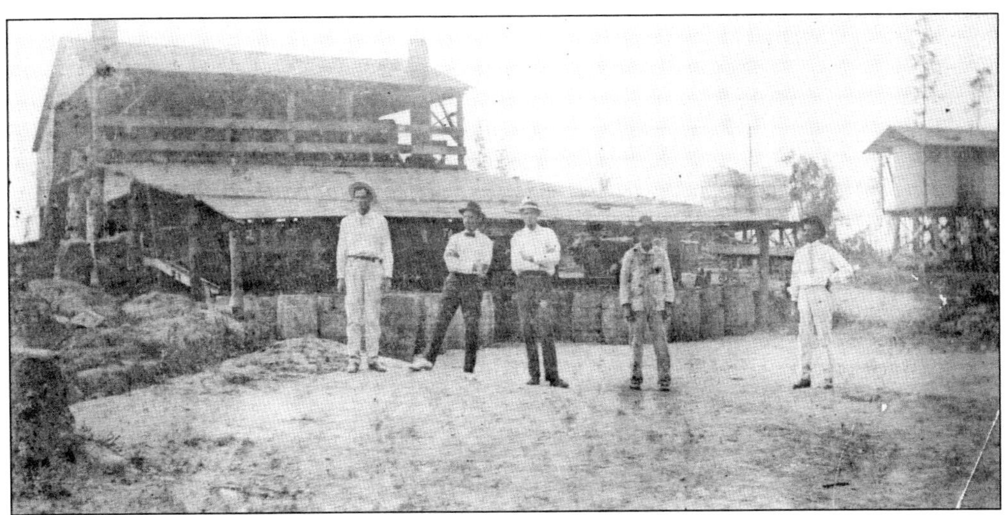

Logging and related industries prospered in northern Evangeline Parish at the turn of the last century. Pine trees would be bled for turpentine, which was distilled in a process similar to making whiskey. The finished product was used for medicinal purposes and in paints. This turpentine distillery, pictured about 1916, was located west of Turkey Creek on what is now known as the Gravel Pit Road. (Courtesy of Jackie Jones.)

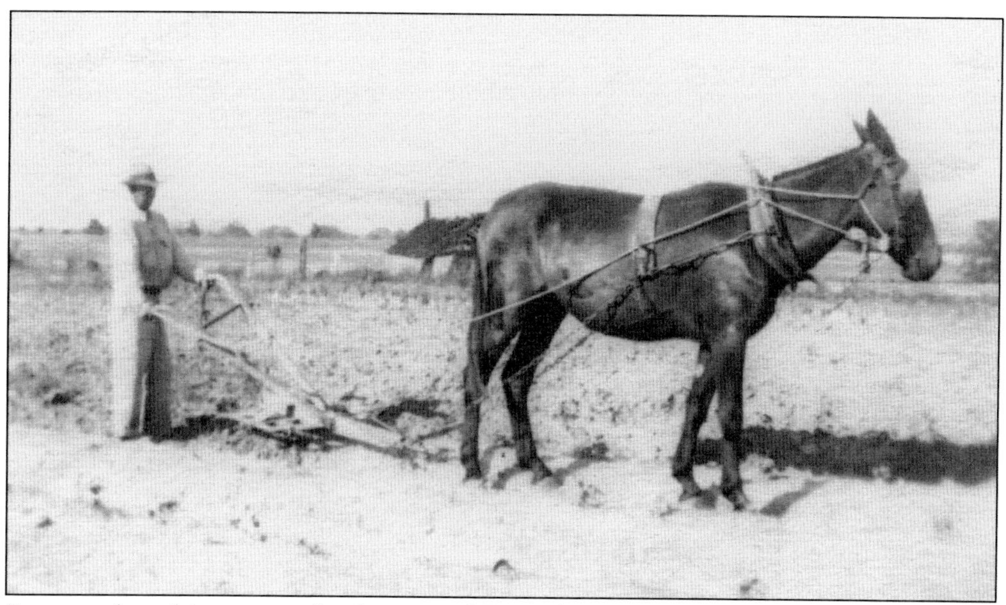

Scenes such as this one were familiar around Evangeline Parish during the first half of the last century. They were so common that it was not often thought worth recording for posterity. Here, Avie Fontenot uses a mule to pull a single-tooth side harrow to prepare his cotton field. The photograph was taken in 1942 near Pine Prairie. (Courtesy of Jackie Jones.)

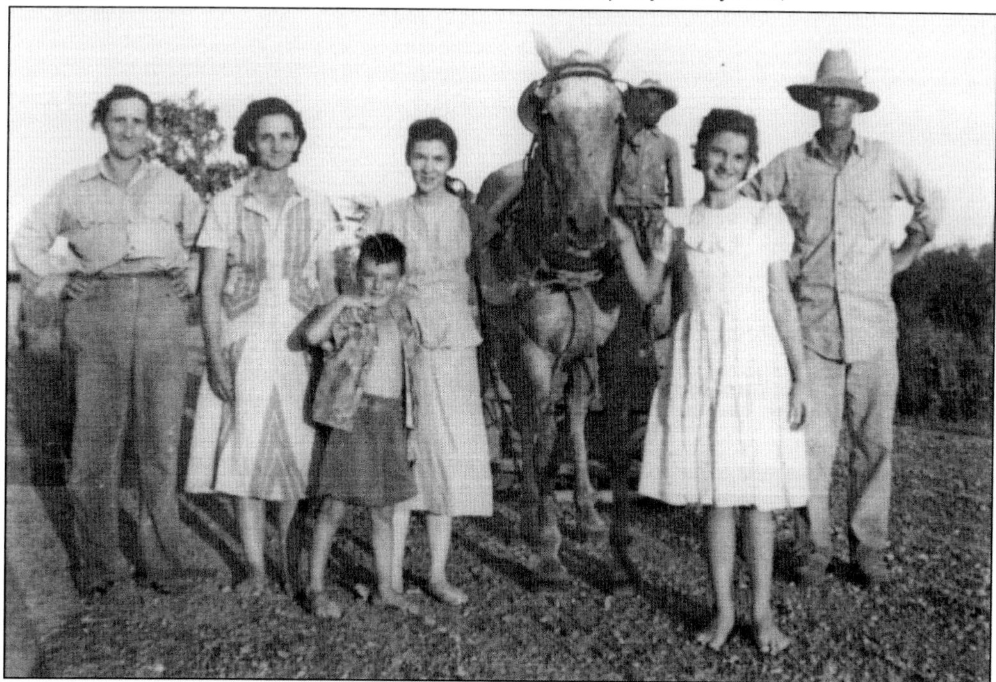

Runnie Fontenot Matte grew up in Belaire Cove, outside of Ville Platte. There were no roads in the Cove at the time. Her family is seen here after a day picking cotton. From left to right are Edna Dupre, Mrs. Noah B. "Regina" Fontenot (mother), Wadness Fontenot (son), Ruby F. Holmes (daughter), Raleigh Griffin (helper and friend), Runnie F. Matte (daughter), and Noah B. Fontenot (father). (Courtesy of Runnie F. Matte.)

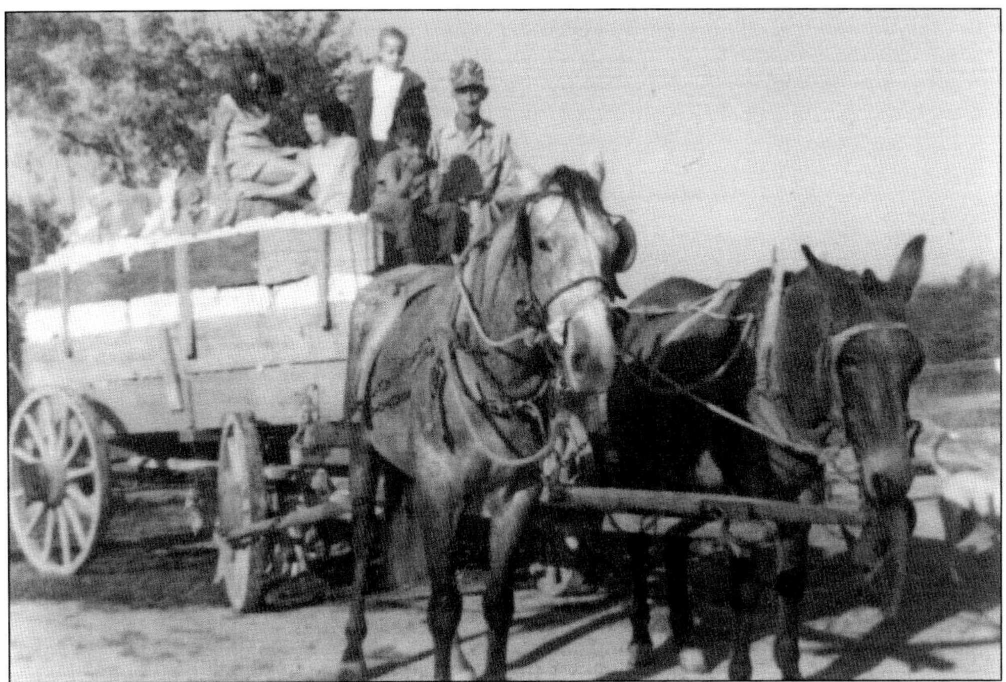

Felix Soileau raised cotton in the Point Blue area for many years before he retired. In the late 1960s, when attempts were being made to reopen the cotton gin in Point Blue, Soileau grew one last crop to support the gin and to allow his grandchildren to get a taste of cotton farming. They are shown here hauling the cotton to the gin. (Courtesy of J.D. Soileau.)

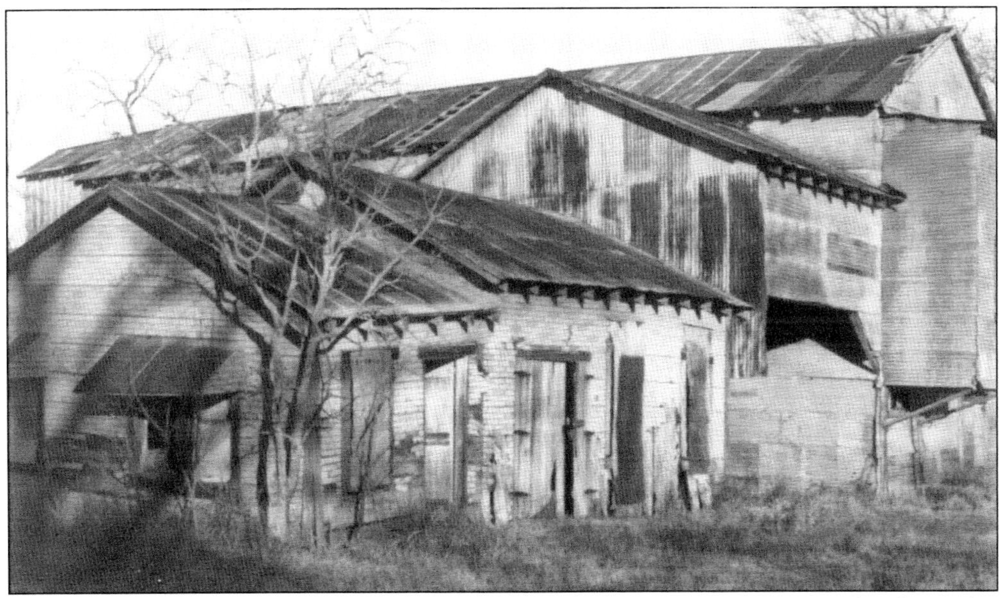

When cotton was the principal crop in Evangeline Parish, cotton gins were a familiar sight. Farmers hauled their crops to the gin in wagons drawn by mules or horses. There, the cotton was weighed and ginned to remove the seeds before being packed into bales for shipment. As cotton declined, the gins went out of business and disappeared. This one in Point Blue burned down in 1995. (Courtesy of J.D. Soileau.)

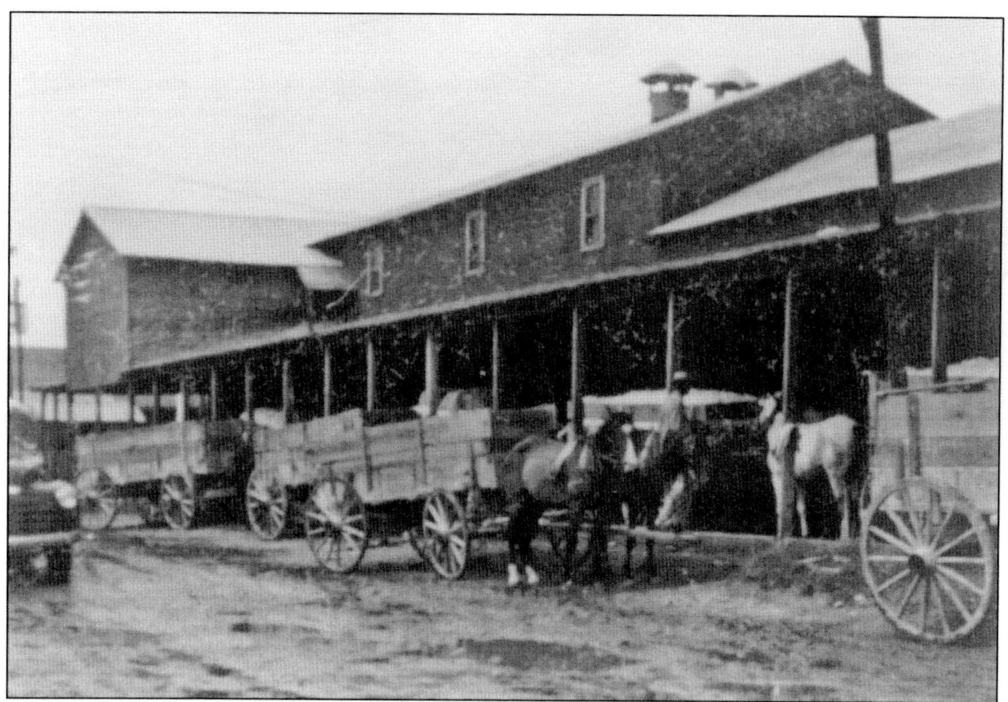

The Service Gin Company was located on West Railroad Street in Ville Platte. It was owned by Clabert Duos and Audley J. Soileau, who also owned cotton gins in Plaisance and Basile. In this 1948 photograph a number of cotton wagons stand under the shed waiting to unload, while empty wagons wait in the yard while their loads are weighed. (Courtesy of Mitzie Duos Cochrane.)

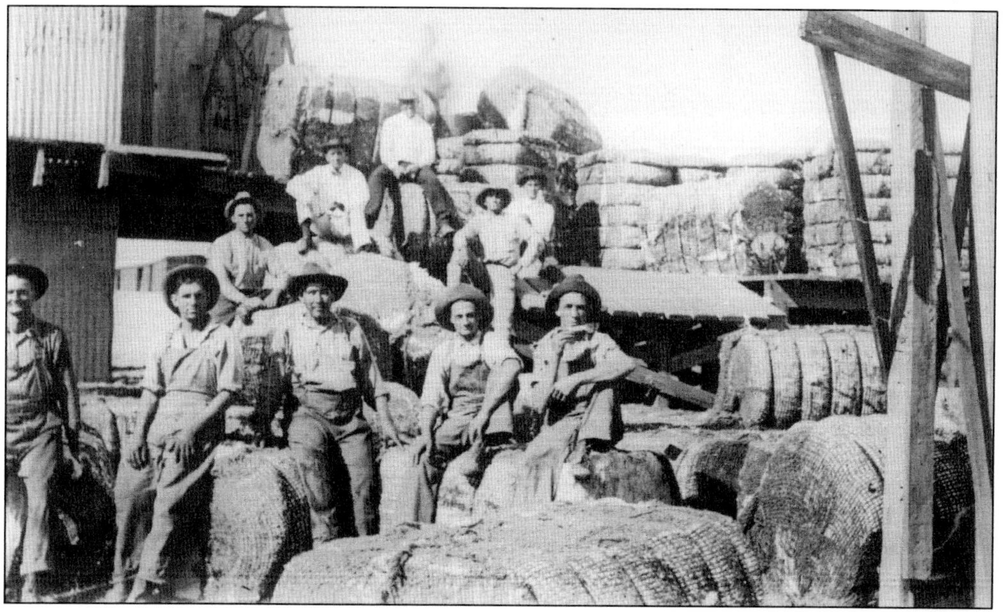

For more than a century, cotton was the principal crop cultivated in Evangeline Parish. From the earliest settlement until well into the 20th century, most farmers in the parish planted cotton. After picking, the cotton was hauled to the local gin to be ginned and baled. The cash received from the sale of the crop supported the family for the next year. (Courtesy of Pam McGee.)

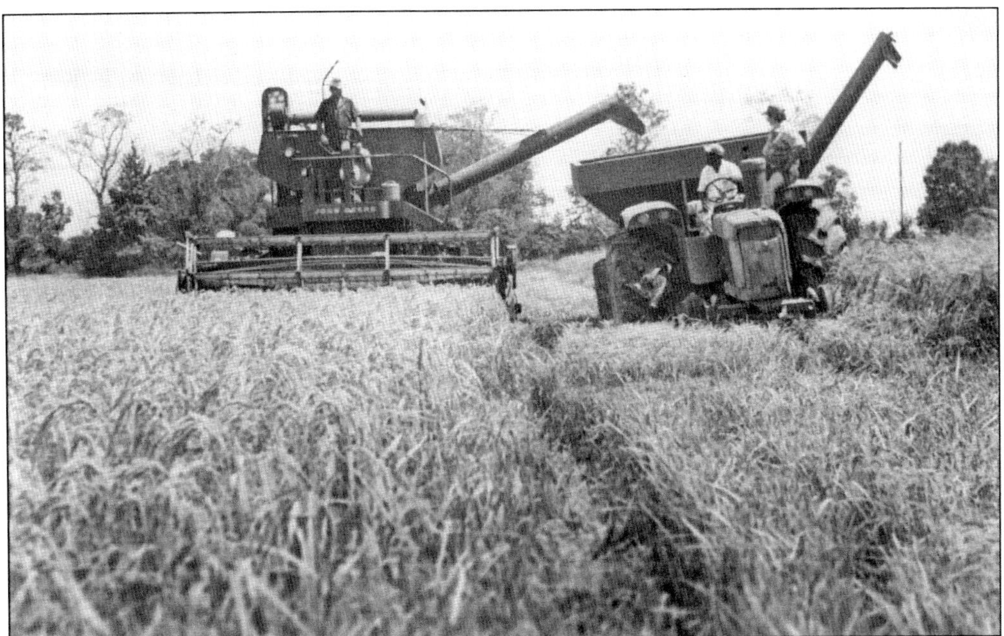

Rice became an important crop in southwest Louisiana in the late 19th century. The flat prairielands, water-retaining clay subsoil, warm temperatures, and abundant annual rainfall provided ideal growing conditions for the crop. Rice fields extend well into Evangeline Parish, and rice is the parish's most important crop both in acreage and value. (Courtesy of *Ville Platte Gazette*.)

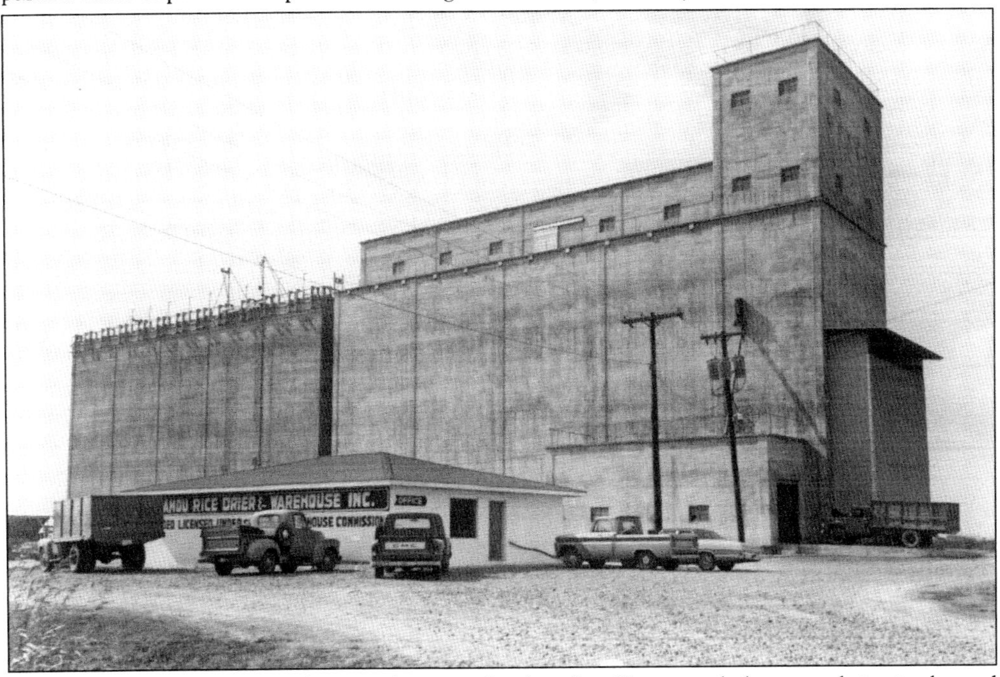

The Mamou Rice Dryer has been in business for decades. Here, newly harvested rice is cleaned and hulled, and some of the moisture removed before it is packaged. At one time, rice mills dotted the landscape of southwestern Louisiana, but consolidation has closed many of the smaller ones. (Courtesy of *Ville Platte Gazette*.)

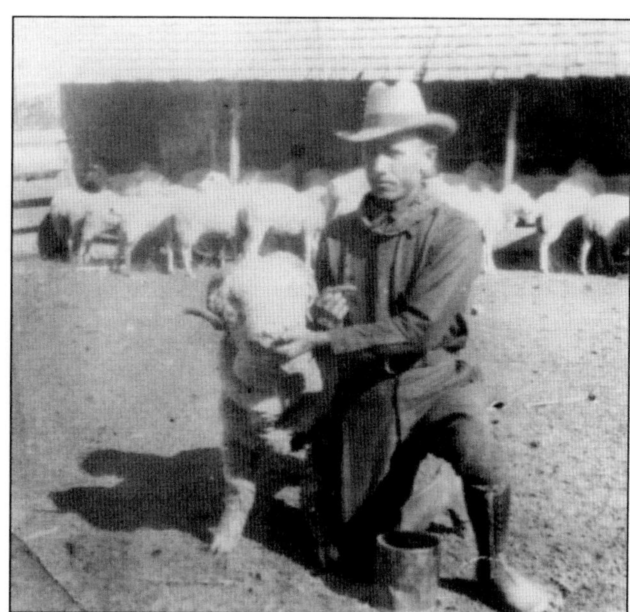

Joe Johnson moved to Caney Creek as a youth to work in his uncle's sawmill. He wanted to be a landowner, so at age 20 he bought his first 200 acres. Eventually he built one of the largest cattle and sheep operations in the area. To improve his stock, he bought this ram in 1939 for $600, about what one of his workers earned in a year. (Courtesy of Barbara Johnson Vautrot.)

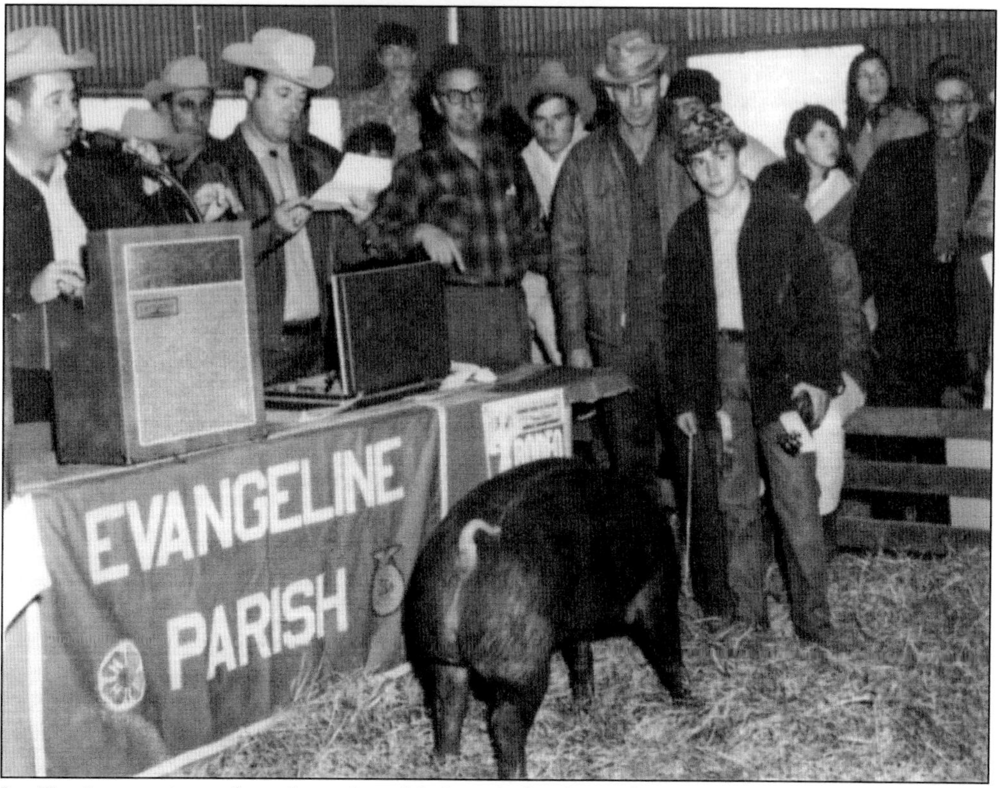

Joe Tate's commission barn hosted weekly livestock sales and an auction each year showcasing animals raised by local 4-H members. The men behind the table are, from left to right, Jennings Tate, Charles "Fuzzy" Guillory, 4-H agent Aubrey Mire, and county agent Newton Jeansonne. Larry Fontenot exhibits his pig as his sisters Lorraine and Linda and retired county agent Charlie Tassin watch on the far right. (Courtesy of Pam McGee.)

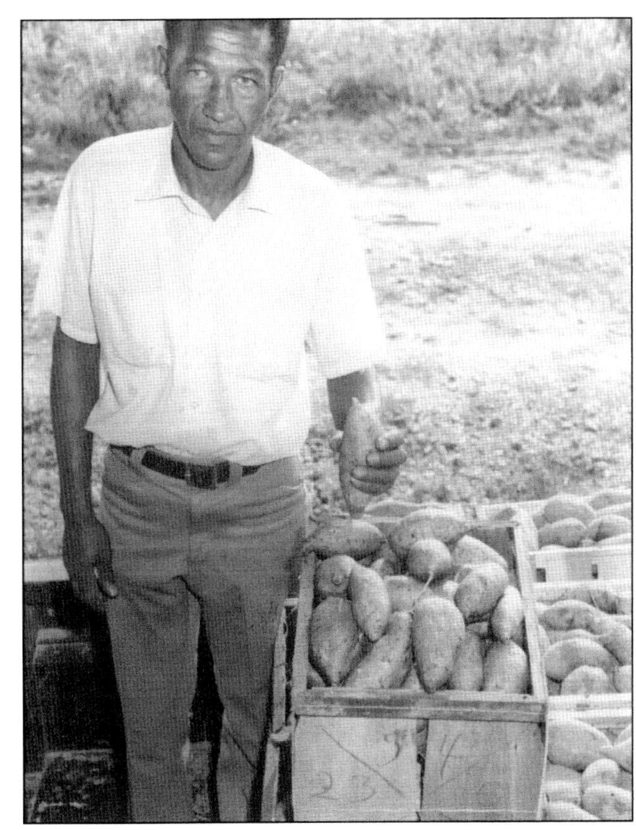

Sweet potatoes were a major crop in Evangeline Parish 30 years ago, with over a million crates harvested. A generation earlier, sweet potatoes were a staple crop for the parish's largely rural population. Delicious, nutritious, and versatile, sweet potatoes are an excellent source of beta-carotene, which the body converts into vitamin A. (Courtesy of *Ville Platte Gazette*.)

Back when sweet potatoes were a major crop in Evangeline Parish, Ville Platte had a canning factory. Here, women pack the peeled and cut tubers into cans, after which syrup would be added and the cans sealed. Sweet potatoes and yams are not related, but the terms are used interchangeably, and sweeter varieties of sweet potatoes are often marketed as yams. (Courtesy of *Ville Platte Gazette*.)

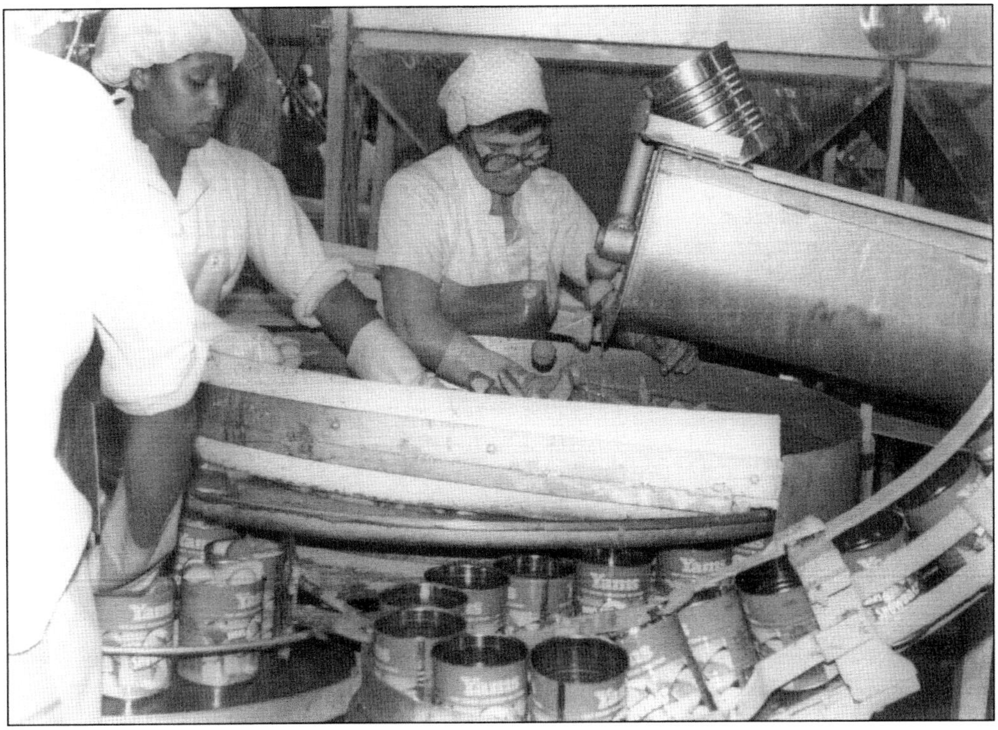

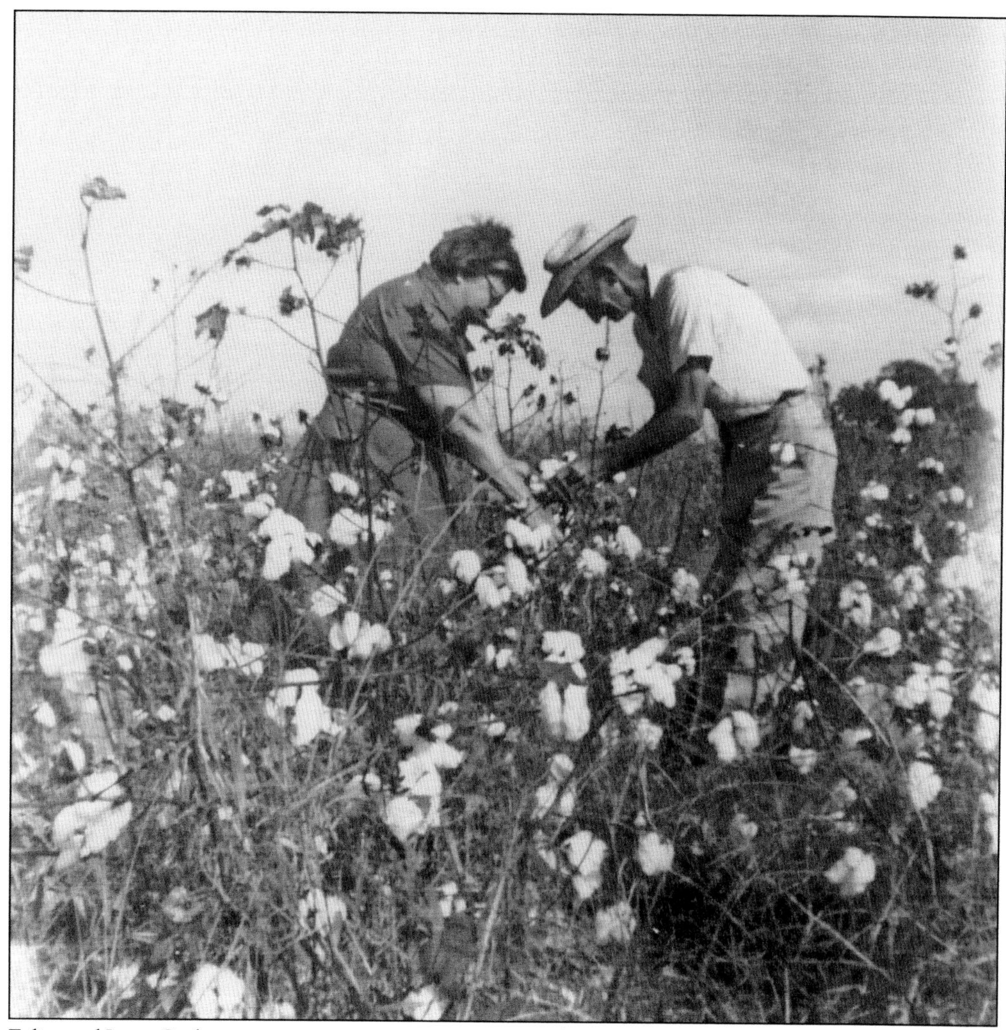

Felix and Lena Soileau grew cotton, sweet potatoes, and corn on their farm near Point Blue. For the harvest, they hired extra help from Ville Platte. Lena worked in the fields along with the men until midmorning, when she would go back to the house to prepare lunch for the workers. After lunch, she returned to the fields and worked until the end of the day. (Courtesy of J.D. Soileau.)

Five

BUSINESSES

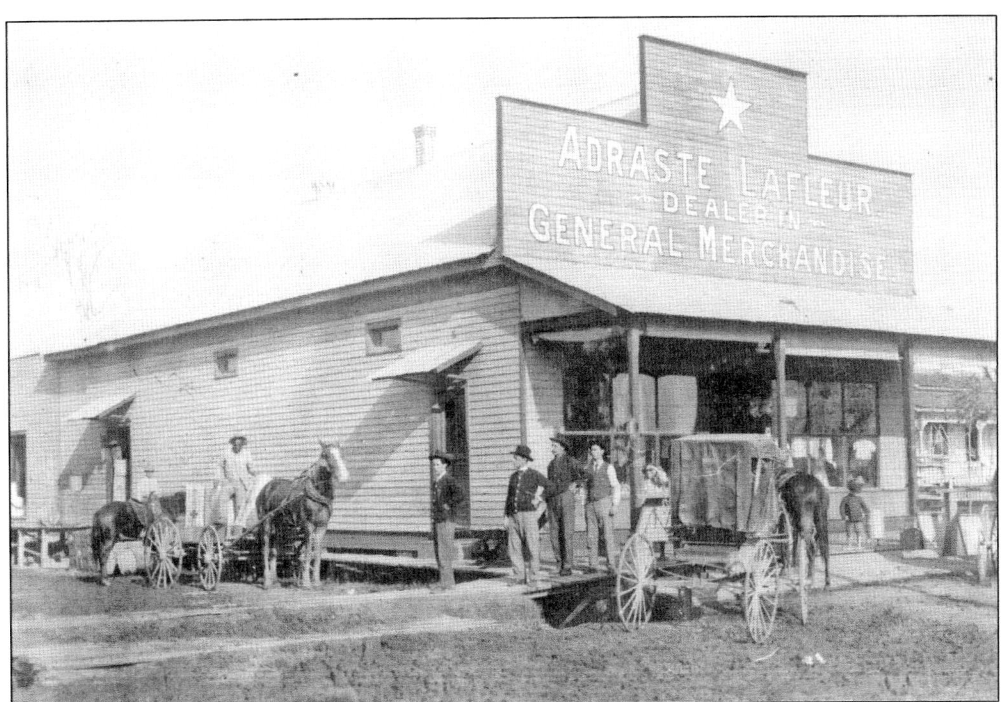

Adraste Lafleur was one of the leaders in the movement to create Evangeline Parish. He went on to serve as its first tax assessor, and at one time served on the police jury. His general merchandise store stood on the corner of Chataignier and Main Streets in Ville Platte. (Courtesy of *Ville Platte Gazette*.)

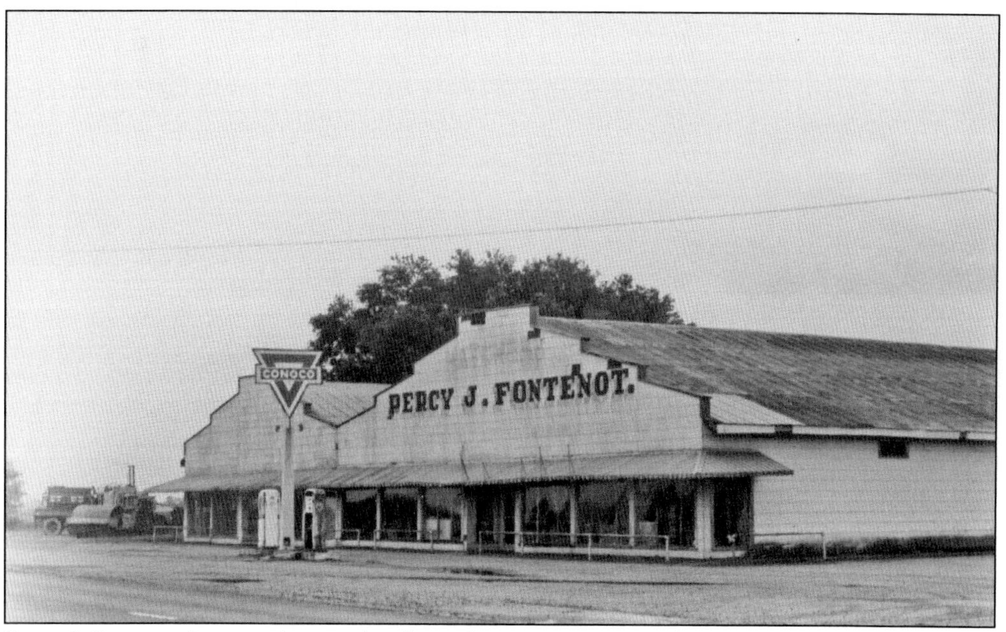

Percy J. Fontenot's general store, bank, and gas station was a fixture near Vidrine for many years. Fontenot got his start selling eggs door-to-door, acquiring the nickname "Poulet." The store was known as Fontenot Hatchery, not because it offered chicks among its wares, but in reference to Fontenot's earlier profession selling eggs. (Courtesy of Center for Louisiana Studies, UL Lafayette.)

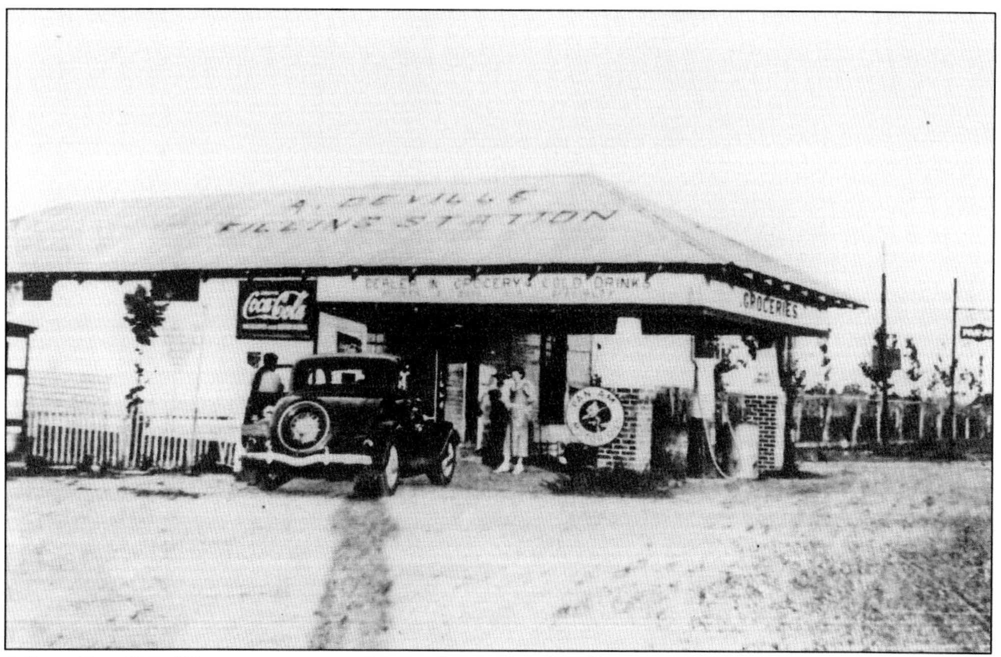

Adeus Deville's filling station was located outside of Ville Platte on US Highway 167. Besides gasoline and motor oil, the establishment sold groceries and cold drinks. It was the forerunner of today's convenience stores, in the days when the highway was still a gravel road. (Courtesy of Kathleen Deville Godchaux.)

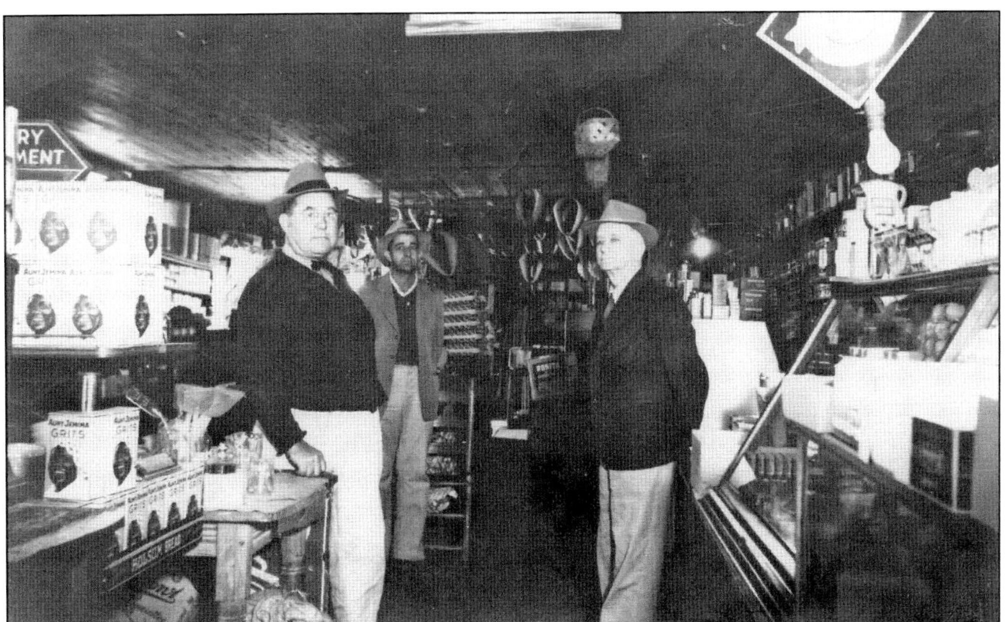

Coreil Hardware Store, located on Main Street in Ville Platte, was more a general store than just a hardware store. It sold foodstuffs as well as tools and farming supplies; it also had buggies for sale out back. The wooden table on the left was used to cut meat. Shown here is John "La Glace" Guillory (far left), Burke Landreneau (second from left), and an unidentified man. (Courtesy of Pam McGee.)

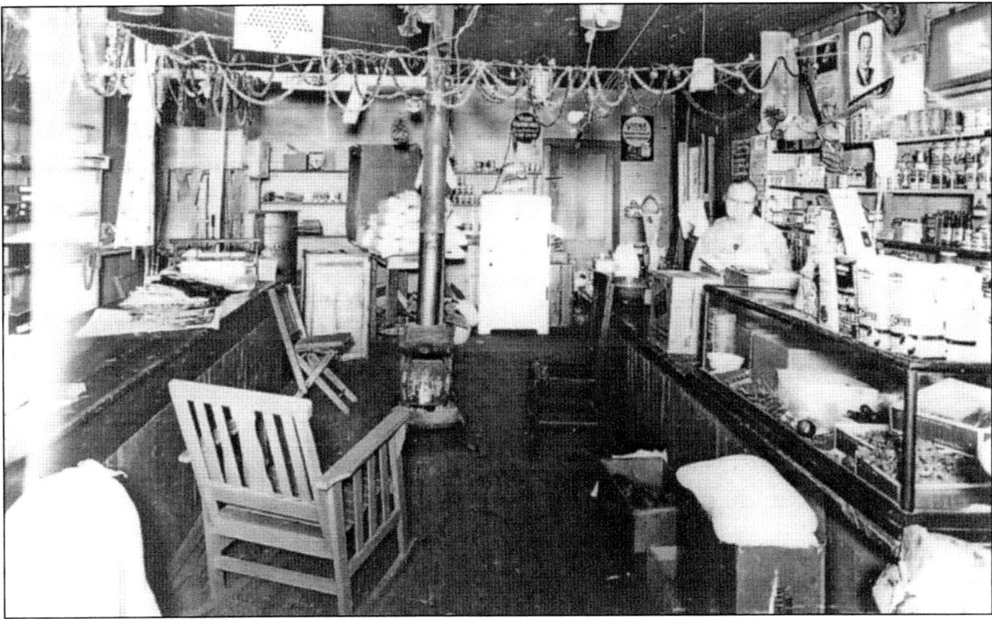

General stores stocked everything neighbors might need, including food and clothing, hardware, furniture and appliances, and even farm implements. An important feature was the stove and the chairs that surrounded it, where locals could gather and exchange news and opinions during the winter when farm work was not pressing. This Pine Prairie store is typical. (Courtesy of Pine Prairie Village Hall.)

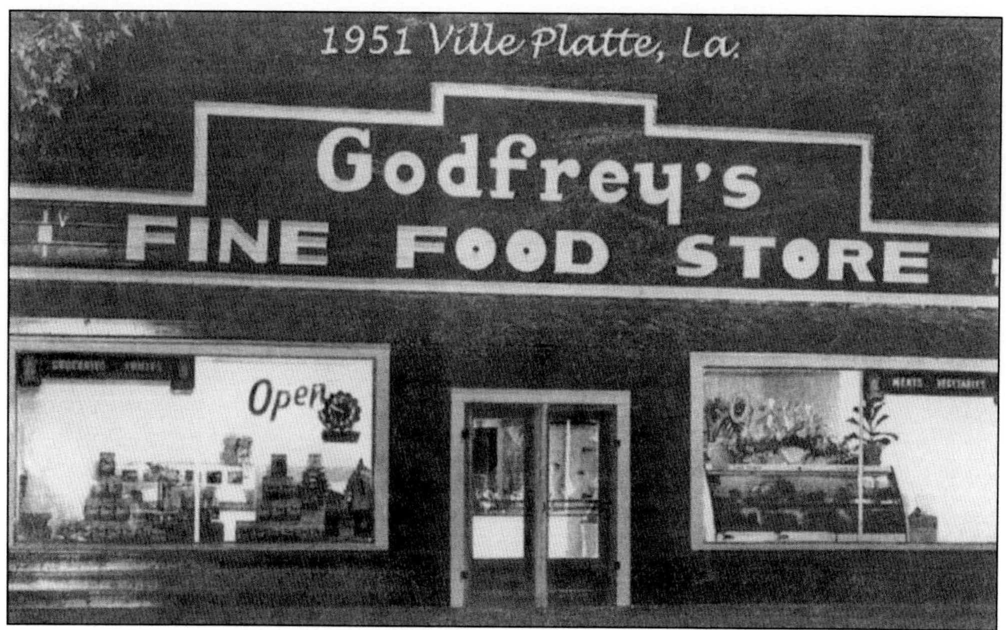

Godfrey's Fine Food Store, owned by Godfrey and Blanche Demoruelle, was located on Main Street, on the western edge of Ville Platte. A grocery store and meat market occupied the front of the building, while two mechanical chicken pluckers occupied the back. The machines could pluck 400 birds a day and were very popular with local duck hunters. Behind the store was a slaughterhouse. (Courtesy of Pam McGee.)

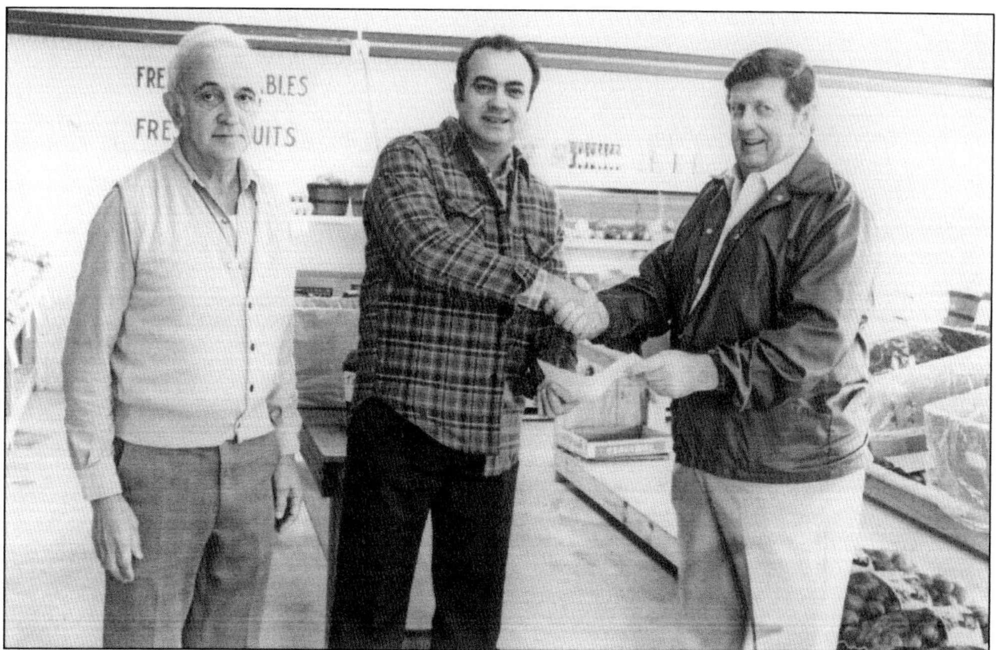

Charlie's Ville Platte Produce, located on Northwest Railroad Avenue in Ville Platte, sold fresh fruits and vegetables. Shown here around 1984 are, from left to right, Edgar "Tee Gar" Ortego, a member of the Evangeline Parish Police Jury; Harold Charlie, the store owner; and Evangeline Parish sheriff Floyd Soileau. (Courtesy of *Ville Platte Gazette*.)

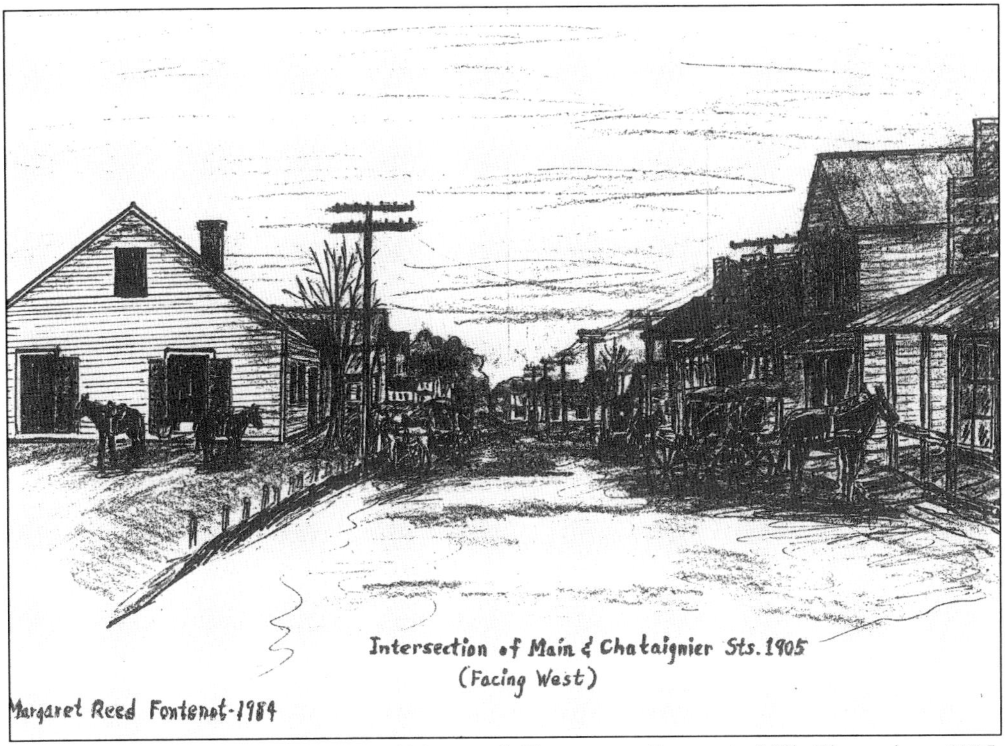

Intersection of Main & Chataignier Sts. 1905
(Facing West)

Margaret Reed Fontenot-1984

This sketch shows the intersection of Main and Chataignier Streets in Ville Platte about 1905. At left is the O'Donnell Building. Beyond it are buildings belonging to the Armand Coreil estate, including a hardware store, warehouse, home, furniture store, café, bar, syrup mill, and blacksmith shop. At right are Adraste LaFleur's store, Albert LaFleur's hardware store, O.E. Guillory's store, Latour's Hat Shop, and the Paul Castenado Hotel. (Artwork by Margaret Reed Fontenot.)

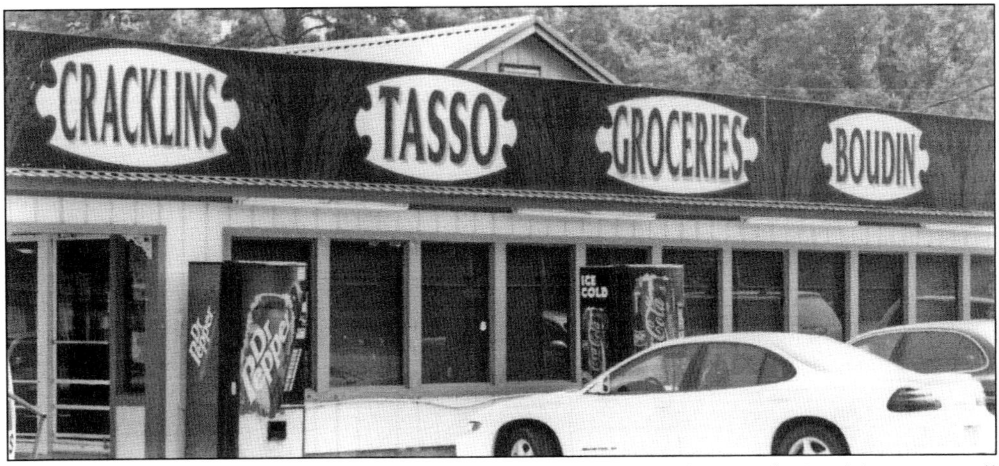

This grocery store in Basile advertises popular local foods made from pork. Cracklins are small pieces of belly fat, deep-fried until crisp and seasoned with salt and red pepper. Tasso is sliced pork, seasoned and smoked, that is used to flavor gumbos, stews, and vegetables. Boudin is a spicy mixture of rice, pork, and seasonings stuffed in a natural casing. (Courtesy of Center for Louisiana Studies, UL Lafayette.)

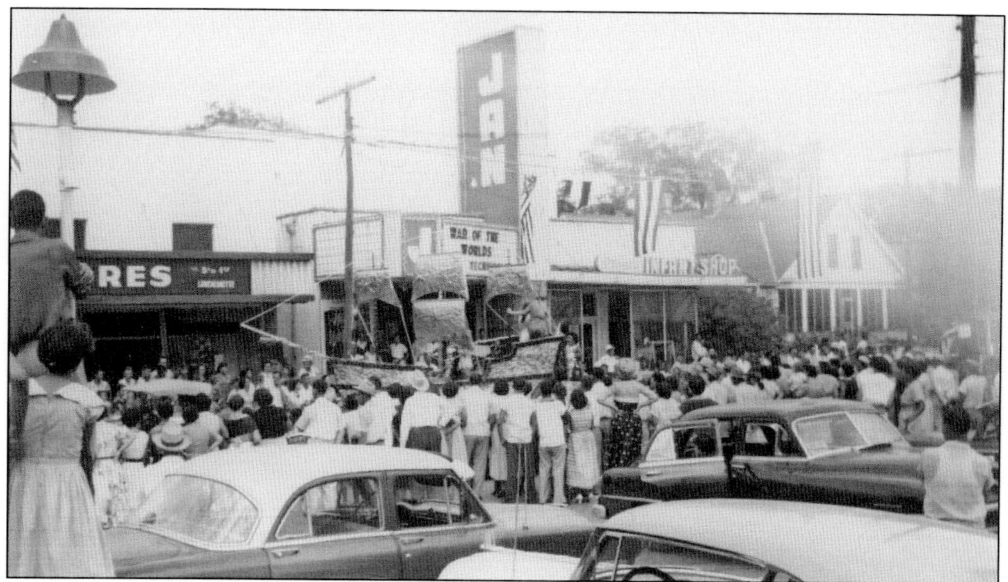

Ville Platte's Main Street is shown in this c. 1954 photograph of an early Cotton Festival parade. On the left is J.W. Lowe's Stores and the Jan Theater. Irene's Baby Shop is right of center, and on the far right is the Rene Derouen residence. The float is a sailing ship made of aluminum foil. (Courtesy of Pam McGee.)

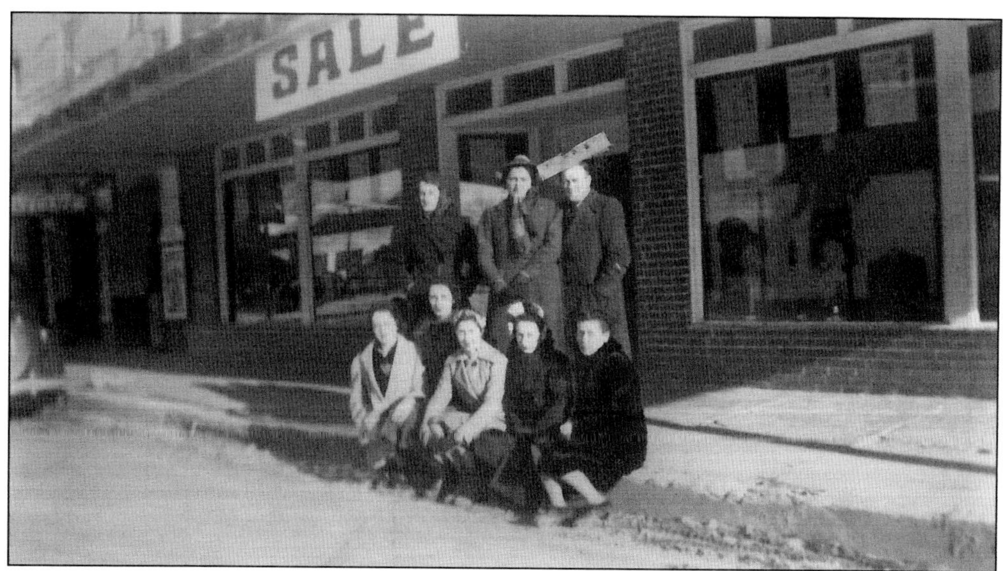

G. Ardoin's was the premier department store in Ville Platte for nearly 80 years. It began as a small general store owned by Alphonse "Mayon" Ardoin. Under his son Guillaume it expanded into a modern department store that spanned a row of buildings. The store burned down on September 27, 1990, when a fire that began across the street in the Evangeline Furniture Store spread. (Courtesy of Kathryn LeBleu Guillory.)

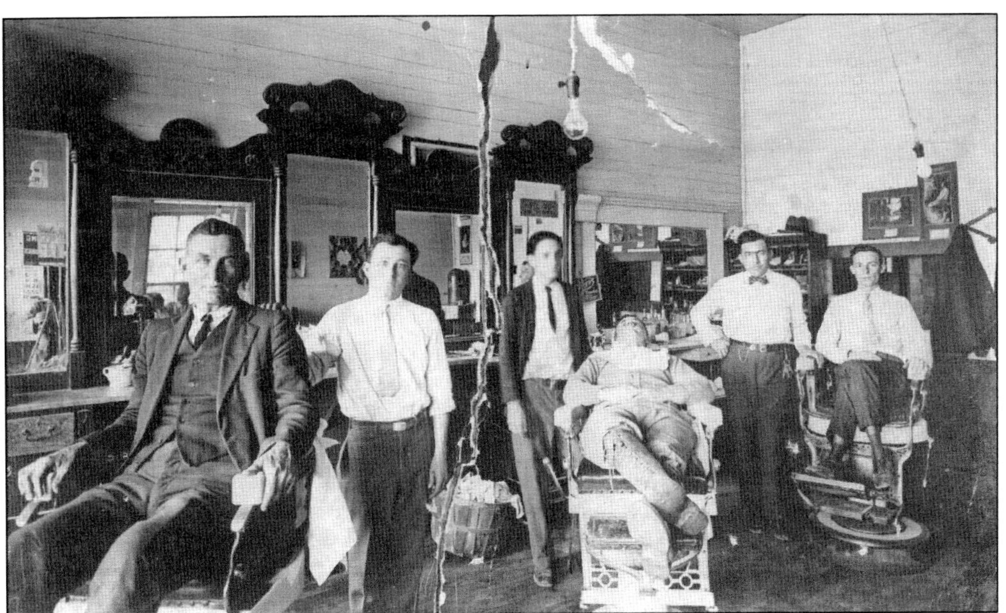

A man could get a shave and haircut at this Ville Platte barbershop, operated by Regile Duos. He could take a bath in the tub in the back room before going to a movie or a dance. While he waited, he could get all the courthouse news and exchange political opinions with the other men in town. (Courtesy of *Ville Platte Gazette*.)

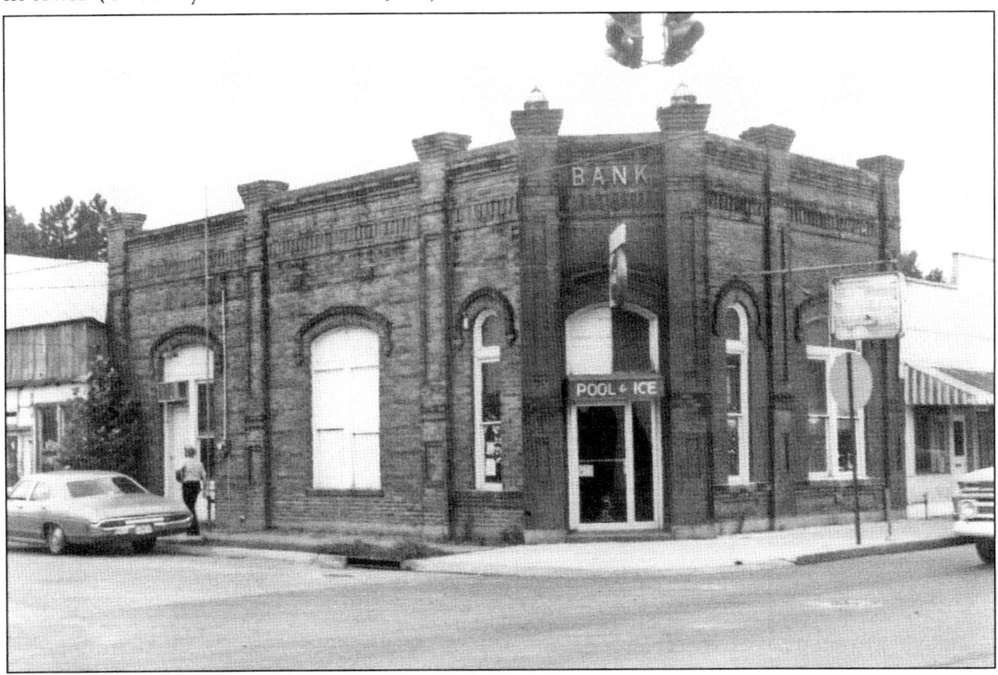

When Evangeline Parish was created and Ville Platte was named its parish seat, the little town began to grow. One of the first signs of the new prosperity was the construction in 1905 of this bank building, the first brick building in town. The structure has had a number of uses over the years, and it still stands on the corner of Main Street and Northwest Railroad Avenue. (Courtesy of Pam McGee.)

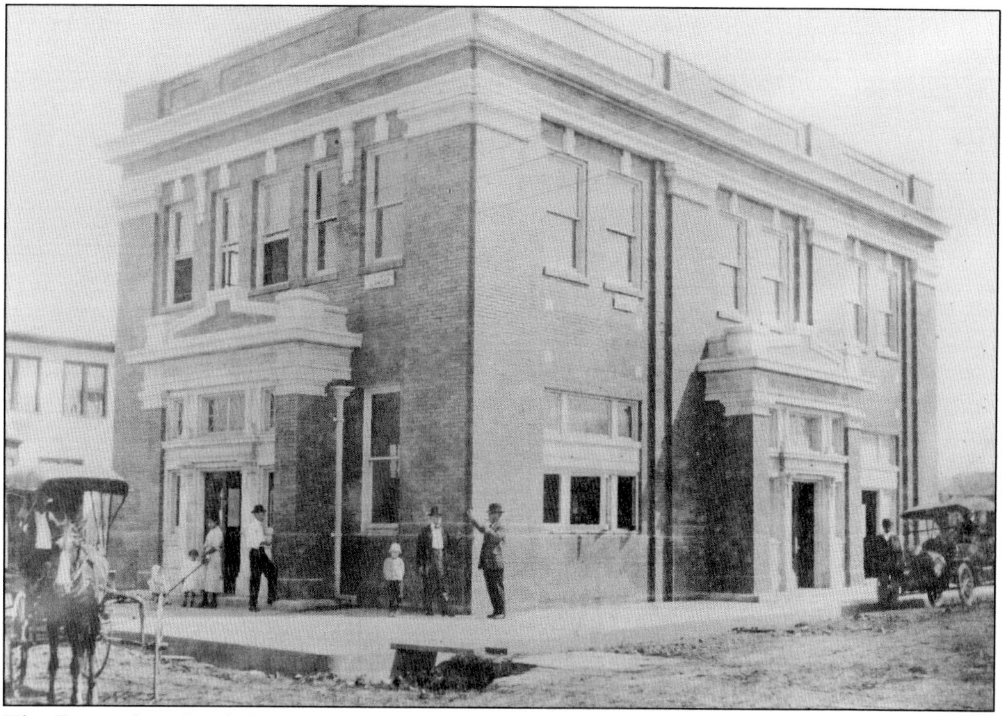

The Evangeline Bank & Trust Company opened in 1912 on the corner of Main and Court Streets in Ville Platte. This handsome red-brick structure was exceeded in grandeur only by the courthouse. The bank is still in operation today, with branches in Pine Prairie, Mamou, Basile, and Chataignier. After the bank moved to more modern quarters in 1977, this building housed city hall and KVPI Radio. (Courtesy of Pam McGee.)

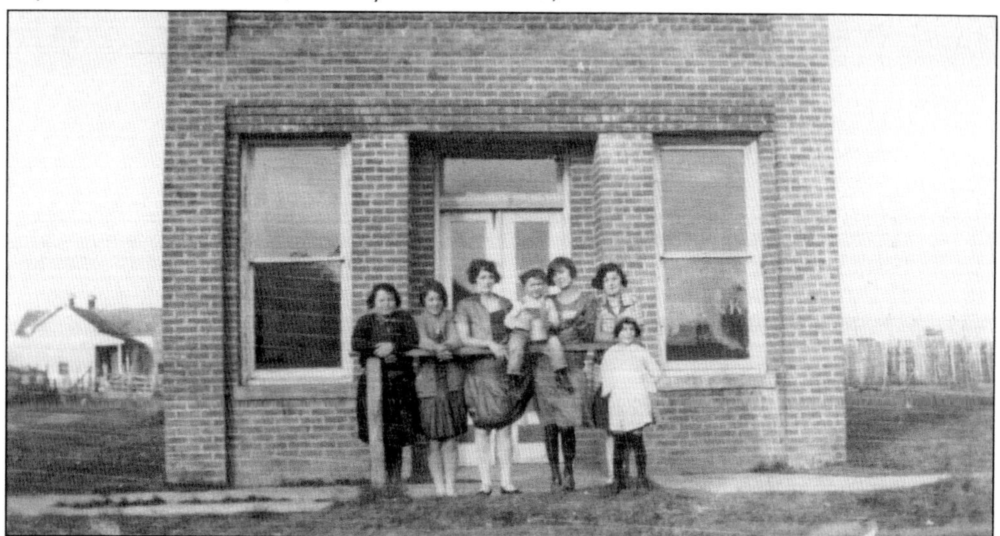

The first bank in Chataignier was a branch of the Evangeline Bank of Ville Platte. It opened in the 1920s in this small brick building. It closed during the Great Depression and never reopened. In the 1970s, the building housed a motorcycle shop. The children shown here in 1928 are, from left to right, Atile Fontenot, Inez Fontenot, Jenneveve ?, Rellum ?, Ament Fontenot, Geraldine ?, and unidentified. (Courtesy of Kathryn Lebleu Guillory.)

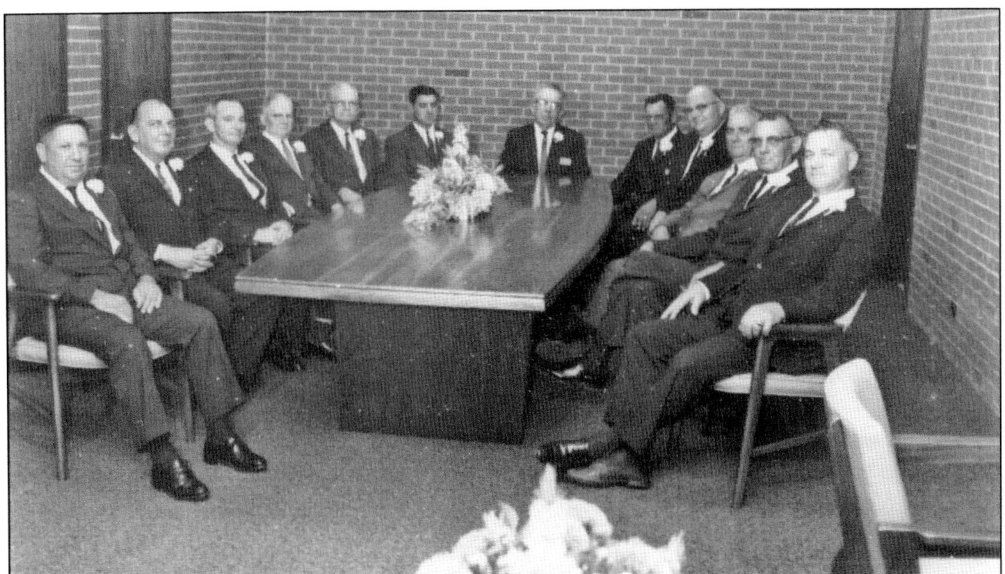

The Basile State Bank opened in 1956 with assets of $933,000. In 1964, the bank erected a new building. The board of directors is pictured here in the new boardroom. From left to right are Cleo Guidry, Sammy Stagg, Wesley Hebert, Melvin Morton, unidentified, Executive Vice Pres. P.J. Baker Jr., Pres. Fulton J. Bacon, Vice Pres. Harry Aguillard, C.L. "Chunky" Hester, Hosea Deshotel Sr., Raymond Klump, and Sidney Pelloquin. (Courtesy Alice Bacon Guillotte.)

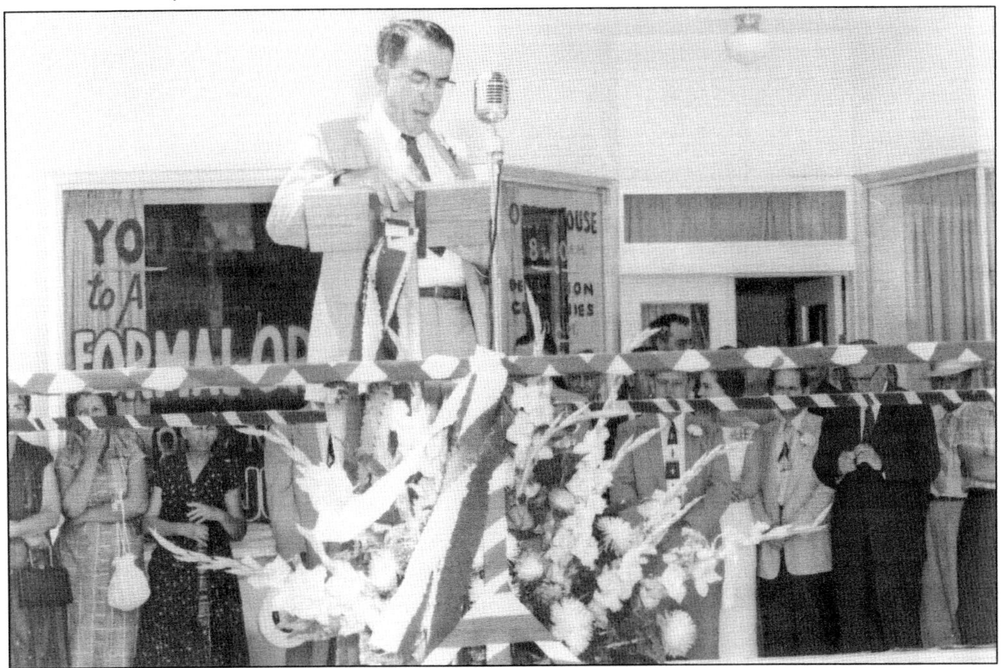

Fulton J. Bacon recognized the need to have a bank in Basile, so he and a group of local businessmen organized the Bank of Basile. The bank opened on July 2, 1956, with Bacon as president. A former educator, he also served on the Evangeline Parish School Board for many years and was its president during desegregation. He is shown here speaking at the bank's grand opening. (Courtesy of Alice Bacon Guillotte.)

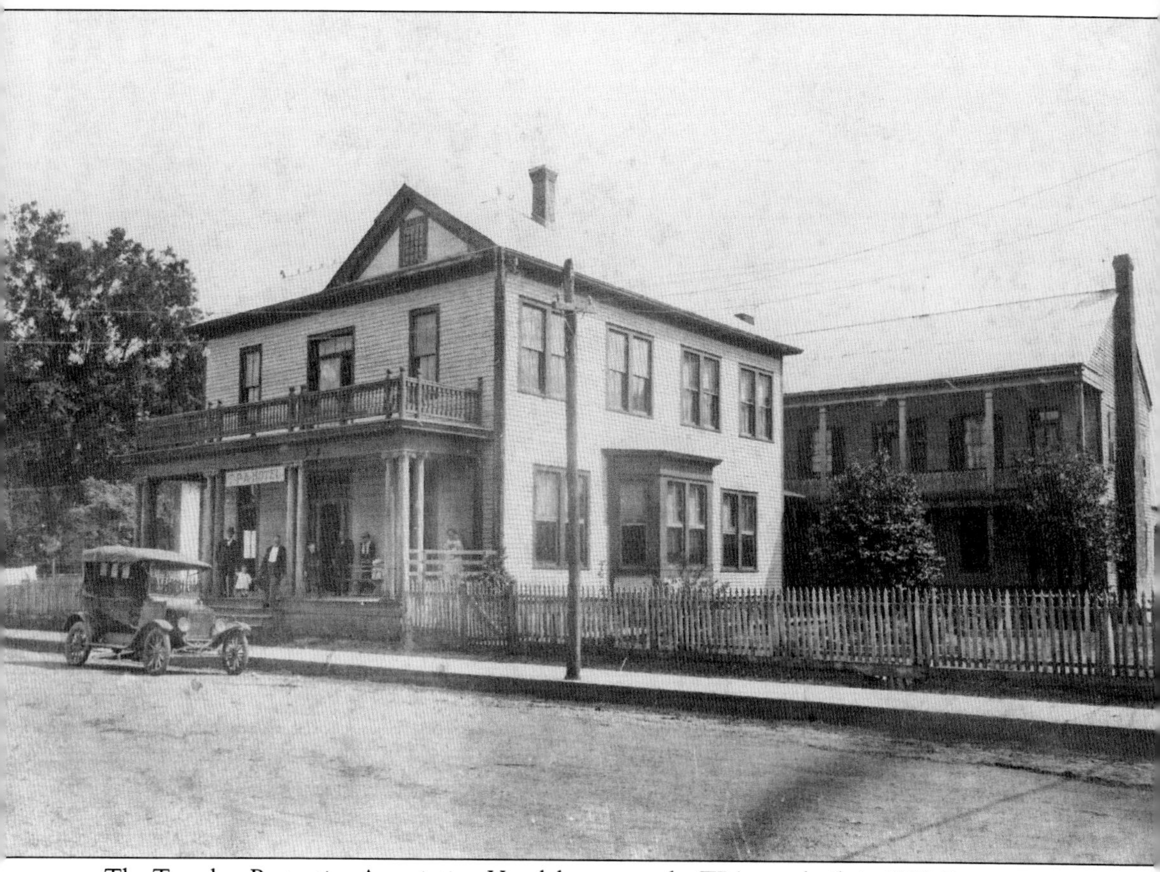

The Travelers Protective Association Hotel, known as the TPA, was built in 1899. For many years it was the leading hotel and a landmark in Ville Platte. LaPearl Ashlock, the wife of *Gazette* editor T.G. Ashlock, operated the hotel, and their home was attached to the back. It had a large dining room where she would serve delicious home-cooked meals to her guests. The TPA was not the only hotel in Ville Platte, but it was considered the leading one. There were at least two others that competed for business. Each hotel would send a buggy to meet trains and try to convince traveling salesmen to stay in their establishment. (Courtesy of *Ville Platte Gazette*.)

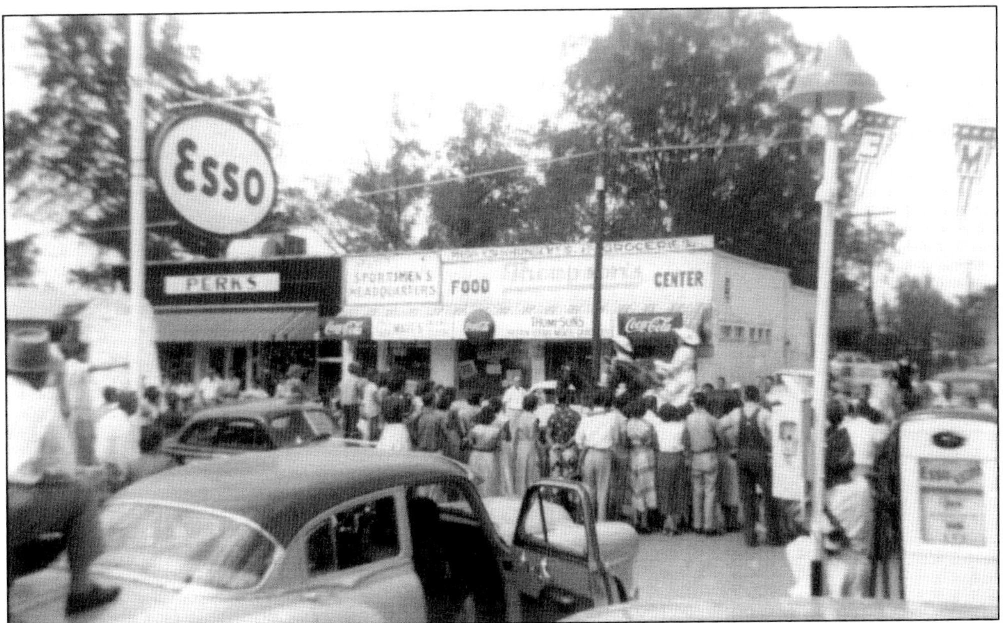

This view of a Fourth of July parade about 1950 shows another section of Ville Platte's Main Street. In the foreground, the Pontiac dealership and Esso station on the corner of Court and West Main Streets were owned by Jim Ardoin, Walter Manuel, and Vic Dupuis. Across the street are Perks, a dress shop run by Mrs. Paul "Perks" Reed, and Marcellus Thompson's Food Center. (Courtesy of Pam McGee.)

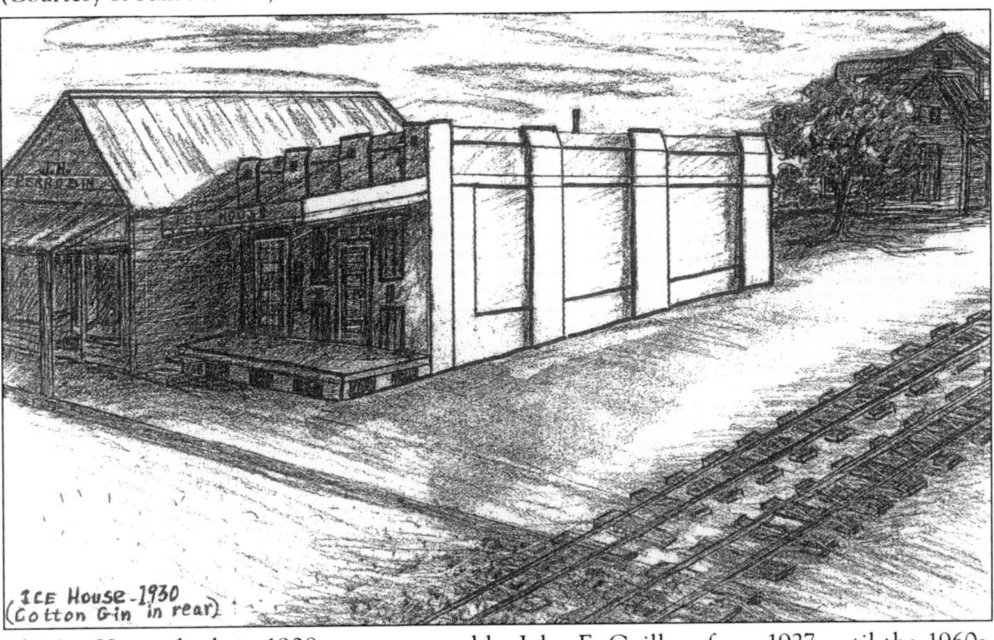

The Ice House, built in 1908, was managed by John E. Guillory from 1927 until the 1960s. Ice was delivered to homes and businesses in a wagon covered with a tarpaulin. Next to the icehouse is J.H. Perrodin's general store. This building was replaced in 1949 with a two-story brick building, still standing today. Farther down the tracks stood a cotton gin. (Artwork by Margaret Reed Fontenot.)

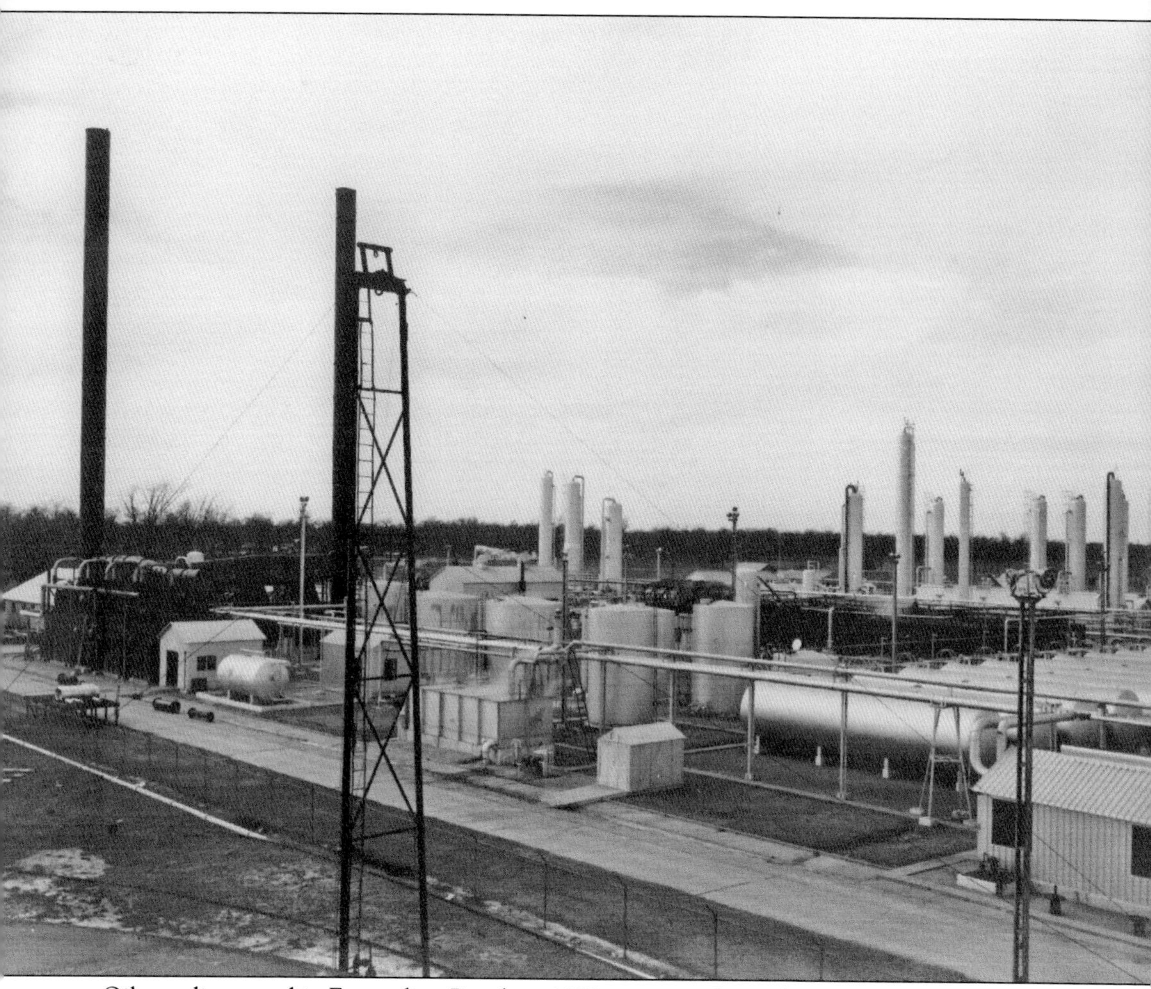

Oil was discovered in Evangeline Parish in 1935; two years later, the Continental Oil Company brought in the first well at Tate Cove. This ushered in a major economic boom for Evangeline Parish and led to the development of other wells in the parish. Over the next 20 years, the Tate Cove field produced 400 billion cubic feet of natural gas and 50 million barrels of oil. At the peak of production, the field employed more than 250 workers on nearly 300 wells. Continental built a camp and a commissary at the oil field for its workers. (Courtesy of *Ville Platte Gazette*.)

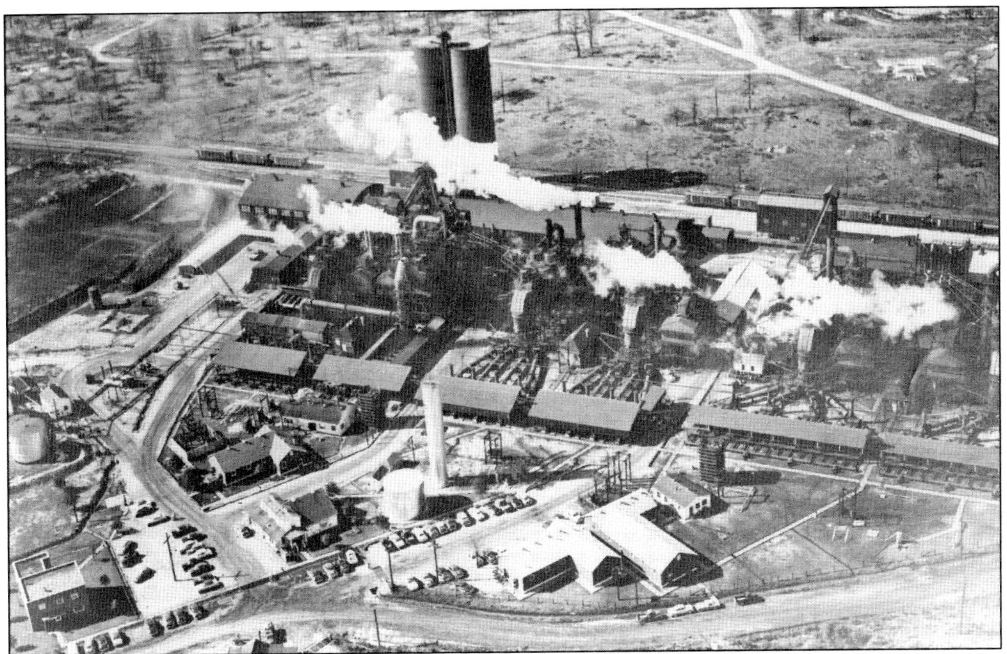

Cabot Carbon Company built this plant in Tate Cove in 1943 to produce carbon black. The firm had a workforce of 54 men. Carbon black is used in manufacturing rubber, inks, and plastics, as well as telephones and phonograph records. Surprisingly, it is also used as a filter to make raw sugar white. The plant is still in operation today. (Courtesy of *Ville Platte Gazette*.)

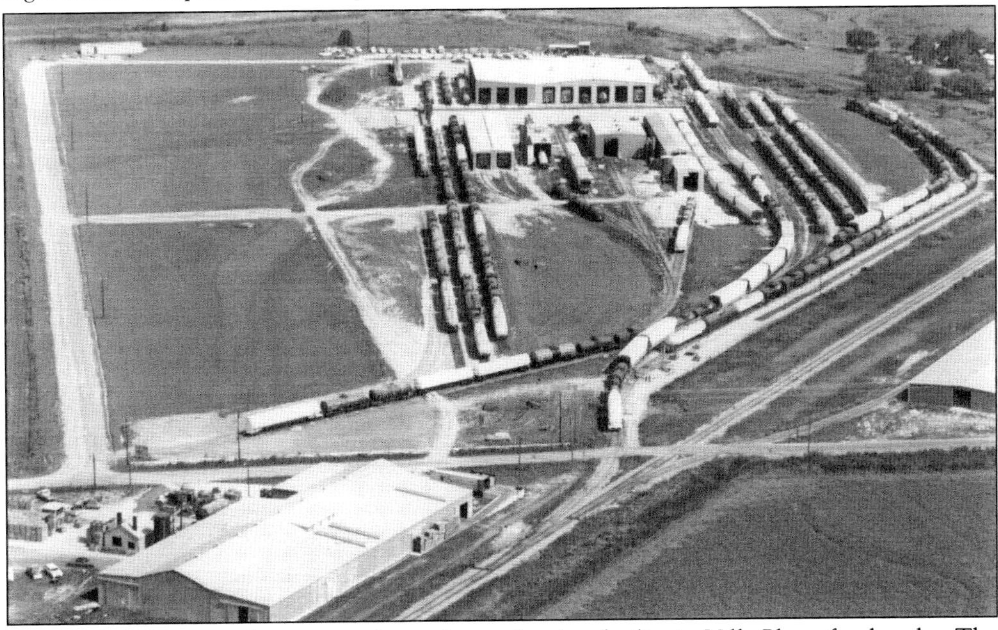

Union Tank Company has operated a tank car cleaning facility in Ville Platte for decades. The facility, still in operation today, is located on Union Tank Car Road, just off Lithcote Road near the railroad tracks. Here, tank cars are cleaned and repainted before being put back in service. The building in the left foreground is the cannery; to the far right is the Evangeline Farmers' Co-op. (Courtesy of *Ville Platte Gazette*.)

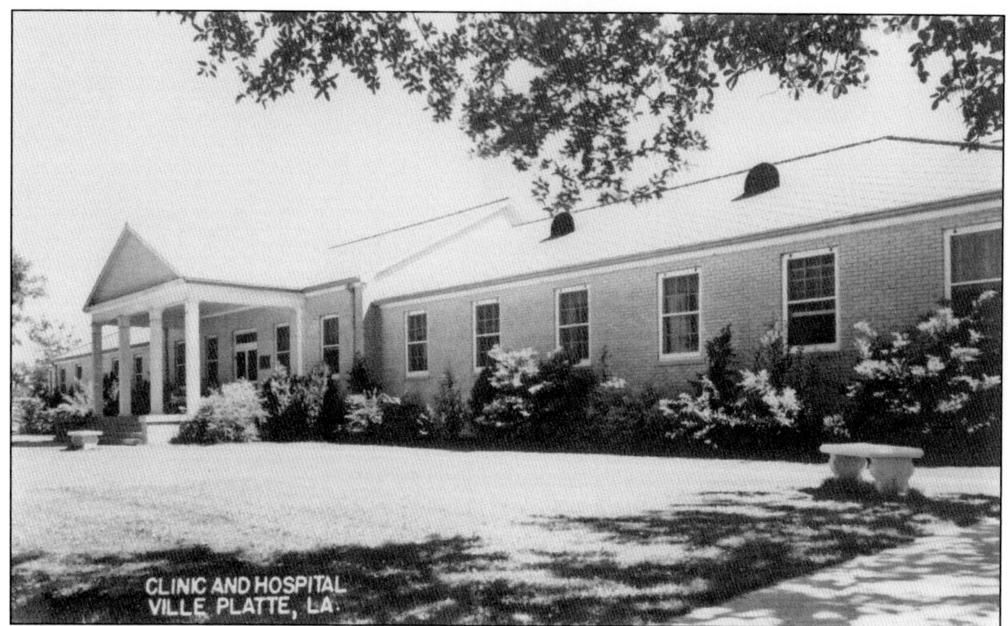

Ardoin's Sanitarium was established by Dr. Yves Ardoin in 1926. Dr. C.L. Attaway joined the practice the following year, and Dr. R.E. Dupre in 1935. The original building, a former residence, was destroyed by fire in 1937. Within months it was replaced by this brick building. After Dr. Ardoin's death in 1944, his partners continued to operate the clinic and hospital under their own names. (Courtesy of Pam McGee.)

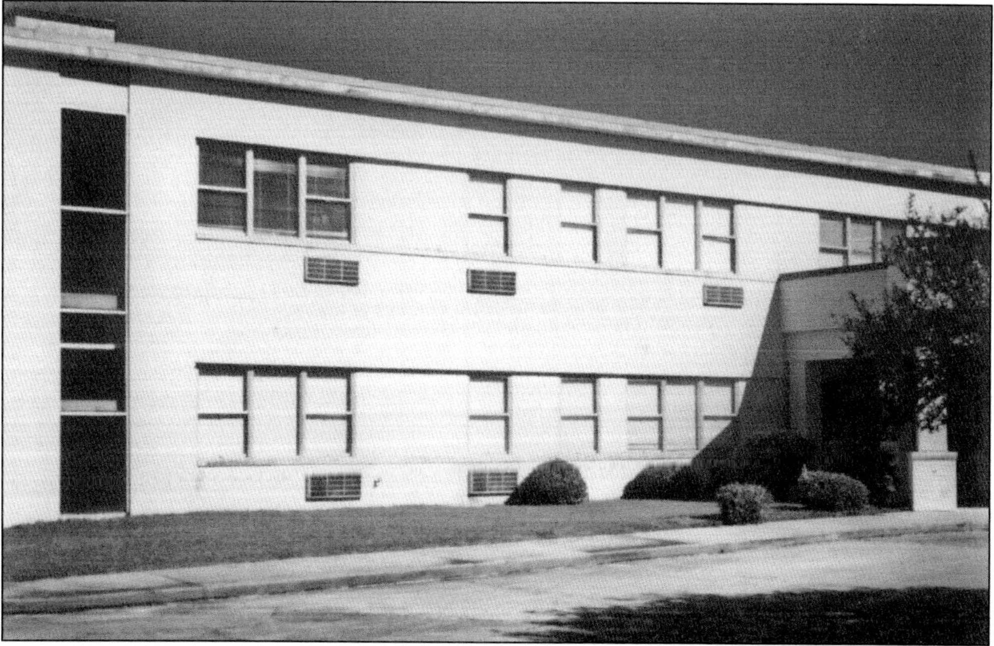

Savoy Medical Center in Mamou was founded in June 1950 by physicians Frank Savoy Sr. and Frank Savoy Jr. At the time, it had 28 beds. Both doctors served the hospital for over 50 years. Today, the facility has grown to 180 beds, with a staff of 50 physicians in a wide range of specialties. (Courtesy of Jean Kiesel.)

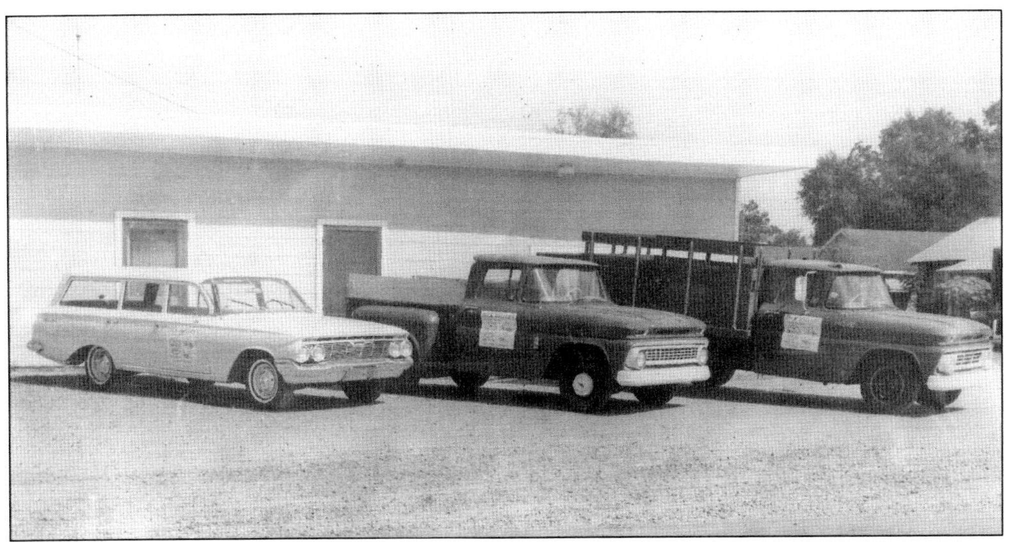

In June 1941, Jack D. Miller opened the original American Inn Restaurant in Ville Platte. There he developed Jack Miller's Bar-B-Que Sauce for customers. In 1955, the product was placed on the open market in south Louisiana and later in other states. The business now is run by Jack's son Kermit, along with Kermit's wife, Sheila, and their son, Christian. (Courtesy of Kermit Miller.)

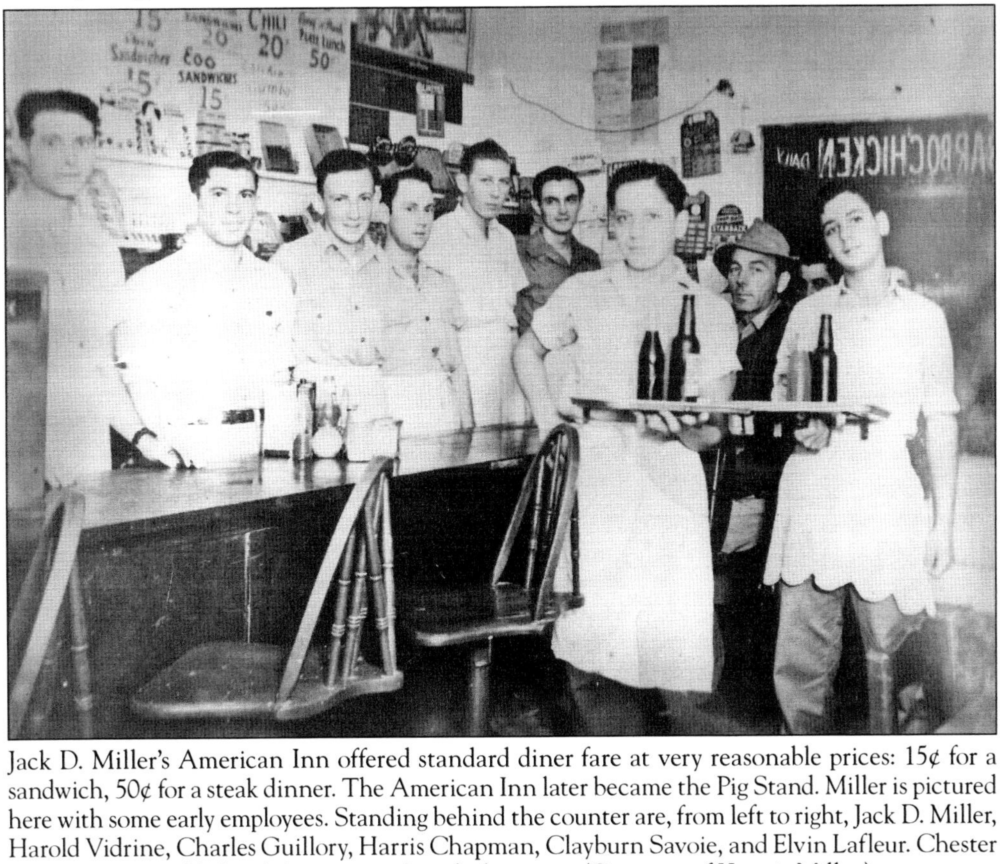

Jack D. Miller's American Inn offered standard diner fare at very reasonable prices: 15¢ for a sandwich, 50¢ for a steak dinner. The American Inn later became the Pig Stand. Miller is pictured here with some early employees. Standing behind the counter are, from left to right, Jack D. Miller, Harold Vidrine, Charles Guillory, Harris Chapman, Clayburn Savoie, and Elvin Lafleur. Chester Guillory is seated behind the two unidentified waiters. (Courtesy of Kermit Miller.)

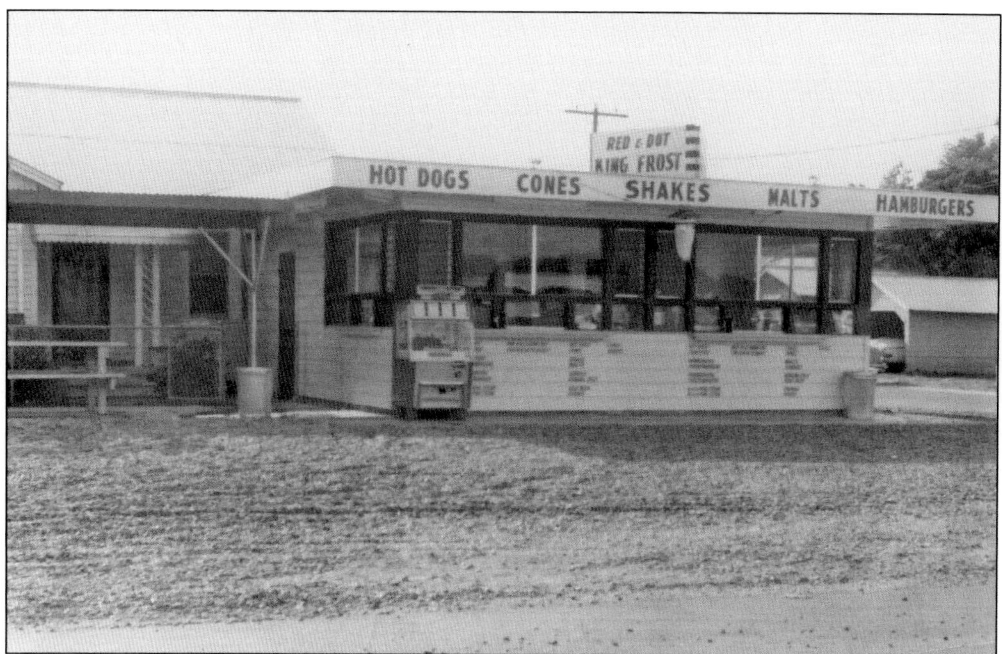

Red and Dot's King Frost Drive-In on Chataignier Road in Ville Platte was owned by Adam "Red" Vidrine and his wife, Dorothy "Dot" Fontenot Vidrine. It was open seven days a week from 8:00 a.m. until midnight, serving a typical drive-in menu of hot dogs, hamburgers, ice-cream cones, shakes, and malts. Naturally, it was a popular hangout for teenagers. (Courtesy of *Ville Platte Gazette*.)

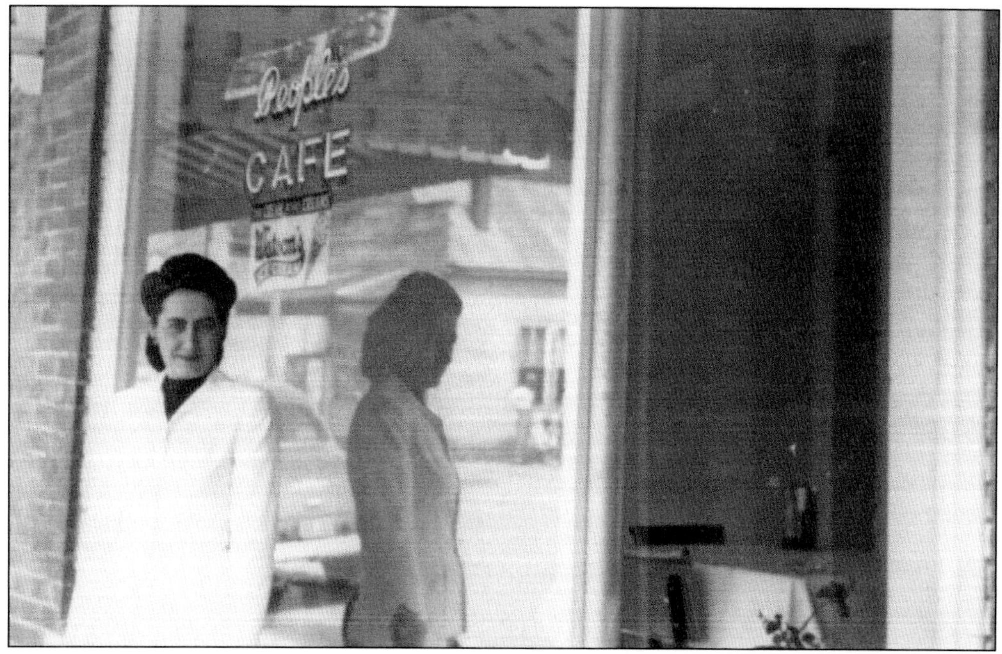

The People's Café, located on West Main Street in Ville Platte, served three meals a day. It was owned by Clabert and Lydie Phillips Duos. After Lydie died in 1939, Clabert hired Winnie Fontenot, shown here, to run the café for $3.50 a week plus room and board. Clabert and Winnie married in 1951 and had three children. (Courtesy of Mitzi Duos Cochrane.)

McDaniel's Grocery, owned by Clester and Anna Dupré McDaniel, opened in the early 1950s on Railroad Avenue in Ville Platte. Besides groceries, the store sold homemade boudin and smoked meats, as well as Army surplus items. A decade later, it became McDaniel's Army Surplus. Shown here on the porch of their home, which was attached to the store, are, from left to right, Clester, J.R., Beryl, Roonie, Neary, and Anna McDaniel. (Courtesy of Sandra Himel.)

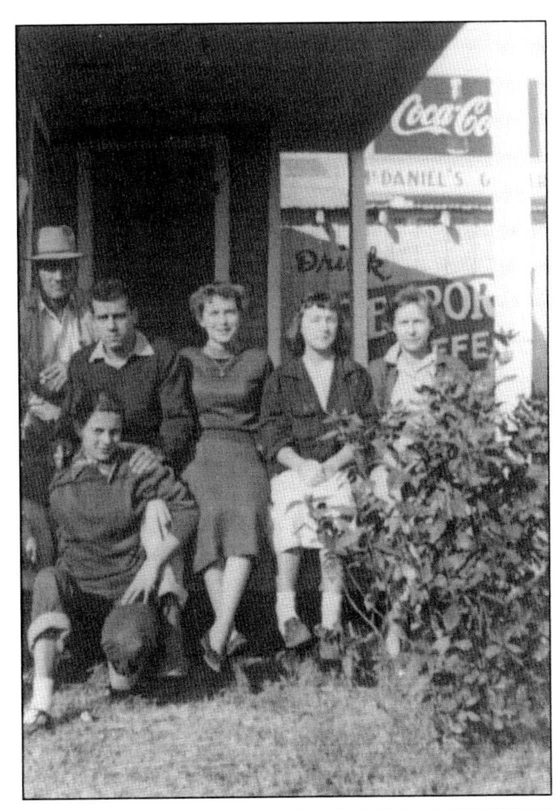

The Iron Pot Roux Company opened in 1953 on a site four miles west of Ville Platte. Owned by Lee Israel (pictured), the company manufactured a single product, canned roux, essential for making many Cajun dishes. Later, the plant made Cousin Ethel's Barbecue Sauce. Today Iron Pot is gone, but Kary's Roux in Ville Platte produces light and dark roux for the convenience of local cooks. (Courtesy of *Ville Platte Gazette*.)

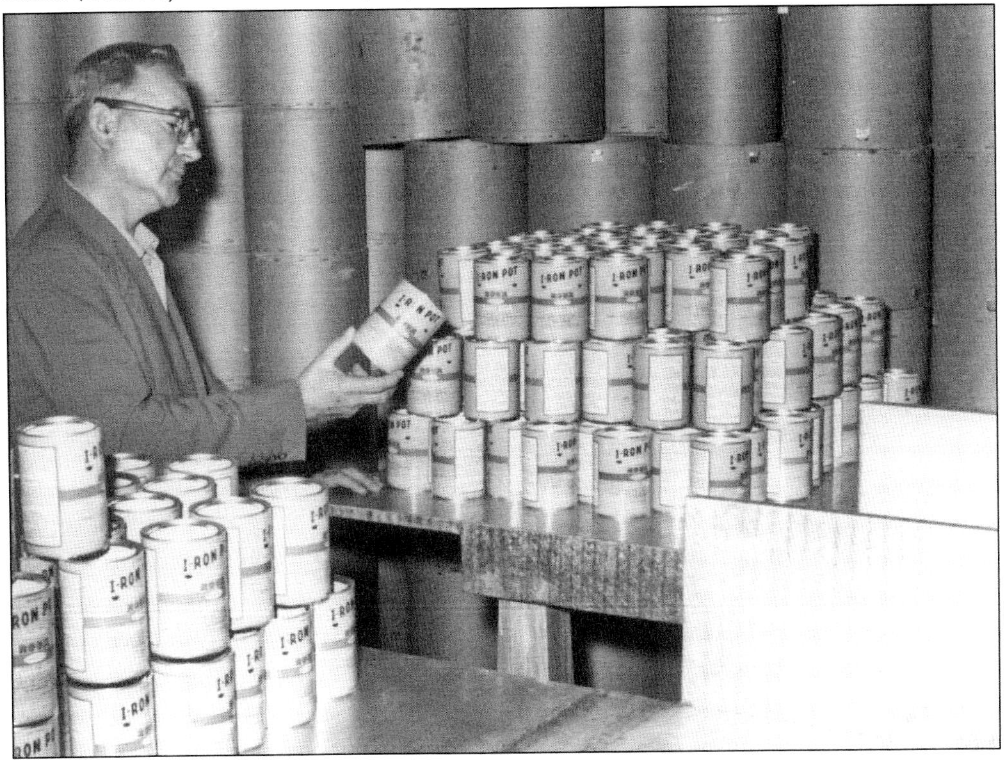

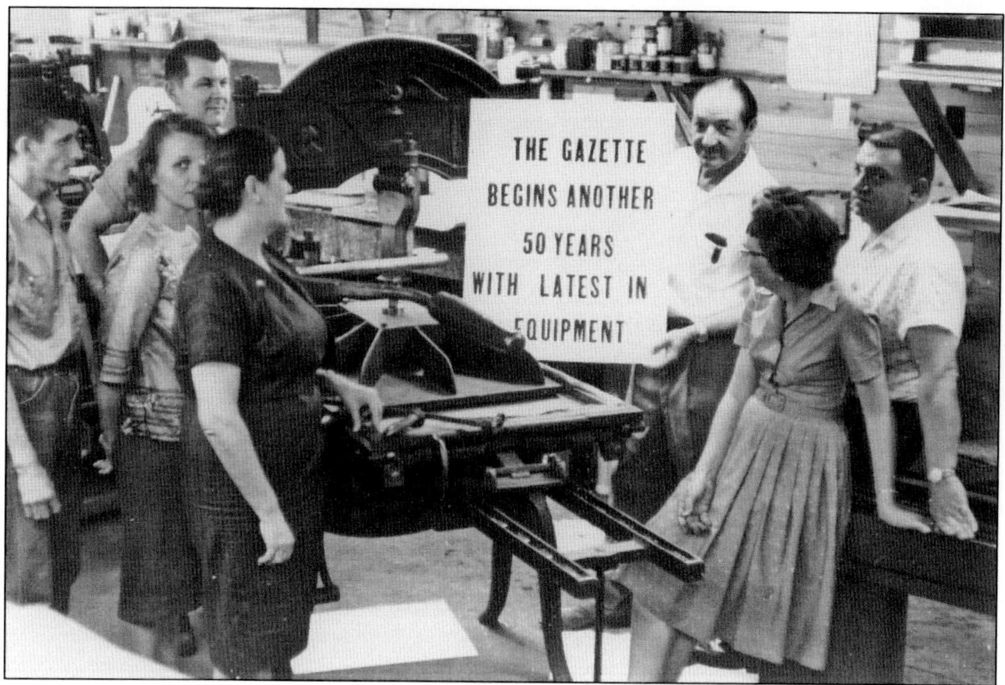

T.G. Ashlock founded the *Weekly Gazette* in 1914 and was its first editor. His son Jules R. Ashlock and his wife, Loretta, started working for the paper in 1932 and took over operations in 1940. They continued to run it until they retired in 1968. The Ashlocks are shown here with *Gazette* staff members in 1964. Jules is holding the sign, and Loretta is at left in the dark dress. (Courtesy of *Ville Platte Gazette*.)

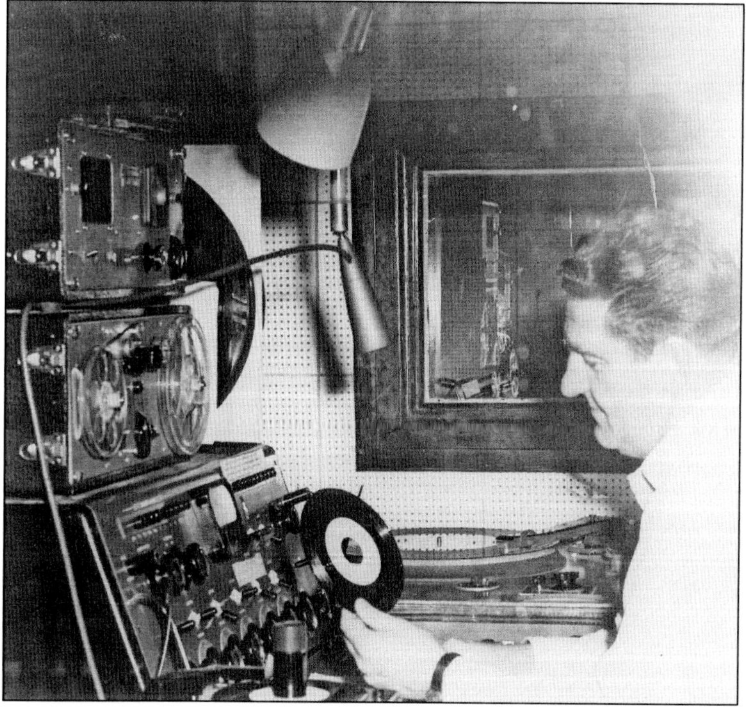

KVPI Radio began broadcasting on an AM channel in 1953 from studios on the second floor of the old Evangeline Bank building. The call letters stand for "Keeping Ville Platte Informed." Since signing on, the station has promoted local Cajun and Creole culture with French-language programming and the music of local artists. Here, sports announcer and DJ Bootsie Cappell broadcasts from the original studio. (Courtesy of KVPI Radio.)

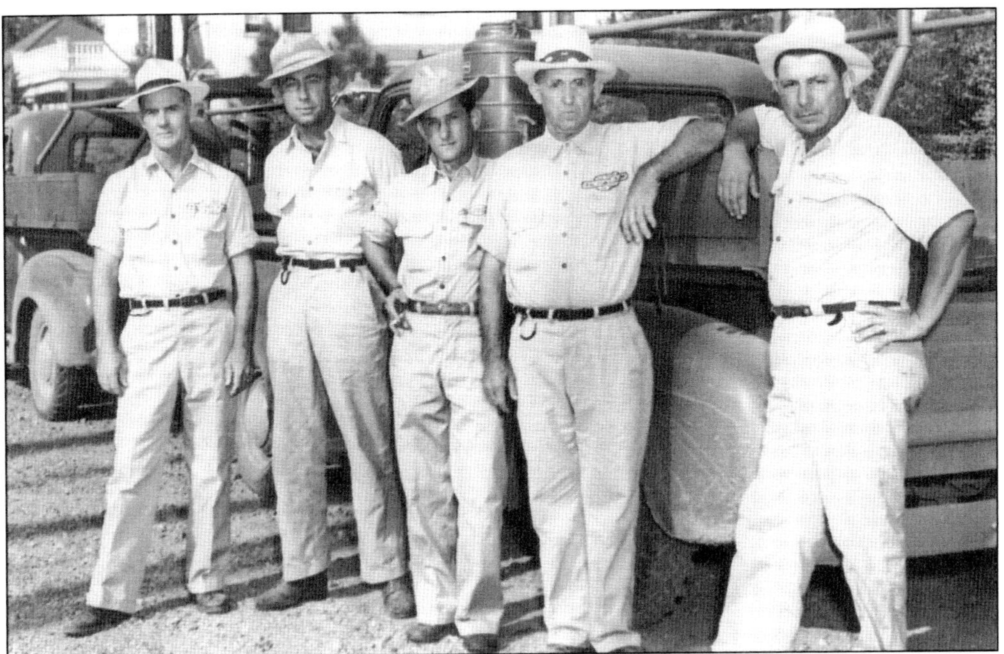

These five men kept electricity flowing in Ville Platte for CLECO, the Central Louisiana Electric Company, in the 1950s. Before the days of bucket trucks, the men had to "hook" the poles: climbing by means of metal spikes driven into the sides of the poles. The men, called "The Untouchables," are, from left to right, Austin Demoruelle, John Lee Fontenot, Wilson Attales, Edward Demoruelle, and Louis Charlie. (Courtesy of JoAnn Burnett.)

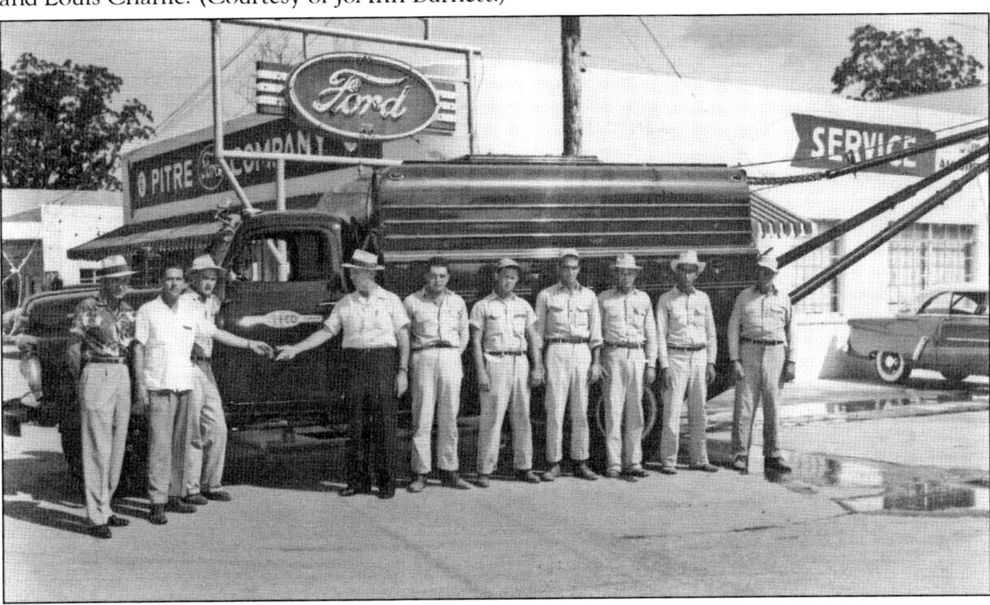

It was big news when CLECO, the local utility company, received a new truck, specially ordered through the Pitre Ford dealership. Shown here are, from left to right, Maurice Pitre, Ford representative S.F. MacArthur, Austin Demoruelle, CLECO district manager Allen J. Lemoine, Jimmy Vidrine, Clay Demoruelle, Elson Fontenot, Dovis Fontenot, Martius Fontenot, and Noah Fontenot. (Courtesy of JoAnn Burnett.)

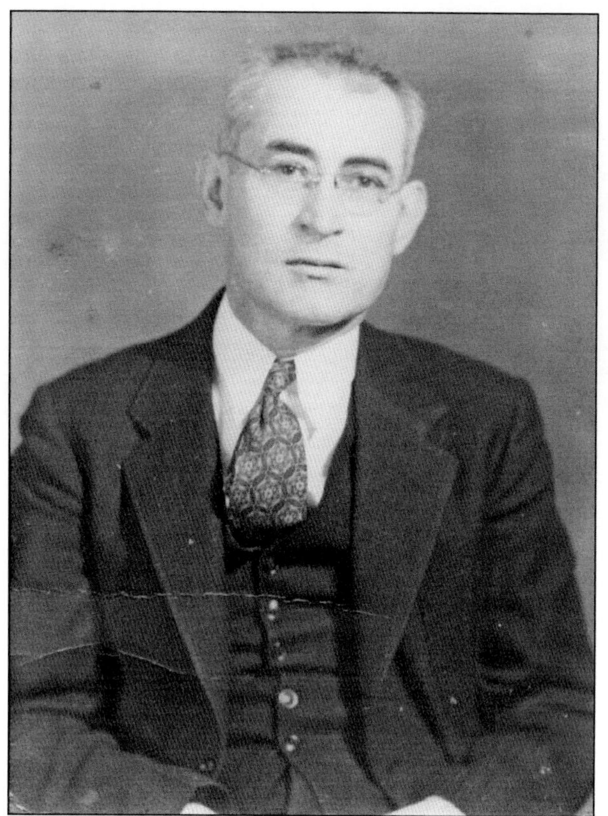

Octave Fuselier owned the Courthouse Saloon and Restaurant, the Rainbow Gardens dancehall, a barbershop, and the Exchange Market across the street from the courthouse. The establishment was open 24 hours a day. In the back room there were card games and slot machines, while a legal "bull pen" met inside the front door of the Rainbow Gardens. (Courtesy of Lynn Landreneau.)

The Rainbow Gardens dancehall stood across the street from the courthouse. It was also known as the fais-do-do. The entrance fee was 25¢ when Octave Fuselier was the proprietor. Only soft drinks were available in the dancehall. Someone who wanted an alcoholic beverage had to leave the dance and go to the saloon, conveniently located in another part of the building. (Courtesy of *Ville Platte Gazette*.)

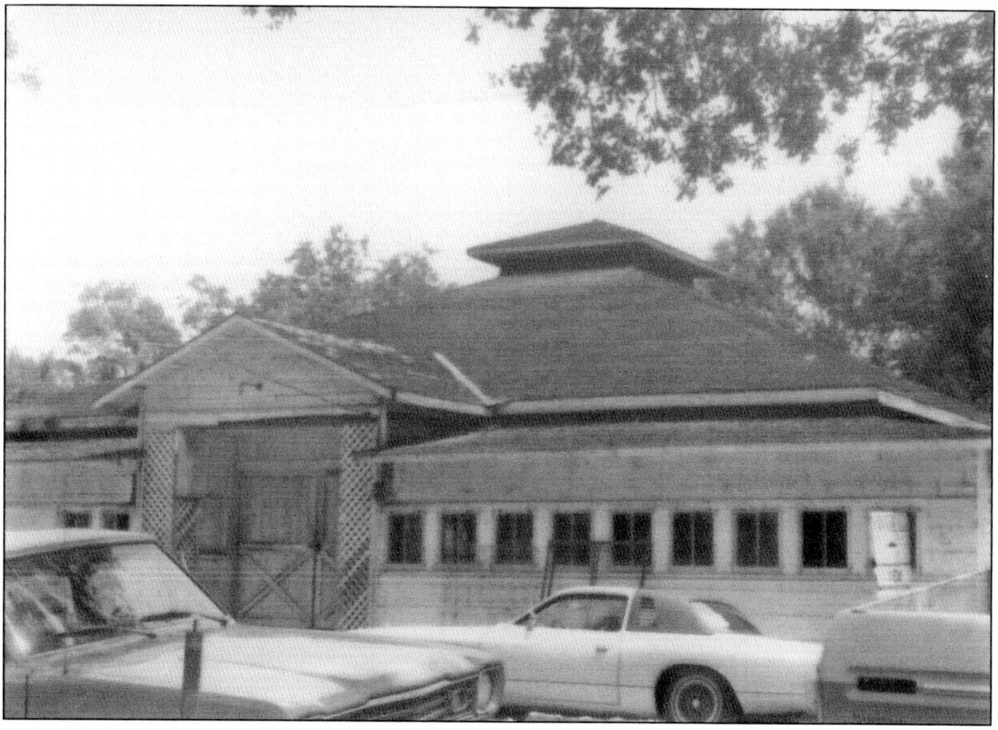

The Evangeline Club, co-owned by brothers Clem and Claude Morein, was located one mile west of Ville Platte. It opened in 1935 and was especially popular with servicemen from nearby bases during World War II. It was known for featuring local bands and was the site of many community functions. The club closed in 1984 and was demolished in 1988, but the memories live on. (Courtesy of Bobby Dardeau.)

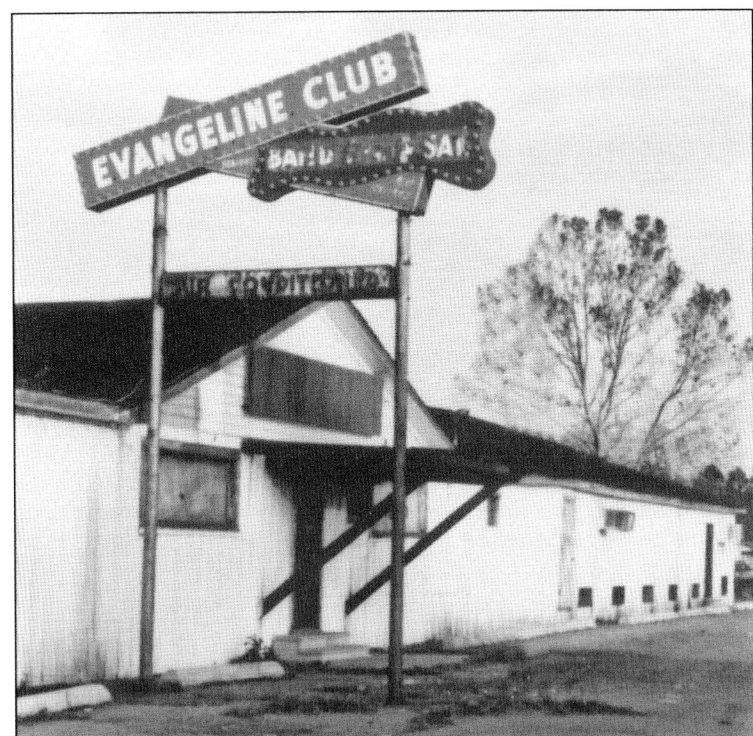

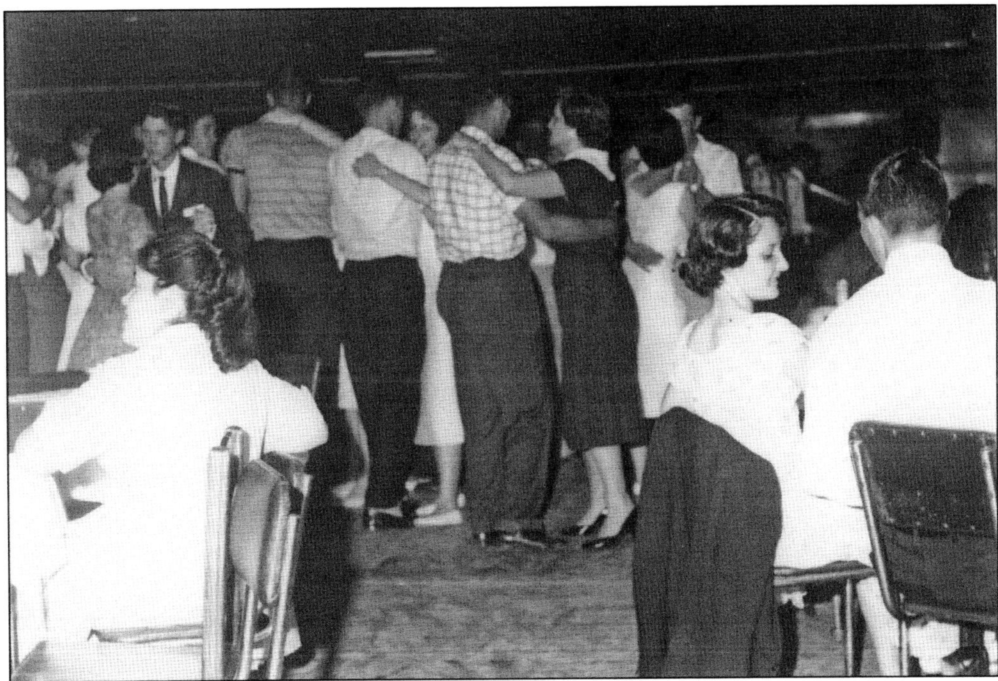

Dancing was a popular activity for young couples. Of all the clubs in Evangeline Parish, and there were many, the Evangeline Club was known for having the most popular bands. The best was the Otis Smith Orchestra, which played there five nights a week and on Sunday afternoons at 5:00 p.m. for many years. (Courtesy of Pam McGee.)

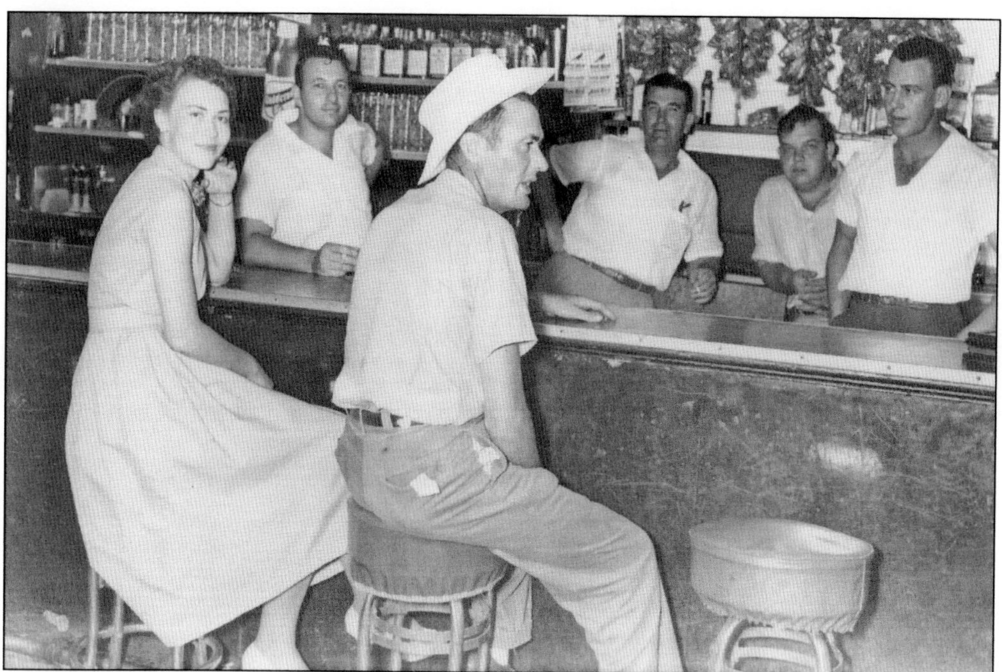

The Evangeline Club boasted a well-stocked bar and a kitchen that offered full-course meals as well as sandwiches and snacks. Shown here are, from left to right, Margie and Floyd Fontenot, "Taxi" Vizinat (in hat), club owner Clem Morein, Merton Soileau, and Don Chapman. The club had live music, featuring some of the best Cajun bands in the area. (Courtesy of Pam McGee.)

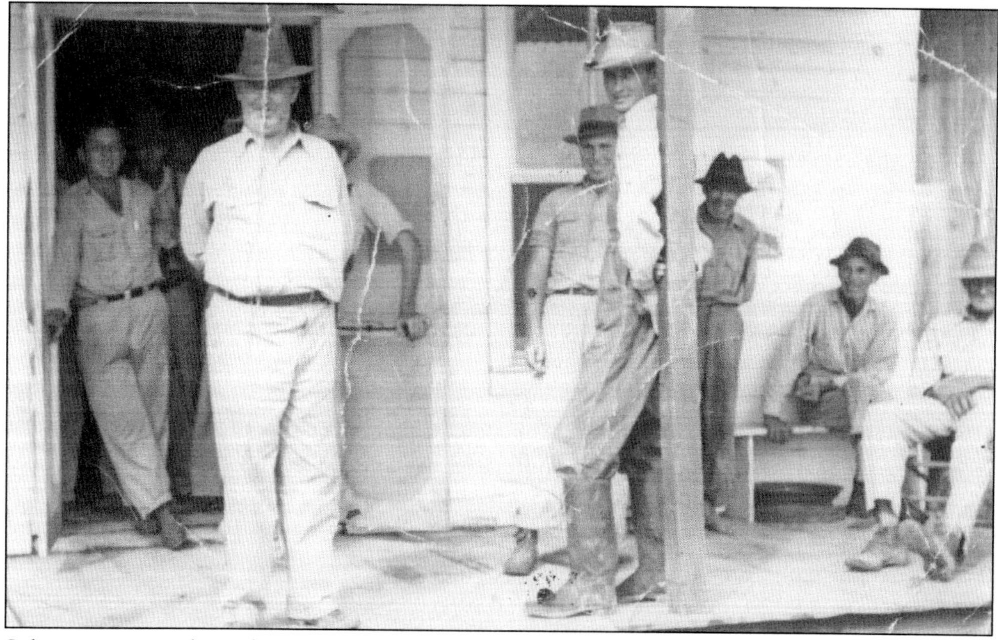

Saloons were popular gathering places where men could go for a drink or to play cards. This one was in Point Blue, a small community between Ville Platte and Chataignier. Pictured in 1942 are, from left to right, Dennis Tremie, the owner, in the doorway; Octave Tate; Evons Guillory, leaning on the post; three men named Fontenot; and Edwin Brunet at far right. (Courtesy of J.D. Soileau.)

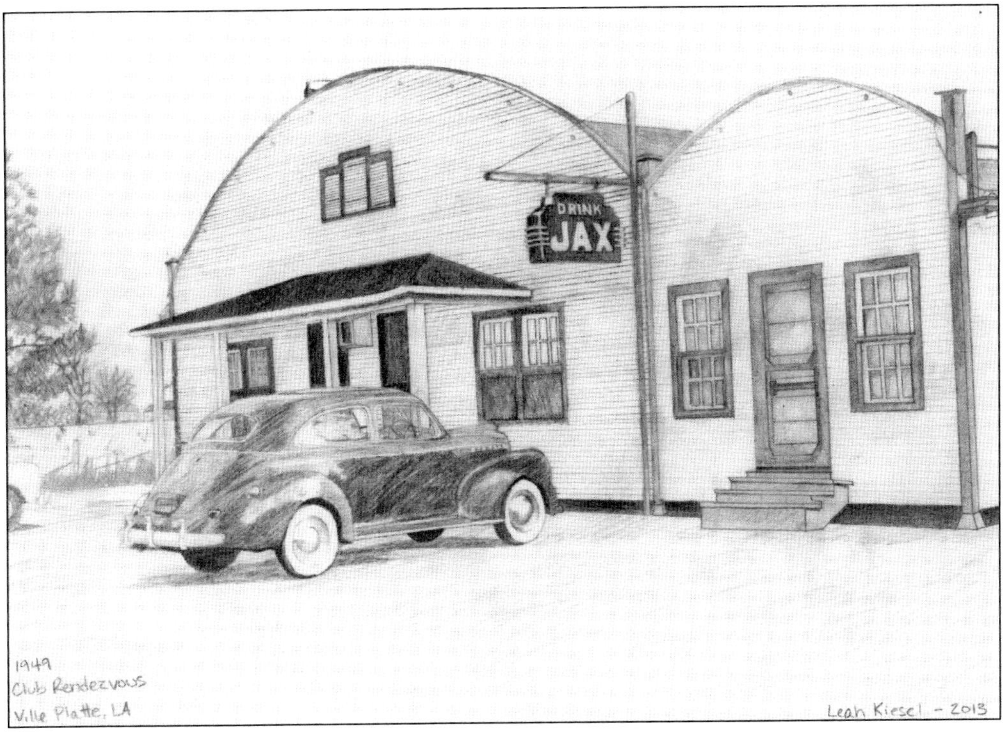

During the 1940s and 1950s, this building housed the Club Rendezvous, owned by Hubert Demoruelle. The Rendezvous was a popular nightclub where locals could hear and dance to big bands and jazz groups. Local talent was often featured there, too. In the back was a card room, with a craps table and slot machines. Later, it was briefly called the Jungle Club, then it became the Kit Kat Lounge. (Artwork by Leah Kiesel.)

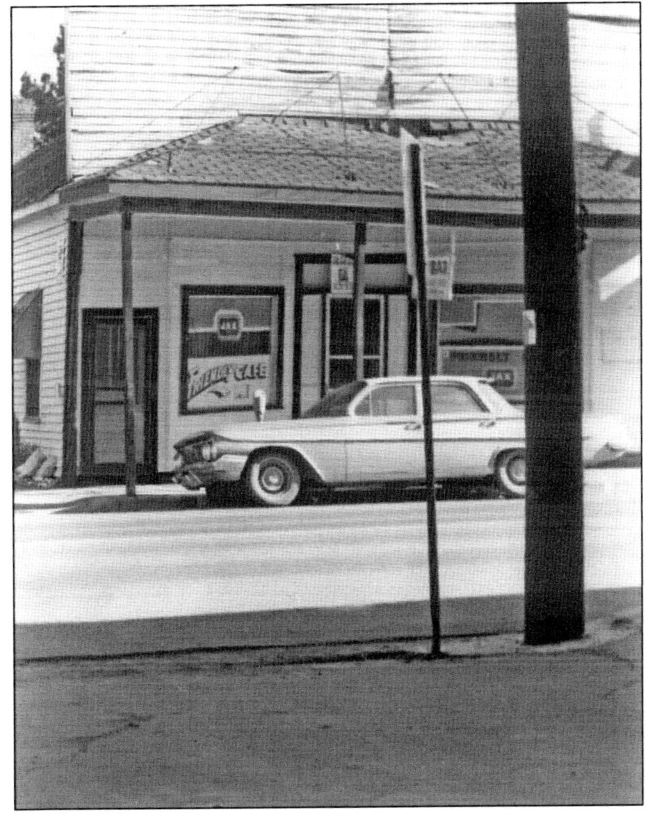

The Friendly Café was one of several cafés in Ville Platte half a century ago, all of which stayed open very late on Fridays and Saturdays to cater to the weekend crowd. People would come to town for business and shopping on Saturday and stay for a little socializing at the clubs. They could get a meal at a café before heading home. (Courtesy of Bobby Dardeau.)

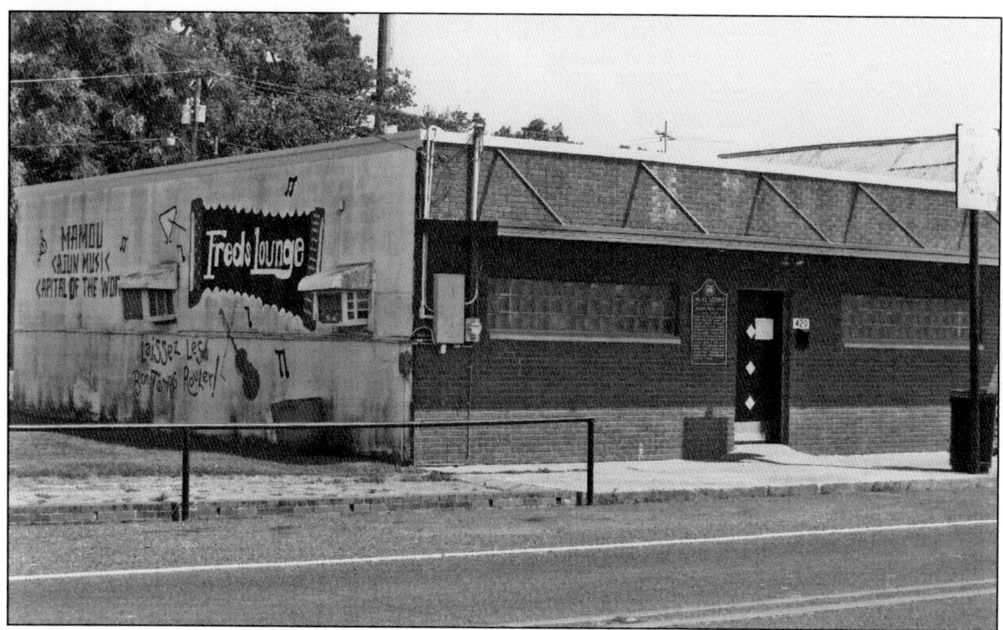

This unimposing building is Fred's Lounge, a fixture in Mamou since 1946, when Alfred "Fred" Tate purchased this old red-brick bar on Sixth Street. Here Fred and his friends Revon Reed and Paul Tate made plans to revive the Courir de Mardi Gras in Mamou in 1950. Reed began broadcasting a live radio program featuring Cajun music from the lounge in 1962. (Courtesy of Jane Vidrine.)

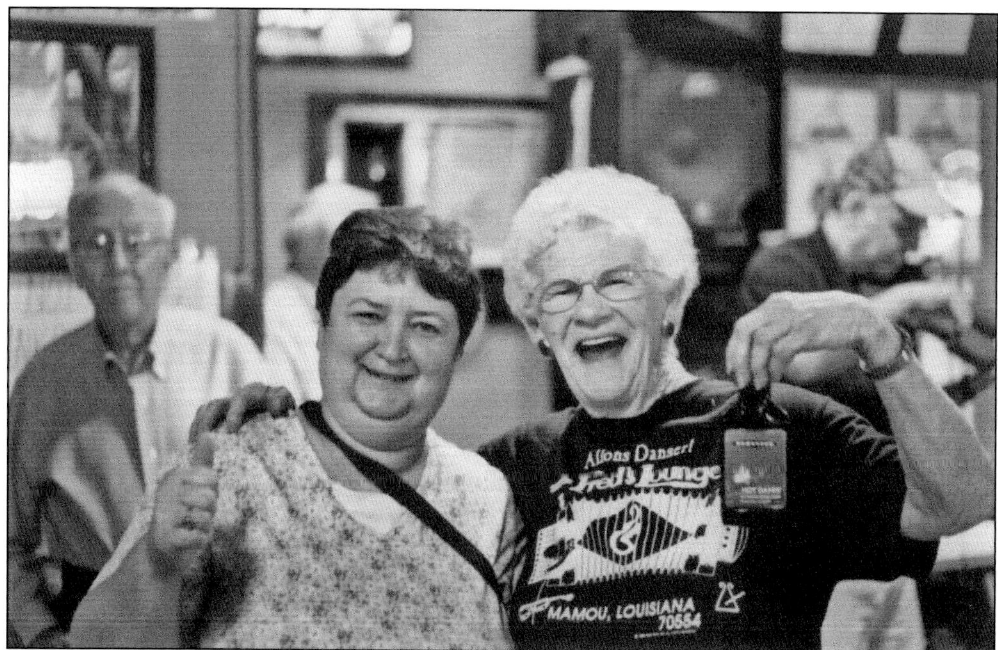

Inside the lounge, it's a different world. After Fred's death in 1992, his ex-wife, Sue Vavasseur, kept the lounge open on Saturday mornings so the broadcasts could continue. She is still active today, passing around trays of boudin, bussing tables, and, here, posing for a photograph with Jane Vidrine (left). Her pocket flask is part of the tradition, too. (Courtesy of Jean Kiesel.)

Six

Recreation

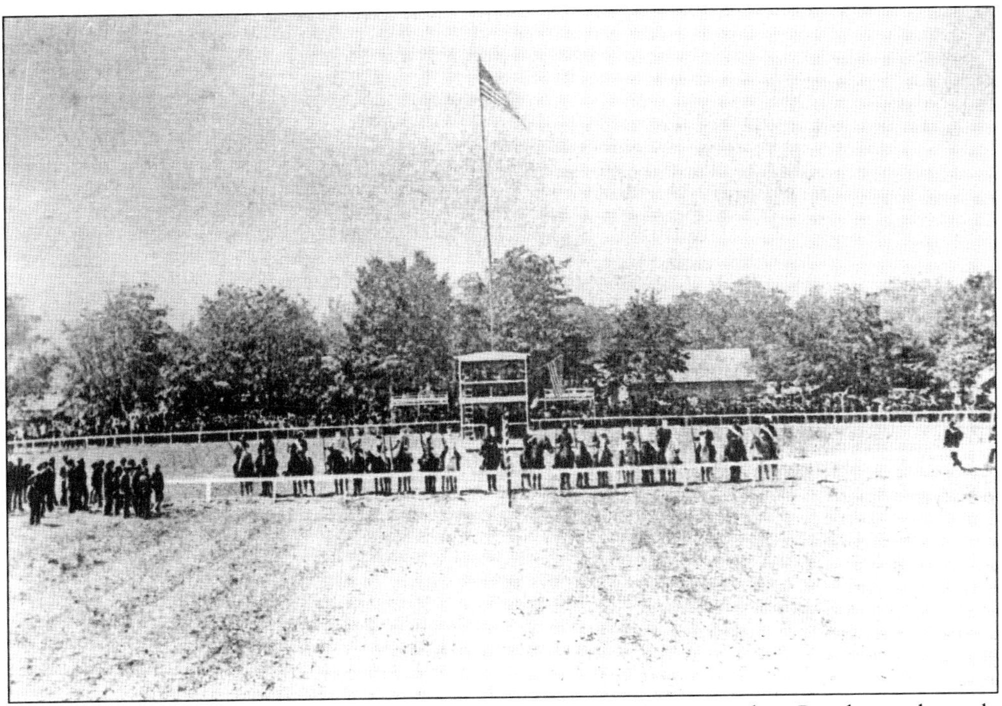

Le Tournoi, a medieval jousting contest, was introduced to the Evangeline Parish area by early settlers including Marcellin Garand, many of whom had come directly from France. It was popular throughout the 19th century. Shown here is the contest held on April 4, 1887, at the intersection of Reed and Main Streets in Ville Platte. (Courtesy of *Ville Platte Gazette*.)

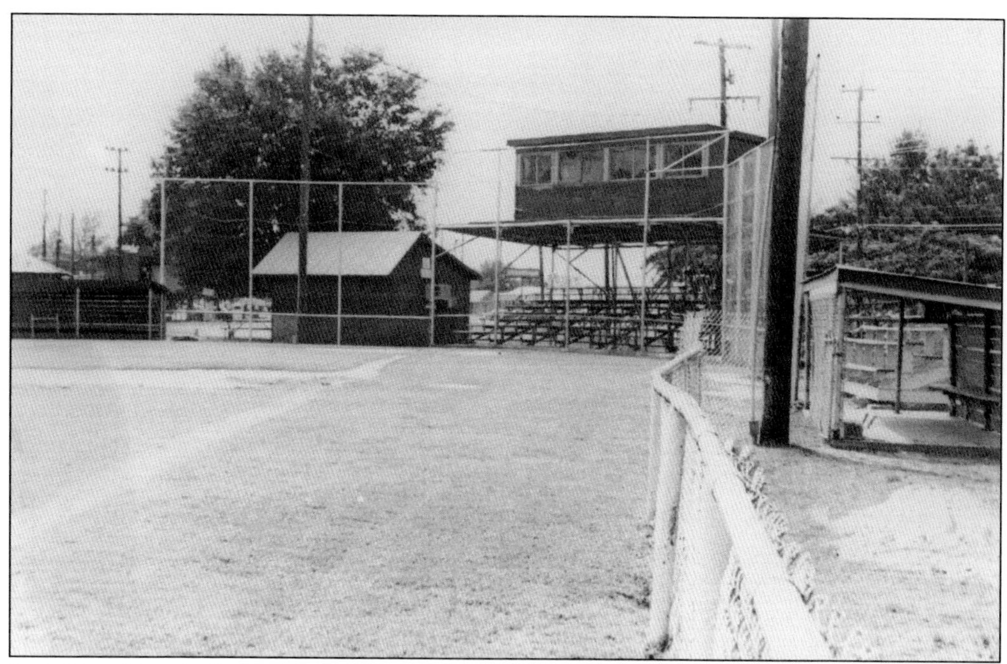

Ville Platte's baseball park has hosted many a youth baseball game in its day. The facilities include a baseball diamond, dugouts for the teams, a concession stand, stadium seating for the fans, and a press box. The facility is about to be replaced by a modern park with multiple fields. (Courtesy of *Ville Platte Gazette*.)

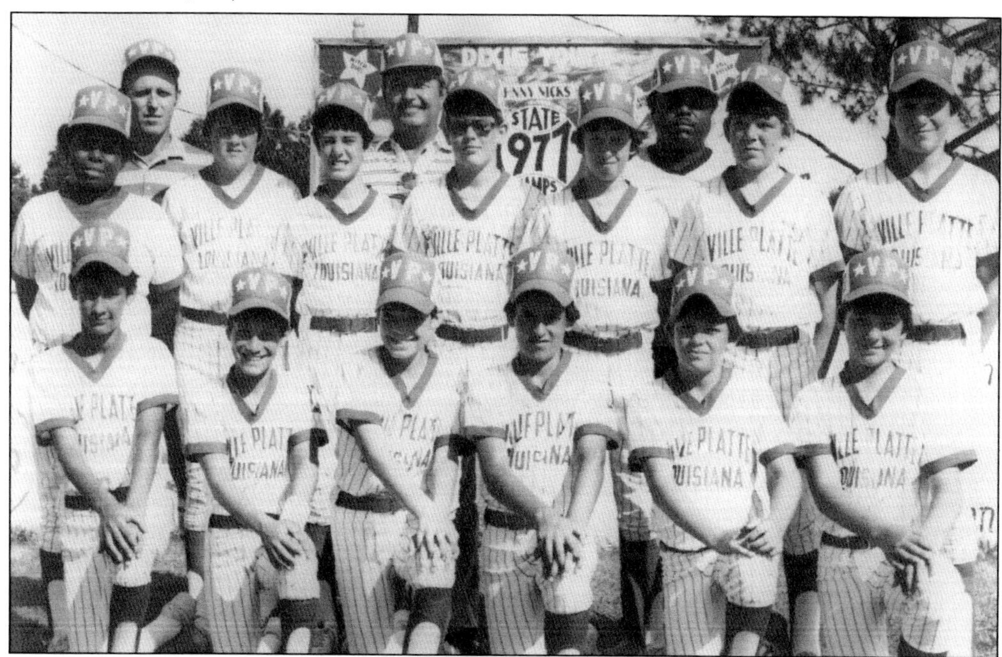

Ville Platte teams have had their share of success playing youth baseball. Many of the boys shown here played on the team for nine- and ten-year-olds that won the state championship in 1977, a few years before this photograph was taken. The sign behind them celebrates that feat. (Courtesy of *Ville Platte Gazette*.)

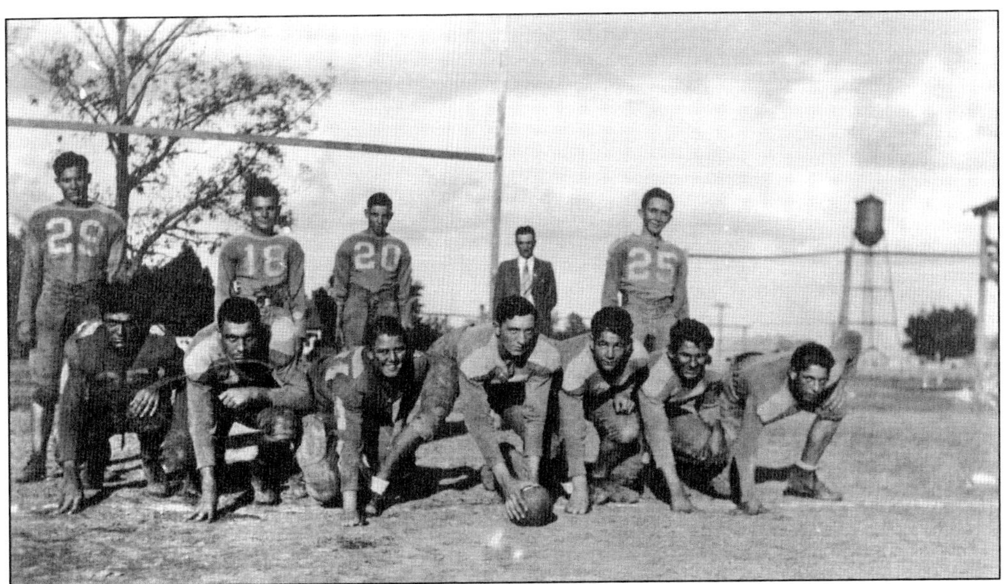

The Ville Platte High School Bulldogs of 1931 are, from left to right, (first row) Linton "Bosco" Phillips, Roy Lafleur, Major Lafleur, Lake Lafleur, "T Ed" Fontenot, Eraste Vidrine, and Dallas Deville; (second row) Wallace "Doo" Soileau, Rodney "T Rod" Duos, Curley "Beasley" Ortego, and Isom Foret. Football was a much rougher game back then. Pads were minimal, helmets were optional, and faceguards were unheard of. Broken bones and black eyes were common. (Courtesy of *Ville Platte Gazette*.)

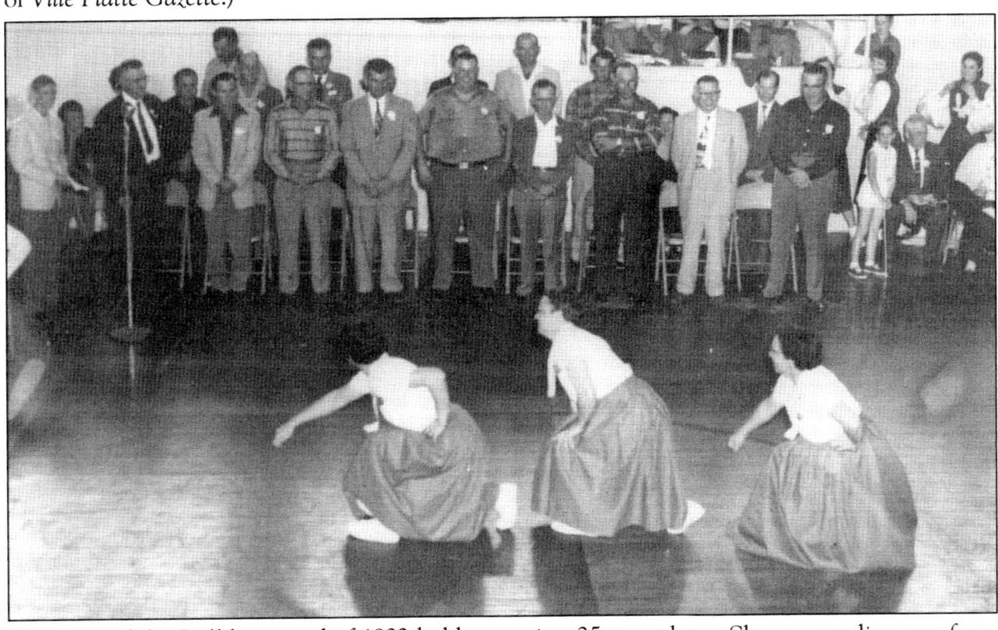

Members of the Bulldog squad of 1933 held a reunion 25 years later. Shown standing are, from left to right, (first row) coach C.A. Soileau, Charles Demourelle, Wilfred Lafleur, Numa Morien, Harold Bordelon, Willie Fontenot, Oscar Sylvester, Dallas Deville, and Eraste Vidrine; (second row) Audley Soileau, Lloyd Fontenot, Drouet Vidrine, Rodney Duos, Lake Lafleur, Clany Soileau, Major Lafleur, and Gilbert Vidrine. The cheerleaders are, from left to right, Verna Ortego, Rose McDaniel, and Mildred Ortego. (Courtesy of Pam McGee.)

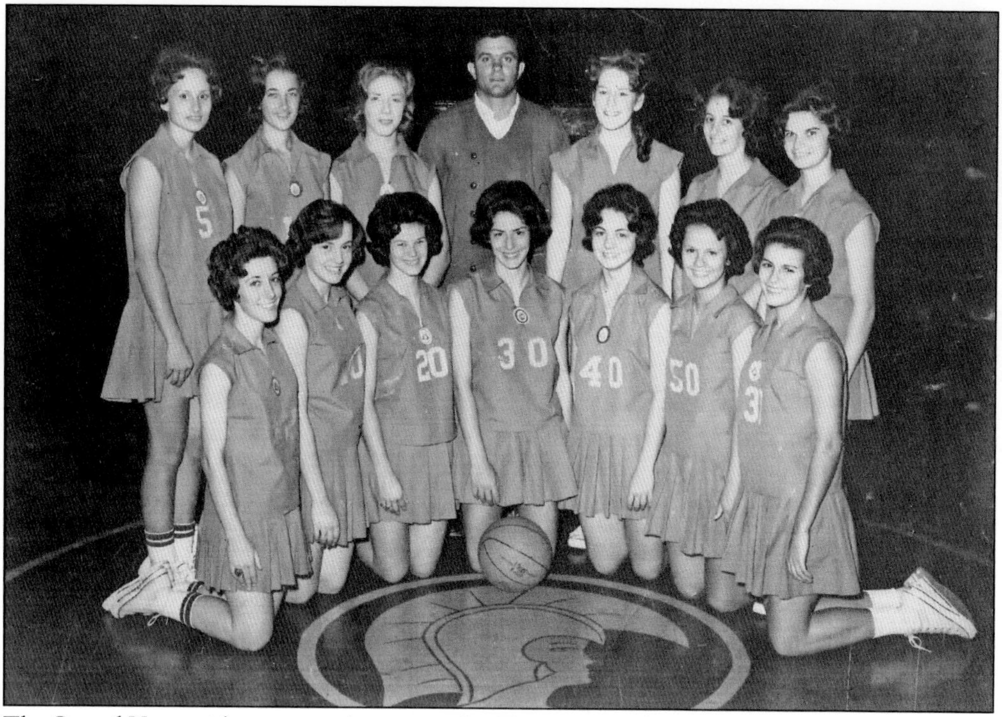

The Sacred Heart girls teams are known as the Trojanettes. The 1962 basketball team posed for this photograph. From left to right are (first row) Barbara Rozas, Cheryl Fuselier, Marlyn Manuel, Johnette LaHaye, Diana Coreil, Cindy Fontenot, and Connie Tatman; (second row) Margaret Davenport, Charlotte Miller, Jonetta Fontenot, coach Steve Brachin, Kathleen Deville, Loretta Veillon, and Patty Ruth Fontenot. (Courtesy of Kathleen Deville Godchaux.)

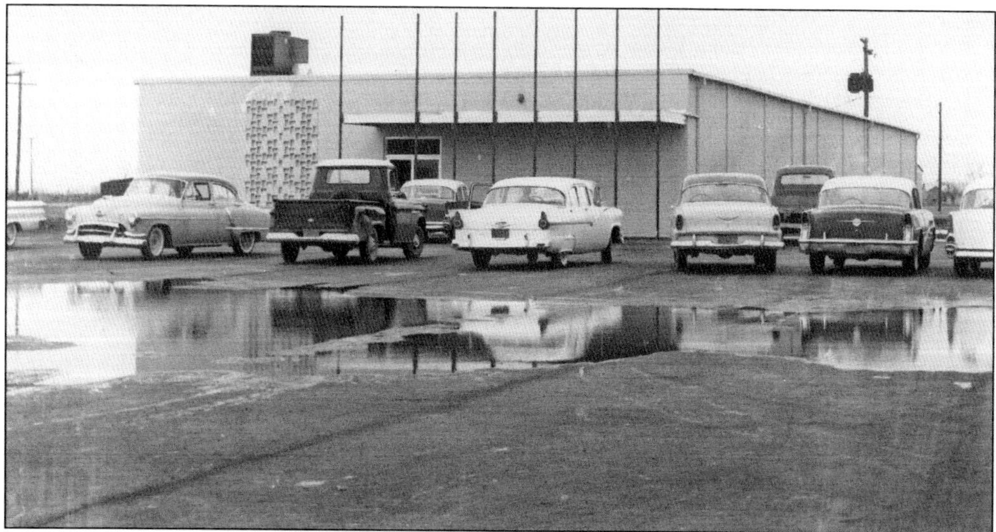

Evangeline Bowling Lanes opened in the Highland Park Shopping Center in Ville Platte in 1960. The first manager was Wilbur Ardoin. The bowling alley had 10 lanes and was open 22 hours a day. (The other two hours were for cleaning.) There were ladies', men's, and mixed leagues. Teams had names like the Legal Eagles, the Pin Splitters, and the Esso-Bees. (Courtesy of *Ville Platte Gazette*.)

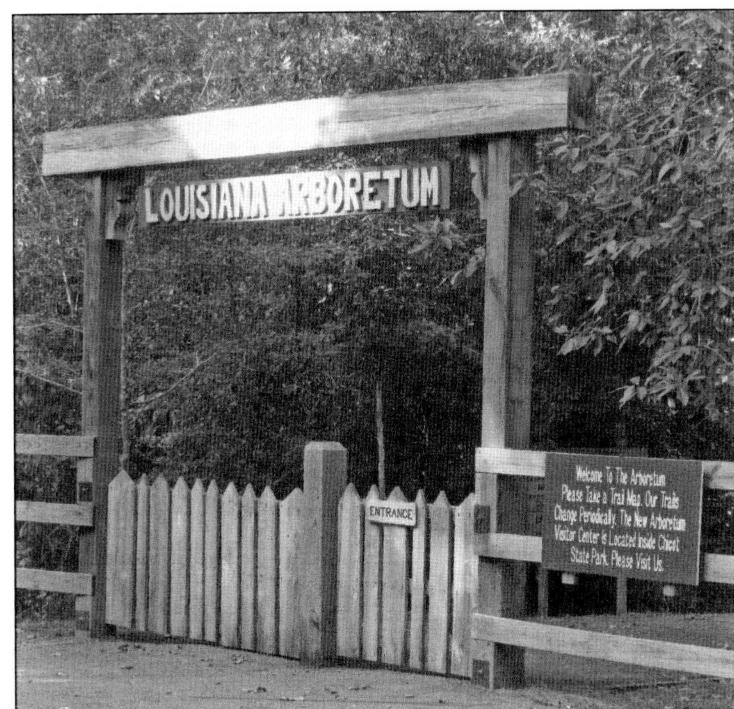

The Louisiana State Arboretum was established in 1961 in Chicot State Park. It was the first state-supported arboretum in the country. Within its 300-plus acres of varying topography is nearly every type of vegetation native to Louisiana except the coastal marsh and prairie. Among the flora are giant beech, magnolia, and oak trees, ferns, and crane fly orchids. Wildlife, too, is abundant. (Courtesy of Jane Vidrine.)

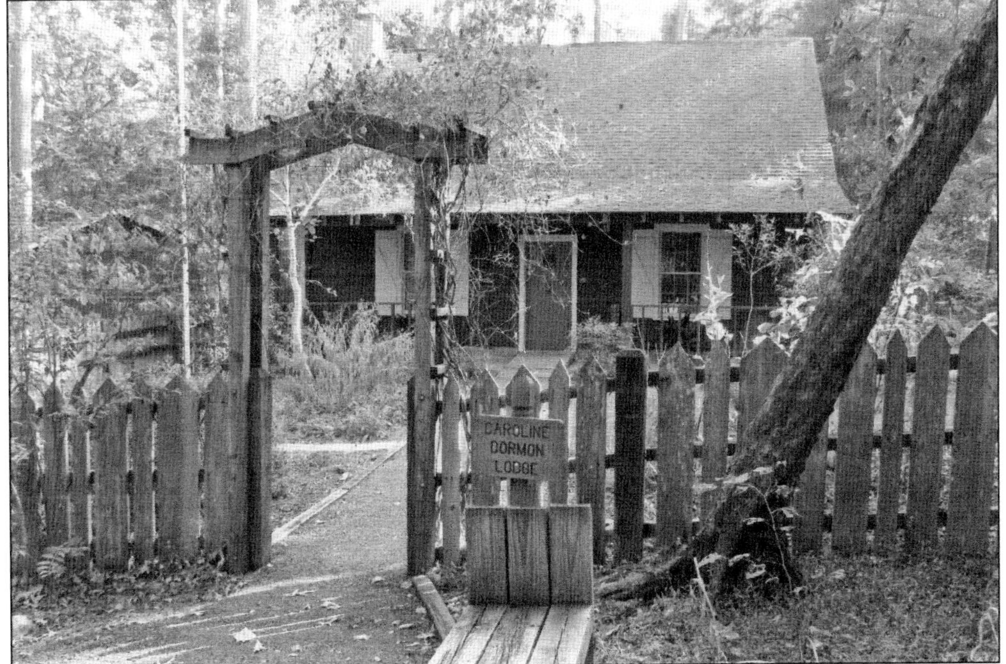

The Caroline Dormon Lodge at the Louisiana State Arboretum houses the visitors' center, a library, and an herbarium preserving native plants that grow on the site. Dormon was a naturalist, conservationist, and author. Among her many interests was the creation of Kisatchie National Forest in central Louisiana. It was she who first proposed establishing an arboretum at Chicot State Park. (Courtesy of Jane Vidrine.)

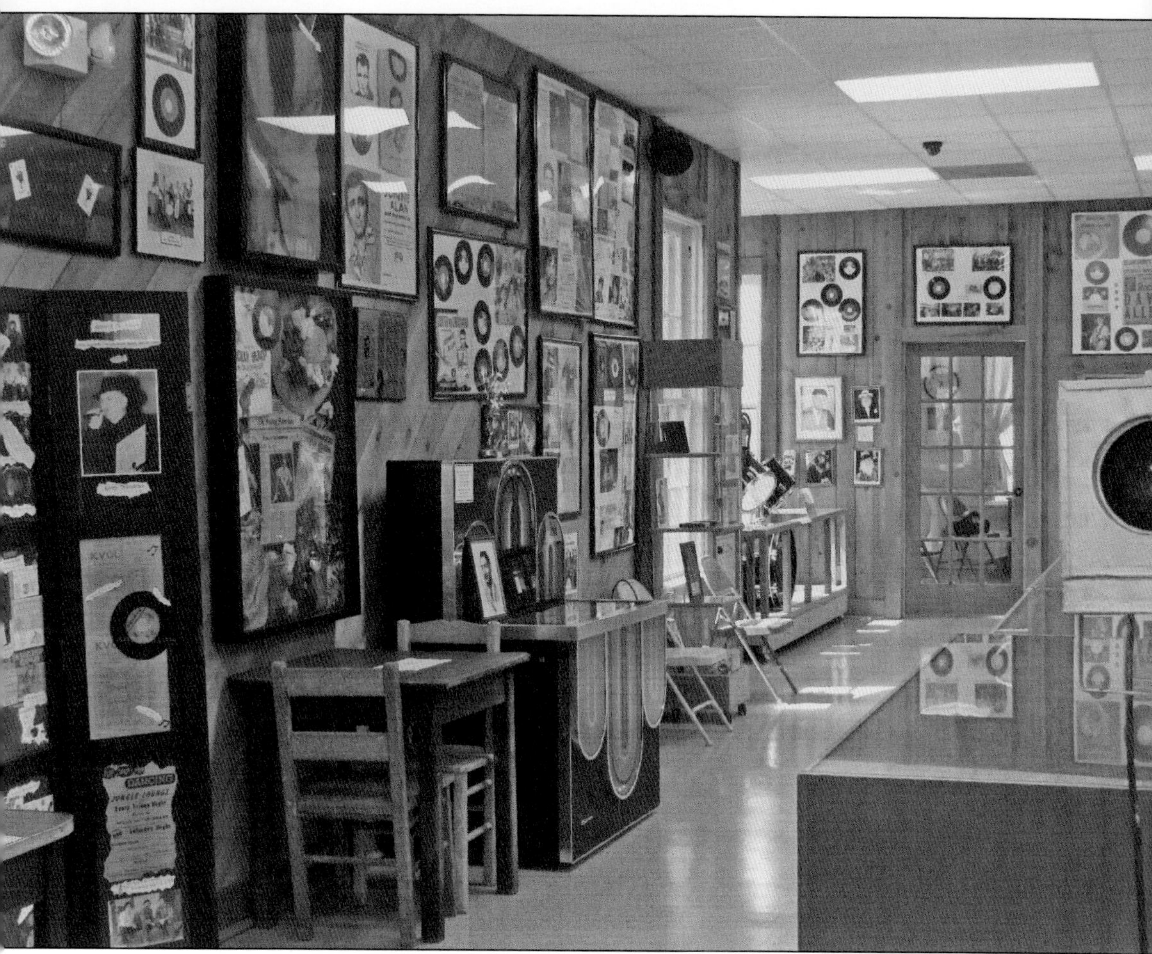

The Swamp Pop Museum in Ville Platte opened in 2010. Swamp pop is a blend of rhythm and blues, country and western, and traditional Cajun and Creole music. The style developed in south Louisiana and was especially popular from the late 1950s to the mid-1960s. One of the labels that recorded swamp pop was Floyd Soileau's Jin label. The genre was wildly popular locally, and many songs made it into the top 100 nationally. The Swamp Pop Museum, housed in the old railroad depot, displays photographs, recordings, musical instruments, posters, and other memorabilia from artists who made swamp pop music. (Courtesy of Jane Vidrine.)

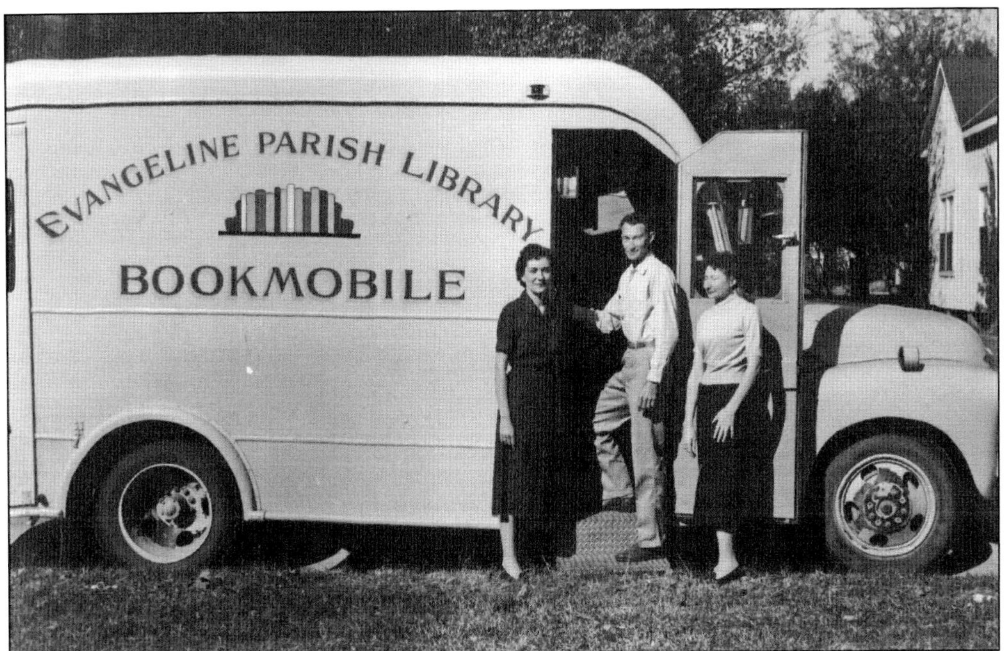

The Evangeline Parish Library had only three branches in 1955, in Ville Platte, Mamou, and Basile. This bookmobile served everybody else, or about half of the library system's 5,000 registered patrons. It made 82 scheduled stops a month. From left to right are Greta B. Fontenot, bookmobile assistant; Leo Smith, driver; and Janet Smith, clerical assistant. (Courtesy of Evangeline Parish Library.)

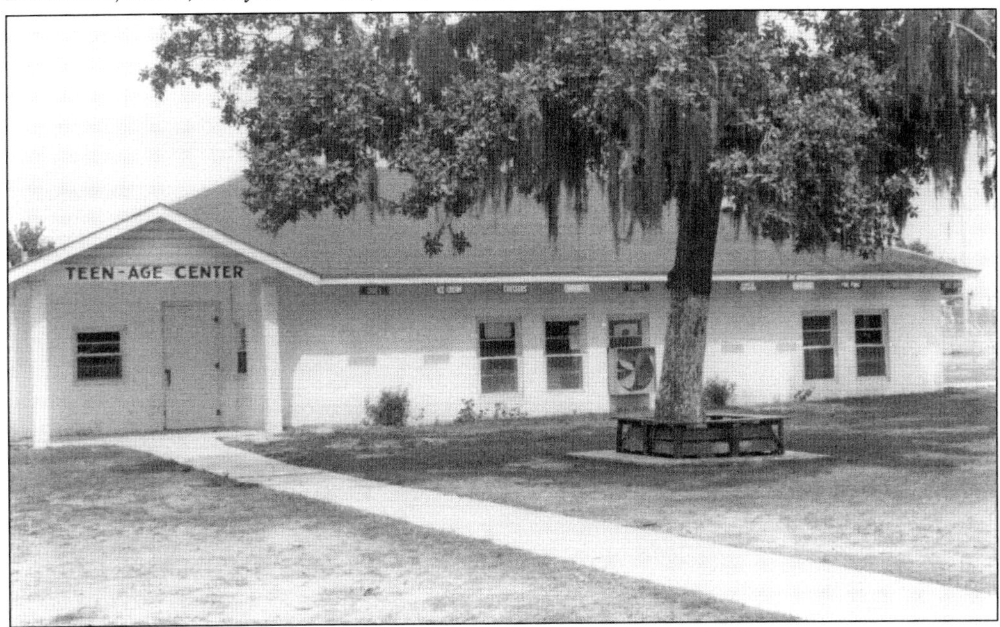

The Teen-Age Center opened in the 1950s in Ville Platte's City Park. Civic clubs got together to erect the building, which had a wooden dance floor and space for tables along the wall. The center offered food and recreation as well as dances. It also served as a meeting place for civic organizations. After the Teen-Age Center burned down, it was replaced by the Civic Center. (Courtesy of *Ville Platte Gazette*.)

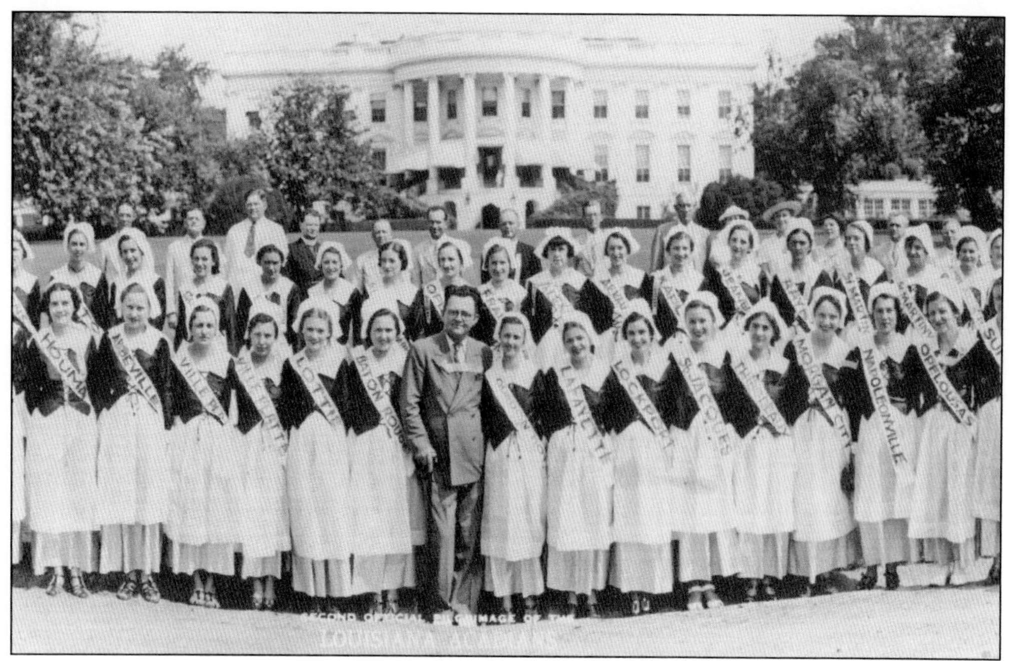

In the 1930s, Cajun entrepreneur Dudley J. LeBlanc spearheaded an Acadian revival in Louisiana. He organized pilgrimages to Acadia in 1930 and 1936, stopping at the White House along the way. The young women in the group wore "Evangeline" costumes, with sashes designating their hometowns. Shown here is part of the 1936 group, with two girls from Ville Platte in the front row on the left. (Courtesy of Pam McGee.)

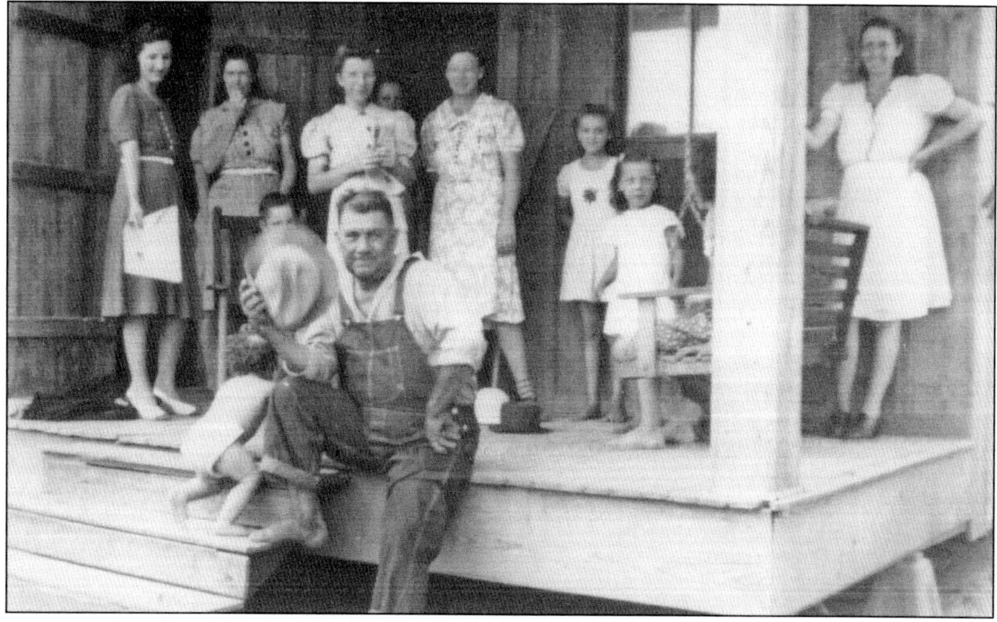

Here, family and friends gather on a porch in Point Blue. Women in the small, close-knit communities of Evangeline Parish enjoyed visiting friends in the afternoon, sharing coffee, and chatting. Standing are, from left to right, Delta Manuel, Edna Vidrine, Eta Aguillard, Mrs. August Manuel, two Manuel girls, and Emily V. Brunet. The man in front is Celestin Fontenot. (Courtesy of J.D. Soileau.)

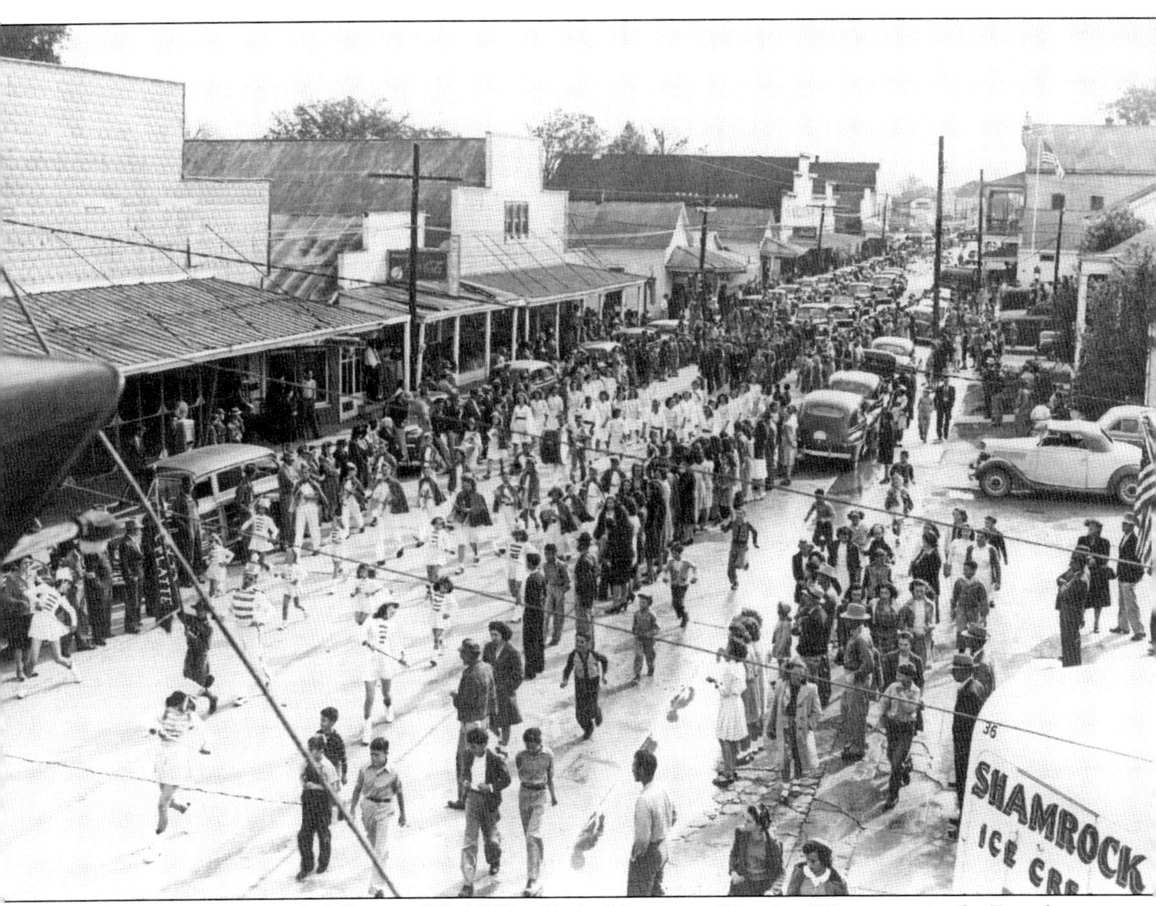

In the years immediately following World War II, the Veterans of Foreign Wars organized a Fourth of July parade each year to honor returning troops. About the same time, local residents revived the tournoi, a medieval jousting competition that was popular in the area in the 1800s, but which had died out before the turn of the 20th century. The tournoi became part of the Fourth of July celebration as well. The parade was held annually for almost a decade until the Cotton Festival was organized in 1954 and absorbed many of the events that had been part of the Fourth of July celebration. In this photograph, the Ville Platte High School marching band leads a group of veterans down Main Street in one of the first parades. (Courtesy of *Ville Platte Gazette*.)

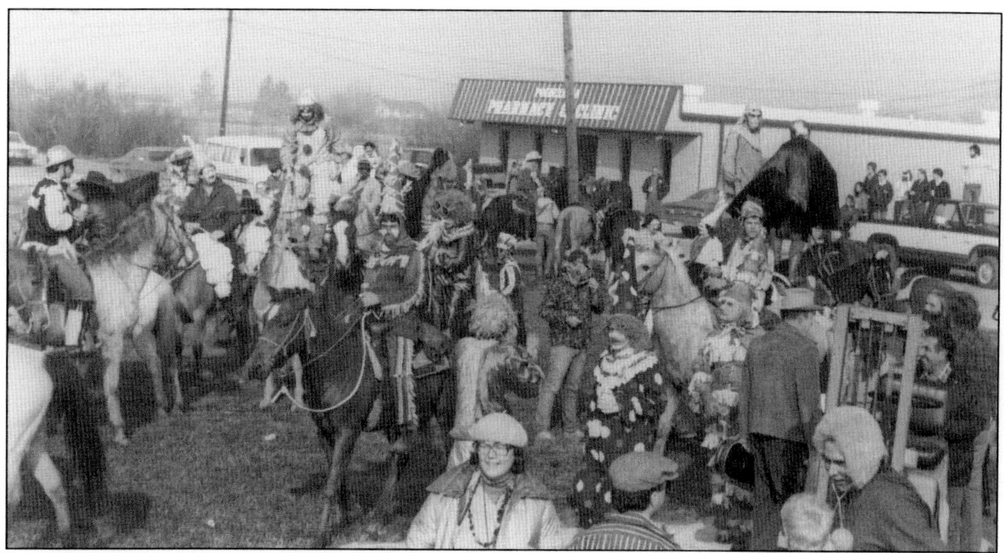

A Cajun Mardi Gras as celebrated in Evangeline Parish has been described as ritualized chaos. A group of costumed and masked men ride through the countryside, collecting ingredients for gumbo to be served to the community that evening. The begging ritual traces back to medieval times. Note that three of the riders are standing on their saddles; such exhibitions of horsemanship are much admired. (Courtesy of *Ville Platte Gazette*.)

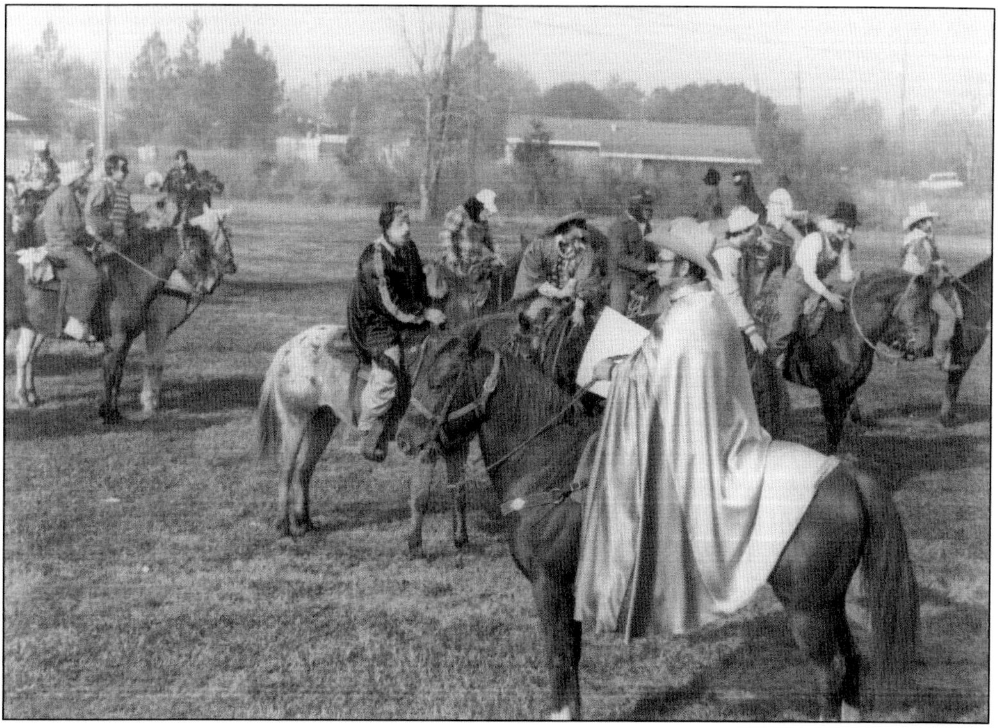

The Courir de Mardi Gras is under the command of the captain, who usually wears a cowboy hat and brightly colored cape, but not a mask. He leads the riders through the countryside and formally asks permission of each household before the riders enter their property. He also ensures that the rules of the celebration are obeyed. His word is law. (Courtesy of *Ville Platte Gazette*.)

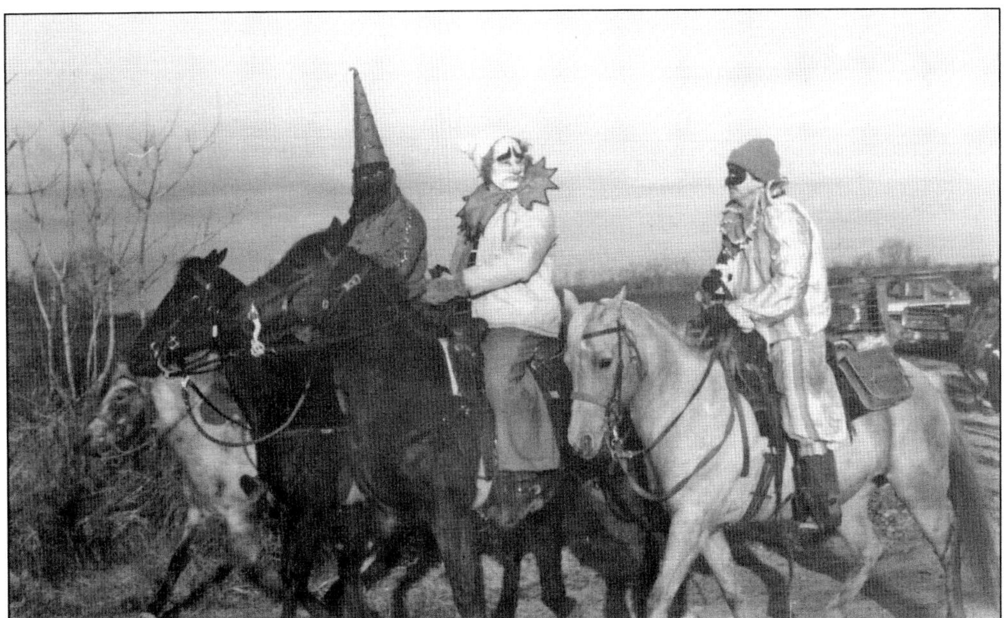

The Mardi Gras run begins early in the morning, with riders bundled up against the cold. All are in costume, with their faces covered. It is important that riders be thoroughly disguised so even family members cannot recognize them. Men often trade horses so they cannot be identified by their mounts. The tall conical dunce's hat is common, parodying medieval noblewomen's headpieces. (Courtesy of *Ville Platte Gazette*.)

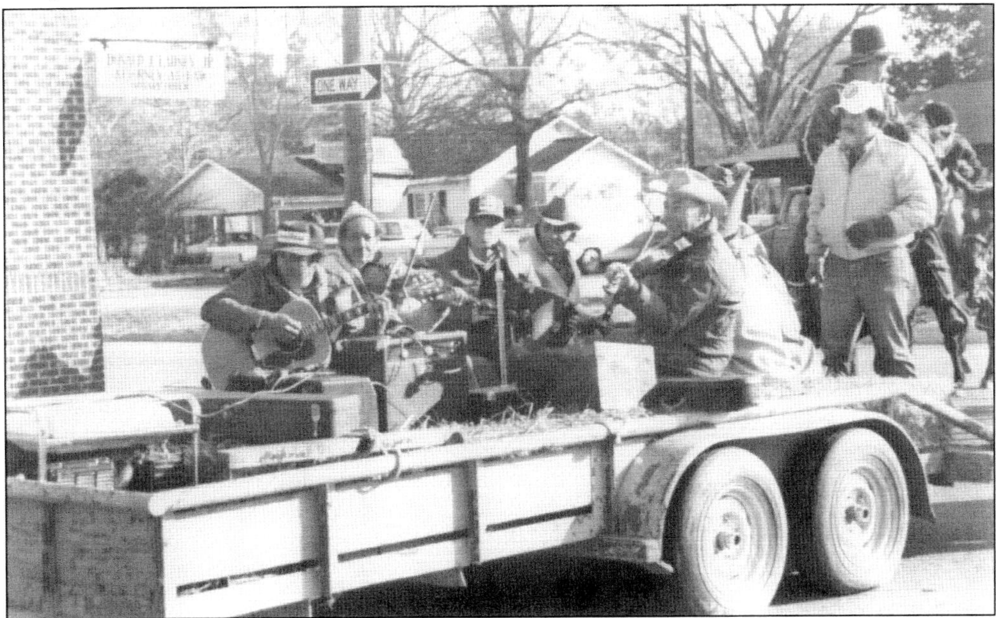

In addition to the riders, participants without horses follow on wagons to take part in the revelry. This wagon carries a Cajun band, which provides musical accompaniment to the festivities. Beer is dispensed in large quantities to the riders from another wagon. This photograph was taken in Ville Platte, before the Courir was suspended there when the city banned alcohol. (Courtesy of *Ville Platte Gazette*.)

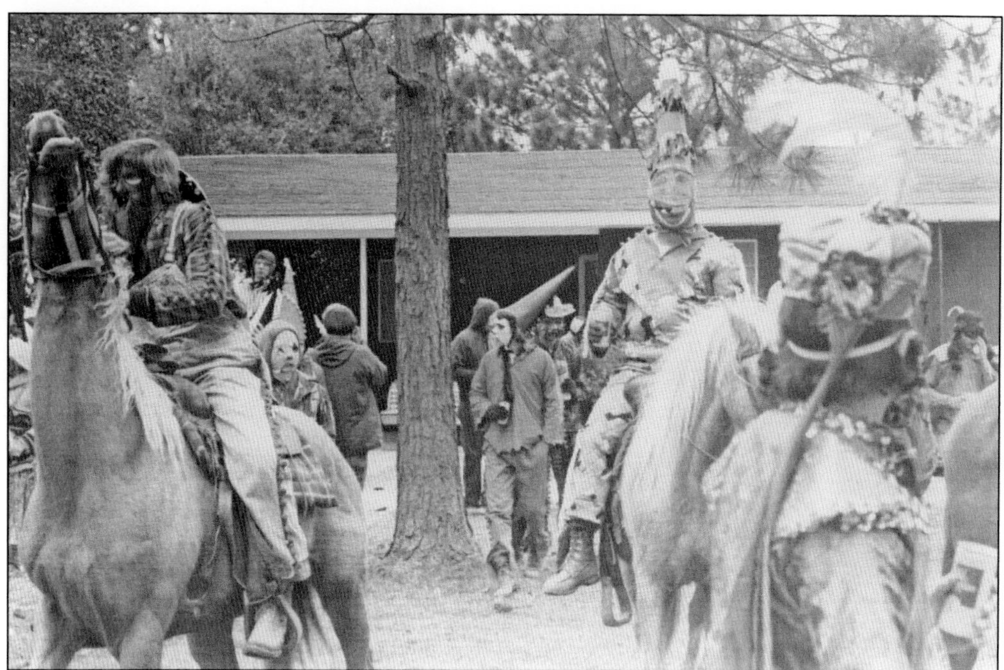

Once permission is granted to come onto the property, riders charge the house as if taking it by assault. They might threaten the residents or pretend to kidnap children. They also perform stunts and generally act up. Once the food gift is acquired, the captain signals that it is time to depart, and the group moves on to the next household. (Courtesy of *Ville Platte Gazette*.)

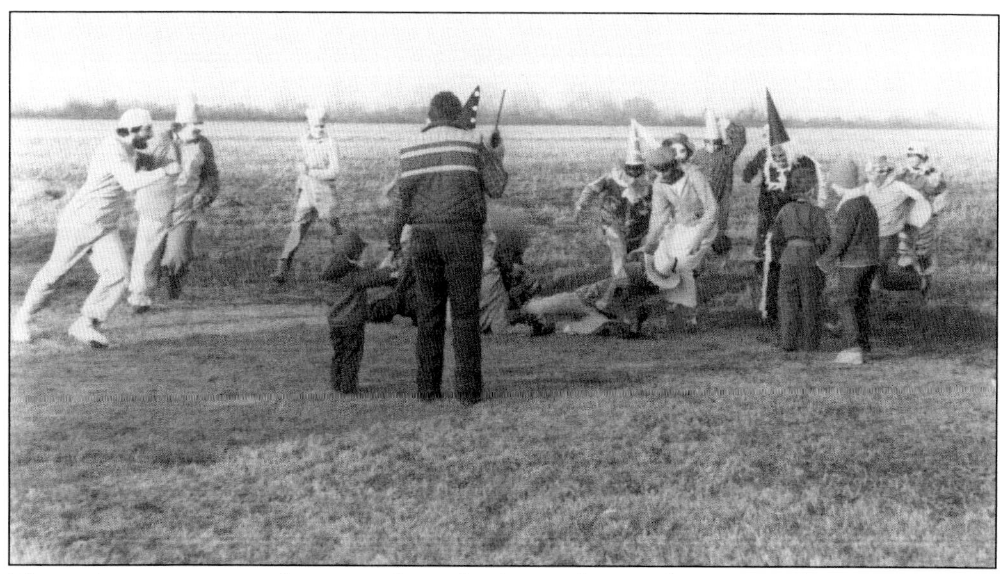

Those who agree to contribute ingredients for the gumbo may donate rice, flour, onions, or oil. But the most highly prized item is a live chicken. The bird is tossed high into the air, and the revelers must chase it down and catch it. As can be seen here, the chase is chaotic and often hilarious. (Courtesy of *Ville Platte Gazette*.)

In the evening, the community gathers to share the gumbo that the men have worked so hard to acquire, riders eating first. The evening ends with a dance, many of the participants in costume and even the youngest taking part. All celebrating ends at the stroke of midnight, for the Carnival season is over and Lent has begun. (Courtesy of *Ville Platte Gazette*.)

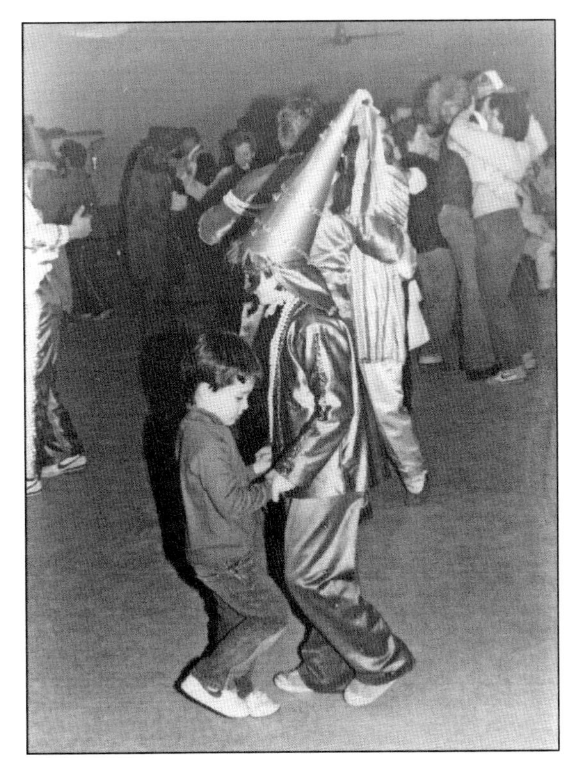

The Dewey Balfa Cajun and Creole Heritage Week has been held every spring since 1990 at Chicot State Park in Evangeline Parish. First organized by Balfa's daughter Christine, the program features concerts and dances each night, and classes and jam sessions during the day for musicians of all ages and skill levels. Here, Dirk Powell (fifth from left) leads a band workshop in 2004. (Courtesy of David Simpson.)

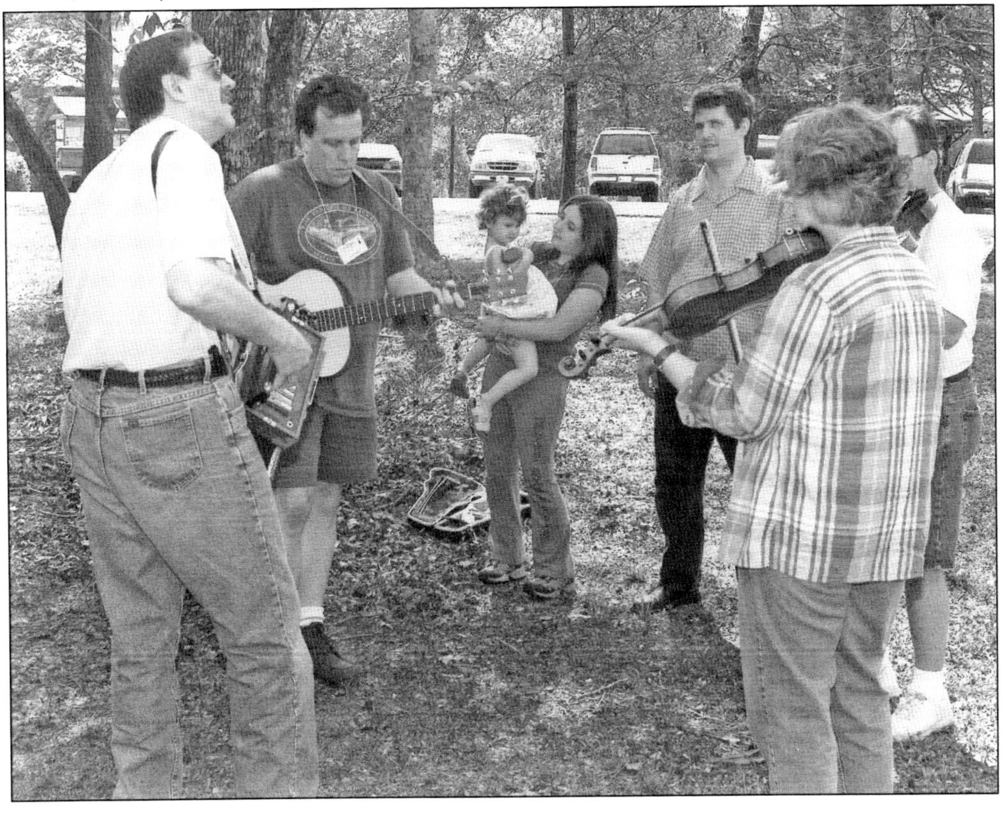

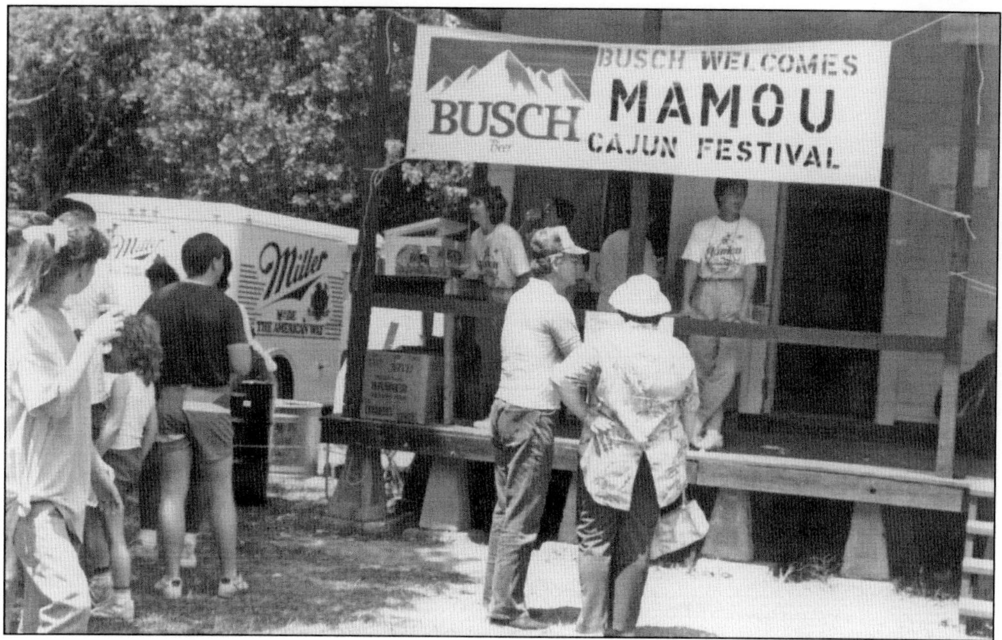

The Mamou Cajun Music Festival was founded in the early 1970s as a way to renew the community's interest in its traditional culture, which seemed to be fading under pressure from modern ways. The festival began as a one-day event featuring local musicians and was sponsored by the Mamou Area Jaycees. (Courtesy of *Ville Platte Gazette*.)

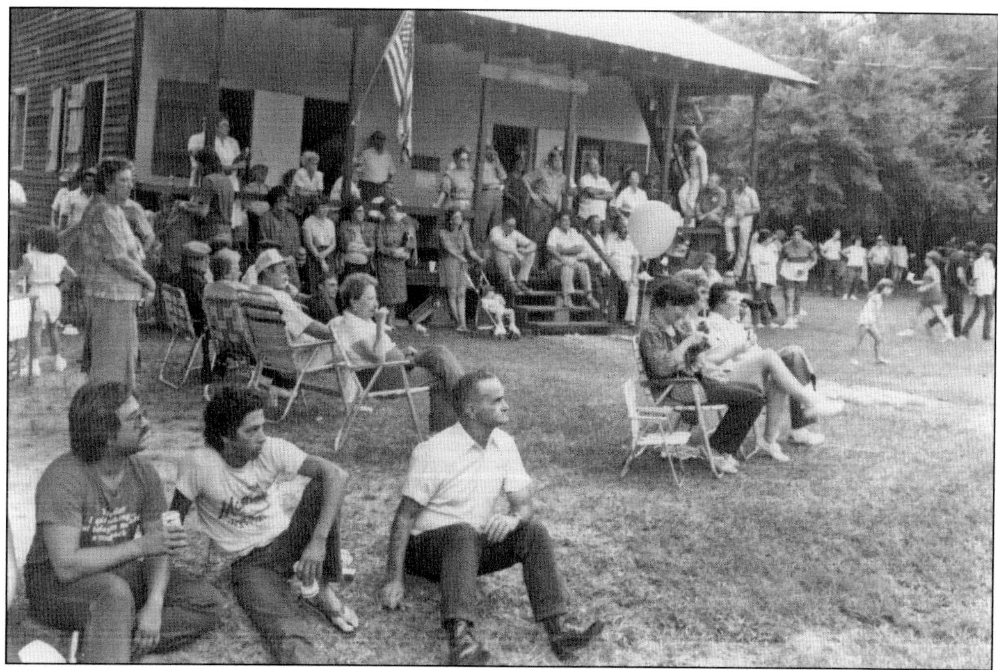

The Mamou Cajun Music Festival soon grew into a two-day annual event. Besides traditional Cajun musicians, the festival features dancing, food, and contests for local citizens and fans from all over the world. Since the early 1980s, the festival has been sponsored by its own organization, which gained nonprofit status in 1985. (Courtesy of *Ville Platte Gazette*.)

Sacred Heart Chapel in Belaire Cove has hosted a Crawfish Cook-Off on the first Sunday after Easter each year since 1990 to raise funds for the church. The featured event is a crawfish étouffée cook-off. The festival includes live music, children's games, a washerboard tournament, concessions, and a live auction. Pictured here is Felton Lejeune and the Cajun Cowboys, who performed at the festival for many years. (Courtesy of Runnie F. Matte.)

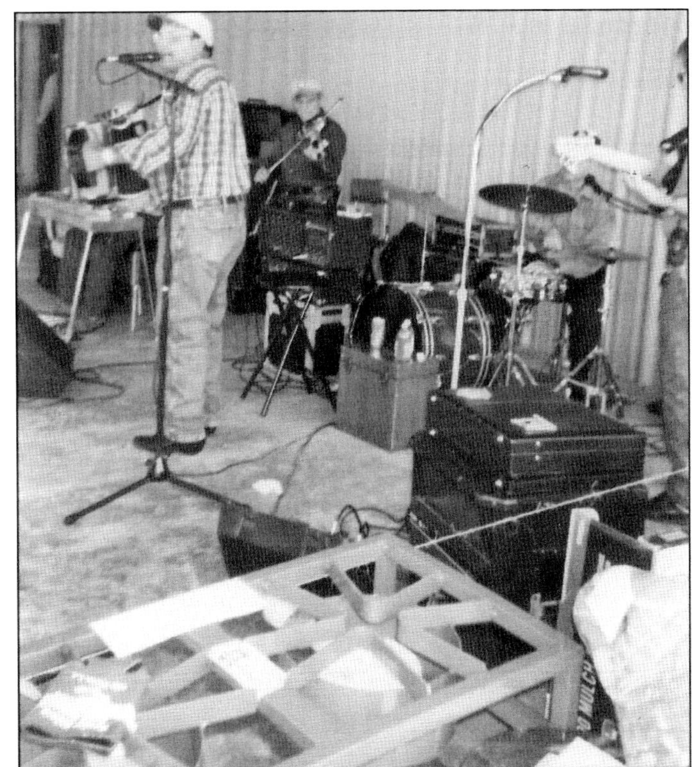

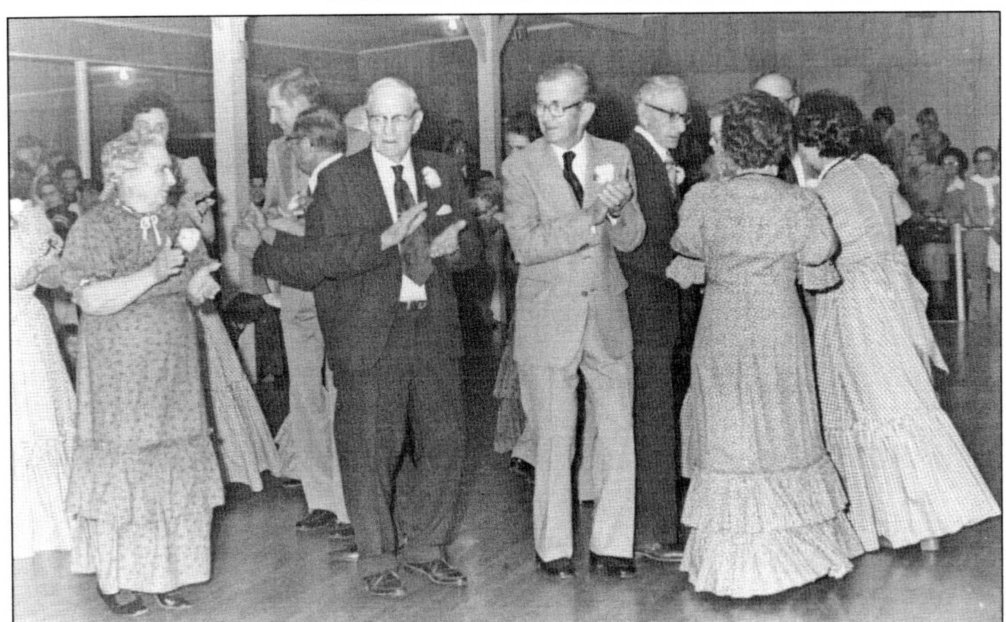

The Louisiana Cotton Festival in Ville Platte opens on Tuesday night with the Contredanse, a French square dance, performed by older members of the community accompanied by a French band. The first contredanse was held in 1962 at the Teen-Age Center. Since 1975, two residents of La Maison de Sante Nursing Home have been crowned Le Roi and La Reine, and they reign over the dance. (Courtesy of *Ville Platte Gazette*.)

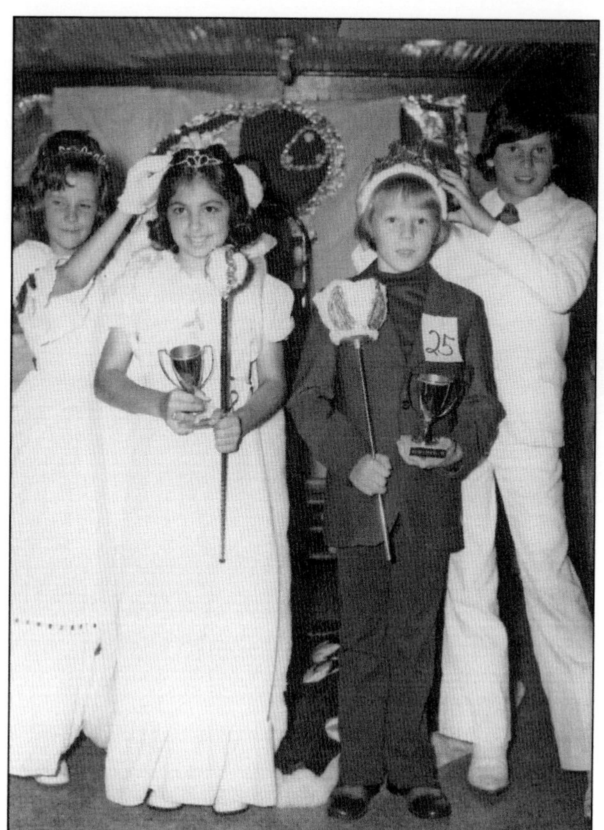

Cotton Festival royalty include Miss Cotton Blossom and King Cotton Boll for pre-teens, sponsored by the Lions' Club Auxiliary. In this photograph, the 1975 Queen Cotton Blossom, Jessica Ann Bordelon, and King Cotton Boll, James Harrington, are being crowned by their predecessors from 1974, Monique Fontenot and Robert Harvey. (Courtesy of *Ville Platte Gazette*.)

The Cotton Pickers are the official entertainers at the Cotton Festival. A new group is chosen each year. Shown here is the group from 1965, the 200th anniversary of the Acadian migration to Louisiana, when the Cotton Festival took an Acadian theme. The members are, from left to right, Susan Johnson, Darlene Zimmer, Sheila Attales, Cindy Buller, Camille Lafleur, Evelyn Guillory, Johnette LaHaye, and Gerry Curole. (Courtesy of Ville Platte Chamber of Commerce.)

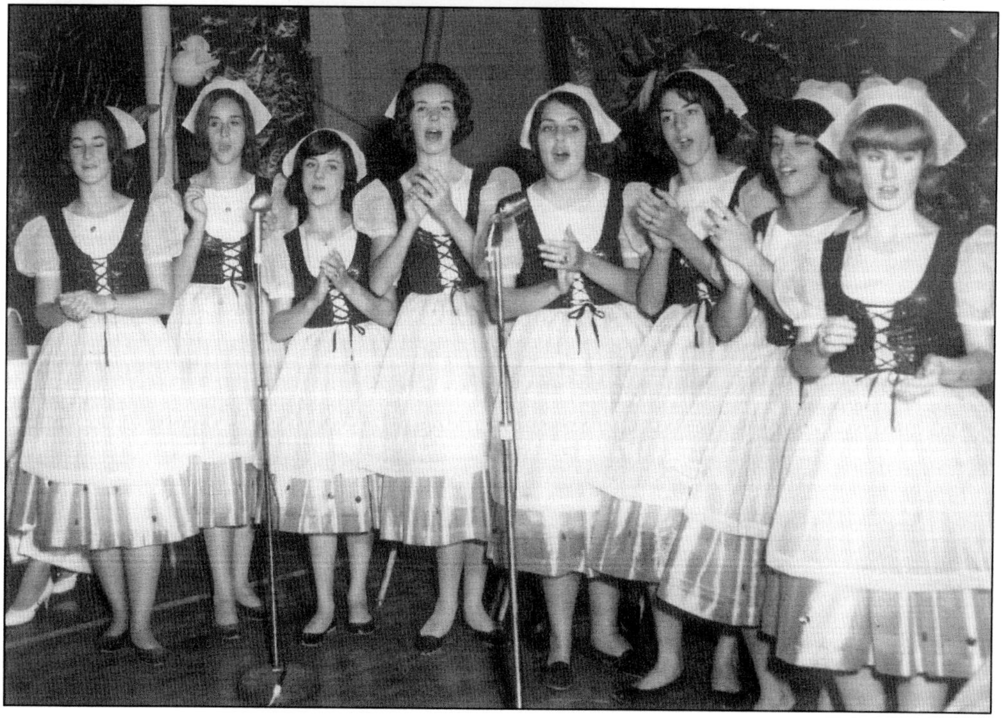

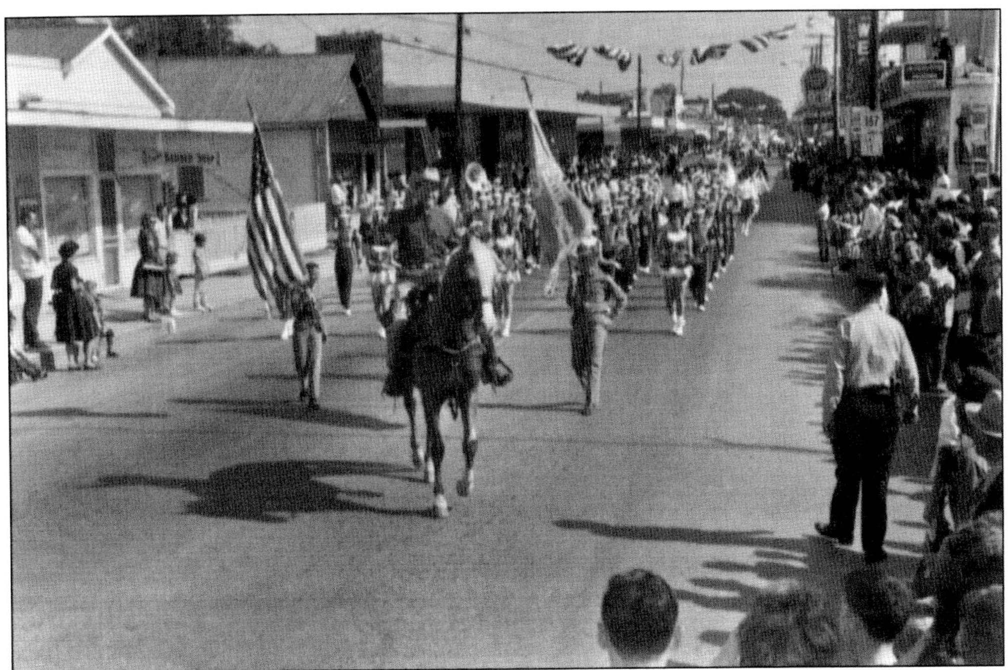

Grand Marshal Jules Ashlock leads the Cotton Festival parade down Ville Platte's Main Street in 1962. Cotton King that year was Dr. Hosea Phillips, a native of Ville Platte and professor of French at the University of Southwestern Louisiana. Queen was Rose Mary Hudspeth, and Colonel Cotton was Henry J. Vidrine, whose grandfather Eloi operated the first horse-drawn gin in Evangeline Parish. The theme for this festival was Camelot. (Courtesy of Ville Platte City Hall.)

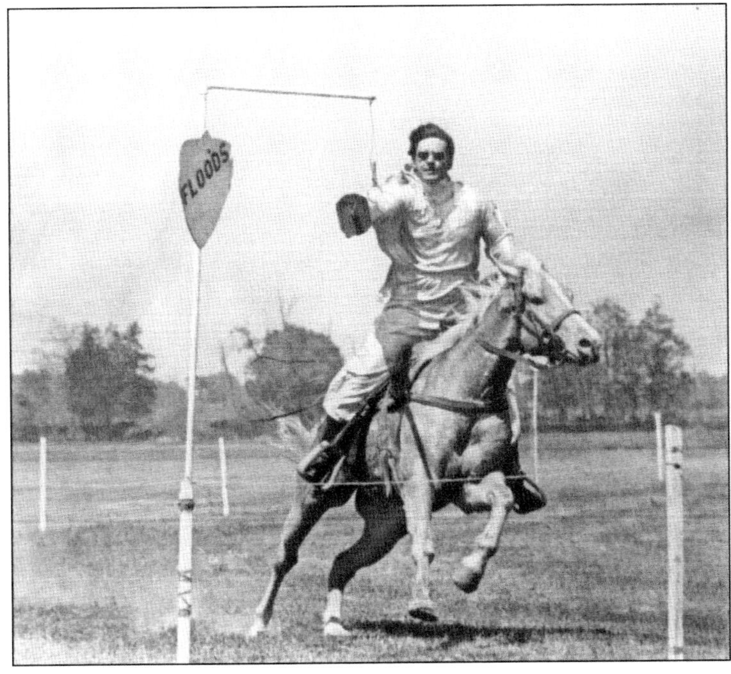

The tournoi was revived after World War II and has been part of the Cotton Festival since 1952. Riders compete on a quarter-mile track, trying to spear seven rings with their lances. The rings represent the traditional enemies of cotton: drought, flood, boll weevil, bollworm, silk, rayon, and nylon. Knights are scored on their speed and accuracy over three heats. Pictured here is 1983 champion Dwayne Fontenot. (Courtesy of *Ville Platte Gazette*.)

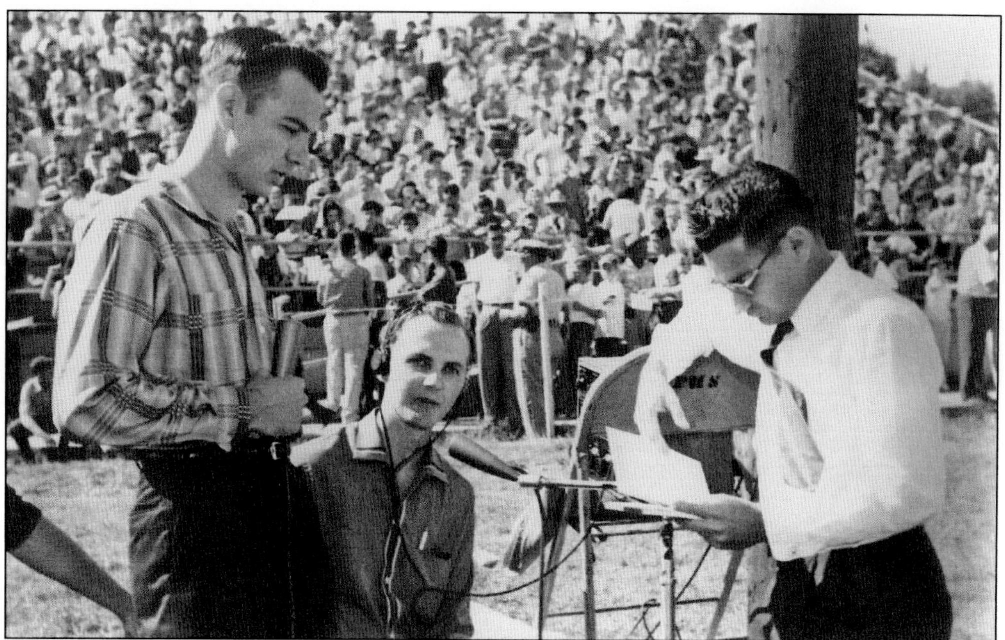

In the early years of the Cotton Festival, the tournoi drew huge crowds. The event was held at the Ville Platte High School stadium, where the bleachers provided plenty of seating. To add to the excitement, Ville Platte's new radio station, KVPI, broadcast the action live from the stadium. Shown here from left to right are John Pitre, Jim Soileau, and Chris Duplechain. (Courtesy of KVPI Radio.)

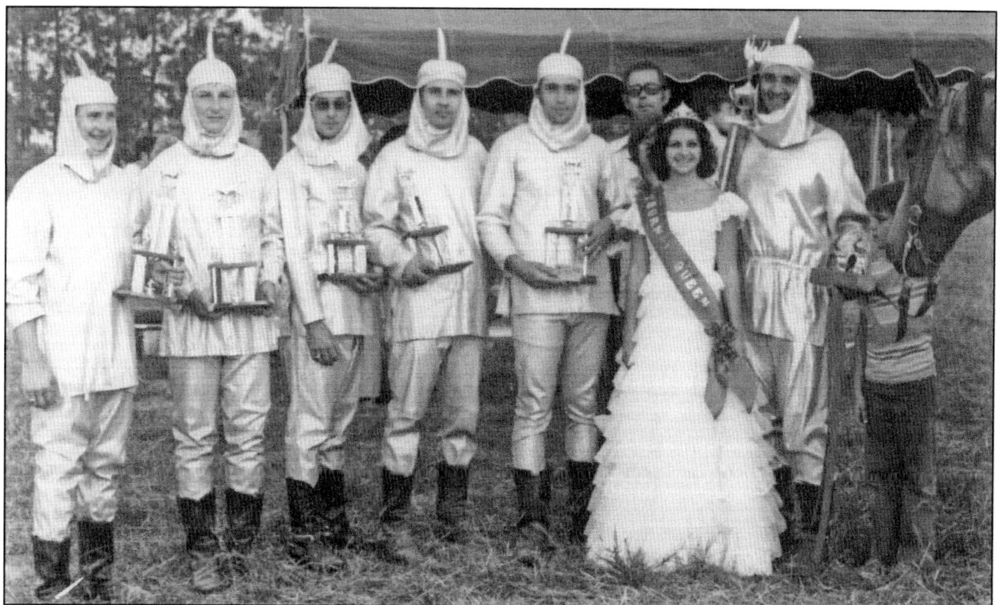

The 1975 Tournoi Queen, Jennifer Fontenot, poses with the tournoi winners. They are, from left to right, John Wayne Johnson of Pine Prairie, sportsmanship; Danny Doucet of Grand Prairie, fastest time; Don Morein of Ville Platte, fourth place; Ollie DeVille of Ville Platte, third place; Bergis Smith of Ville Platte, second place; and Berkman Veillon of Eunice, Tournoi Champion. (Courtesy of *Ville Platte Gazette*.)

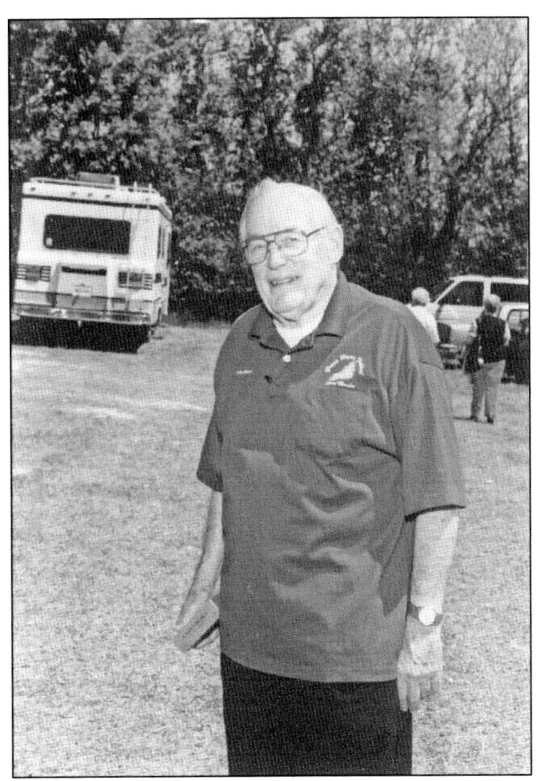

Pine Prairie has hosted the Boggy Bayou Festival each spring since 1986. Events include concerts, a queen's pageant, competitions in nail-driving, joke-telling, and boudin-eating, carnival rides, arts and crafts exhibits, and a Sunday morning Catholic Mass. Father Leslie Prescott, pastor of St. Peter's Catholic Church, helped found the Boggy Bayou Festival and Prairie Manor nursing home, and served as president of the nursing home board. (Courtesy of Bernice Ardoin.)

Proceeds from the Boggy Bayou Festival benefit Prairie Manor, the local nursing home. Here, festival board members pose in the early 1990s, when the festival moved to its present location south of town off Heritage Road. From left to right are Rayford West, Rachel Guillory, Billy Campbell, Sandra Book, Father Leslie Prescott, Queen Casey Landreneau, Ray Foreman, Bernice Ardoin, and Hazel Veillon. (Courtesy of Bernice Ardoin.)

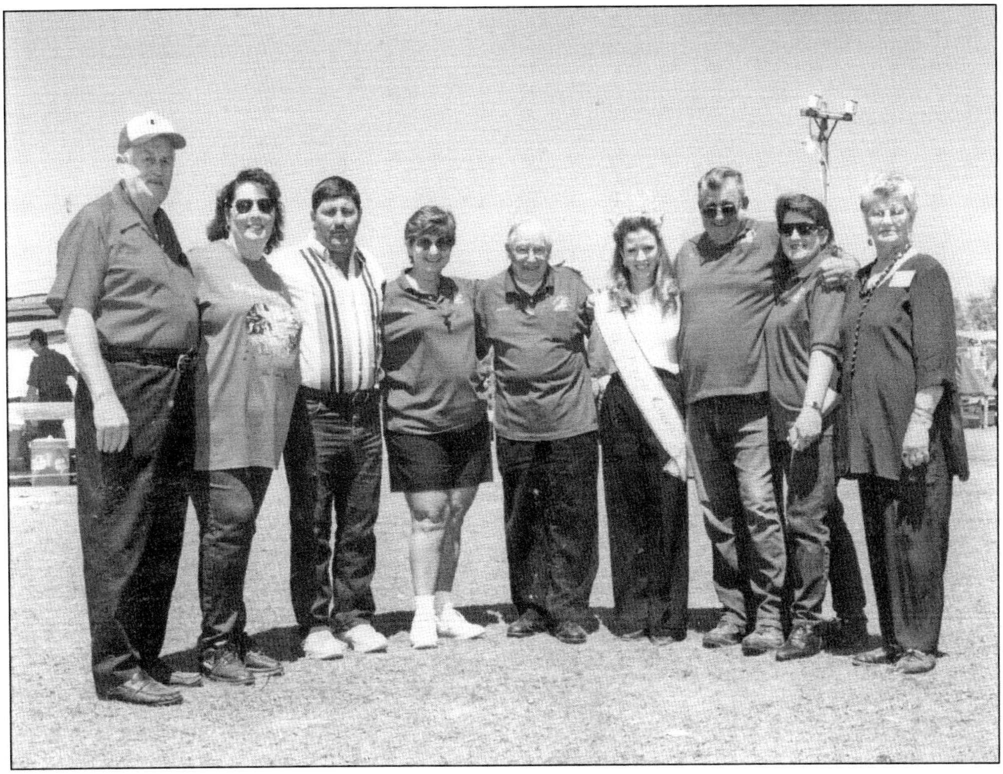

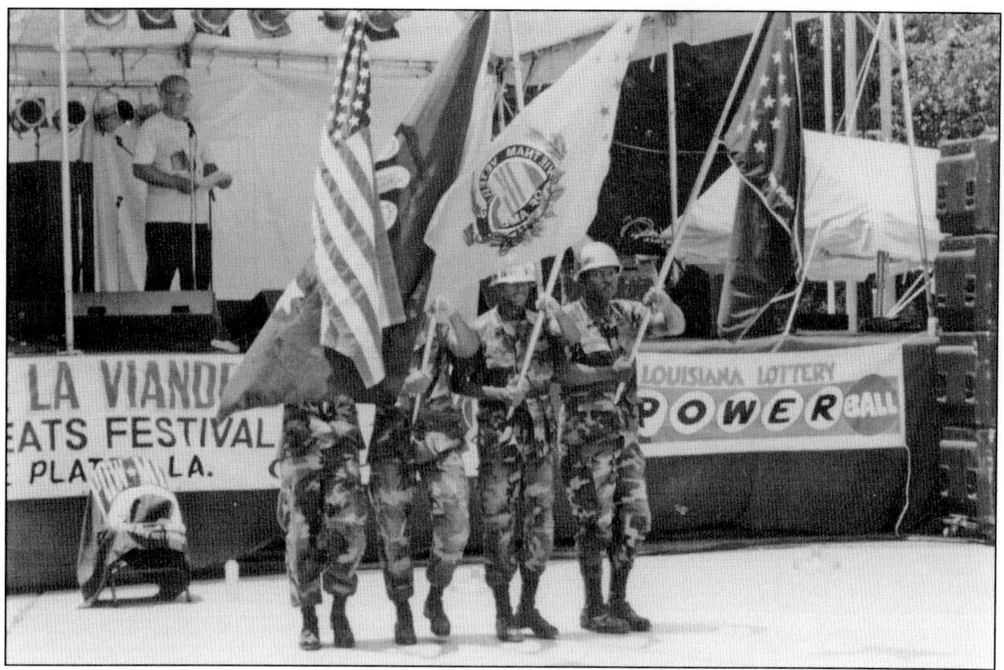

The Vietnam Veterans of America Evangeline Chapter No. 632 began organizing in February 1992 and received its charter that August. Since 1993, the chapter has sponsored Le Festival de la Viande Boucanée, or Smoked Meat Festival, in Ville Platte to raise funds to support needy families and individuals and for other civic projects. (Courtesy of Vietnam Veterans of America Chapter No. 632.)

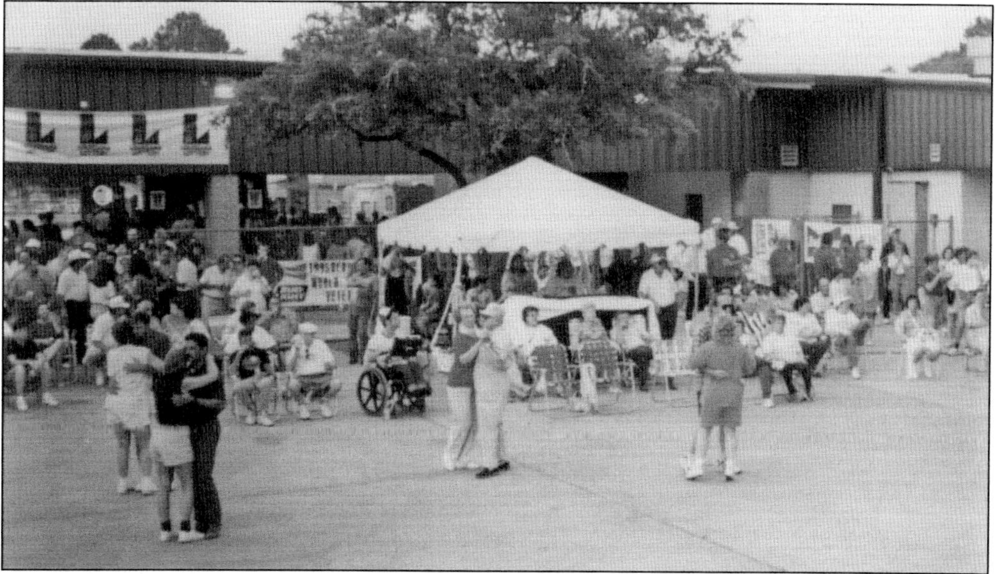

Held over a three-day weekend in June, the Smoked Meat Festival features live music, the World Championship Smoked Meat Cook-Off (with amateur and professional divisions), cooking demonstrations, exhibits of traditional arts and crafts, a working smokehouse, military performances and exhibits, and a beauty pageant. In its 20-year history, the festival has come to rival the Cotton Festival in popularity. (Courtesy of Vietnam Veterans of America Chapter No. 632.)

Bibliography

Ancelet, Barry Jean, Jay Edwards, and Geln Pitre. *Cajun Country*. Jackson, MI: University Press of Mississippi, 1991.

Bonnes Nouvelles. Ville Platte, LA: Bobby Dardeau, publisher.

Gahn, Robert Sr. *A History of Evangeline Parish, Its Land, Its Men and Its Women Who Made it a Beautiful Place to Live*. Baton Rouge, LA: Claitor's Publishing Division, 1941.

Landreneau, Mary Lynn F. *The Louisiana Cotton Festival, 1953–1992*. Ville Platte, LA: self-published, 1992.

Oubre, Claude F. *A History of the Diocese of Lafayette*. Strasbourg, France: Editions du Signe, 2001.

Prairie Pioneers, Some Founding Families of Evangeline Parish, Louisiana. Ville Platte, LA: Evangeline Genealogical and Historical Society, 2011.

Smith, Ramona A. and Kathleen M. Stagg. *Sacred Heart Catholic Cemetery, Ville Platte, Louisiana, 1864–1992*. Ville Platte, LA: self-published, 1993.

————. *Le Vieux Cimetière: The Old Ville Platte, Louisiana Cemetery: 1852–1990*. Ville Platte, LA: self-published, 1991.

Thompson, Mabel Alice. *Looking Back: A Narrative History of Bayou Chicot*. Ville Platte, LA: self-published, 1983.

Ville Platte Gazette. Ville Platte, LA.